SOUNDS BEYOND

KEVIN C. KARNES

SOUNDS
BEYOND

———

Arvo Pärt and the 1970s
Soviet Underground

The University of Chicago Press   CHICAGO AND LONDON

The University of Chicago Press, Chicago 60637
The University of Chicago Press, Ltd., London
© 2021 by The University of Chicago
All rights reserved. No part of this book may be used or reproduced in any
manner whatsoever without written permission, except in the case of brief
quotations in critical articles and reviews. For more information, contact
the University of Chicago Press, 1427 E. 60th St., Chicago, IL 60637.
Published 2021
Printed in the United States of America

30 29 28 27 26 25 24 23 22 21   1 2 3 4 5

ISBN-13: 978-0-226-80190-2 (cloth)
ISBN-13: 978-0-226-81540-4 (e-book)
DOI: https://doi.org/10.7208/chicago/9780226815404.001.0001

Library of Congress Cataloging-in-Publication Data

Names: Karnes, Kevin, 1972– author.
Title: Sounds beyond : Arvo Pärt and the 1970s Soviet underground /
    Kevin C. Karnes.
Description: Chicago : University of Chicago Press, 2021. | Includes
    bibliographical references and index.
Identifiers: LCCN 2021017525 | ISBN 9780226801902 (cloth) |
    ISBN 9780226815404 (ebook)
Subjects: LCSH: Pärt, Arvo—Criticism and interpretation. | Underground
    music—Soviet Union—History and criticism. | Music—Estonia—20th
    century—History and criticism. | Music—Soviet Union—Religious aspects.
Classification: LCC ML410.P1755 K37 2021 | DDC 780.92—dc23
LC record available at https://lccn.loc.gov/2021017525

♾ This paper meets the requirements of ANSI/NISO Z39.48-1992
(Permanence of Paper).

CONTENTS

Note on Translations, Transliteration, and Pronunciation *vii*
Note on Recordings *ix*
List of Musical Examples and Figures *xi*

ONE. Spaces Beyond: An Introduction *1*

TWO. A Beginning: The Riga Polytechnic Disco, 1974–76 *34*

THREE. Tintinnabuli and the Sacred *51*

FOUR. Ritual Moments: The RPI Festivals, 1976–77 *79*

FIVE. Tallinn 1978 *106*

SIX. Aftersounds: Bolderāja, Sergiyev Posad,
and a Train to Brest-Litovsk *121*

Acknowledgments *141*
Appendix: Key Premieres and Early Performances of
Pärt's Tintinnabuli-Style Works, 1976–78 *145*
Notes *147*   Sources *175*   Index *187*

TRANSLATIONS, TRANSLITERATION, AND PRONUNCIATION

Unless otherwise noted, all translations from non-English languages are my own. Where published translations exist, I have consulted them and I cite them along with the original-language sources of my own translations. Russian names and sources are transliterated using a simplified version of the Library of Congress (LC) system, omitting ties and diacritical marks. When individuals have other preferred or widely used Romanizations of their proper names (Alexei Lubimov), I use those in the text but use LC Romanizations in the notes and source list (Aleksei Liubimov), giving alternate spellings in parentheses where I feel they are necessary or helpful. In Latvian, the letter š is pronounced like the English *sh*; the name Hardijs Lediņš is pronounced, basically, as "Hardeez Ledinsh," with stress on the first syllable of both given and family names.

RECORDINGS

To read a book about music without listening along would be a partial experience at best, and I hope that readers will listen to everything they can of the works discussed here. Many are commercially recorded and widely available (King Crimson's 1974 album *Red*, for instance), and I do not point readers in any particular direction when it comes to finding them. In the case of Pärt's work, I refer where possible to the canonical recordings on the ECM label, made in collaboration with the composer beginning with *Tabula rasa* in 1984 (ECM New Series 1275). Where recordings of works by Pärt or others are harder to track down, I point to their locations in the notes: to websites, to moments in a film, or to shelf marks for the handful of recordings that can still only be heard by visiting the archives of Estonian Radio (Estonian Public Broadcasting) in Tallinn. Fortunately, the vast majority of the music discussed in this book can be purchased or found online.

MUSICAL EXAMPLES AND FIGURES

EXAMPLES

3.1. Pärt, funeral (*matus*) music for the film *Colorful Dreams* (1974) *52*

3.2. Pärt, sketch for the opening of *Calix* (vocal lines only) *58*

3.3. Pärt, opening measures of the *Gloria* from the *Missa syllabica* *65*

4.1. Martynov, *Passionslieder* (1977), measures 17–28 *97*

6.1. Lediņš, *Kuncendorf's China Notes* (1978), opening measures of track 2, "Abschied" *128*

FIGURES

1.1. Flyer for the Festival of Contemporary Music at the Student Club of the Riga Polytechnic Institute, 1977 *3*

1.2. Concert program for the official Tallinn premiere of Pärt's *Tintinnabuli* suite, 1976 *8*

1.3. Vladimir Martynov and Arvo Pärt in Tallinn, November 1978 *11*

1.4. Ilya Kabakov, *Graph of Hope and Fear* (1983) *14*

1.5. Erik Bulatov, *Dangerous* (1972–73) *16*

1.6. Collective Actions Group, *Action 16: Ten Appearances*, February 1, 1981 *18*

2.1. Hardijs Lediņš behind the turntable at an RPI discotheque, mid-1970s *35*

2.2. Lediņš's discotheque at the RPI Student Club (formerly Anglican Church), mid-1970s *46*

3.1. Pärt, page from *Modus* (1976) *53*

3.2. Pärt, compositional sketch for *Modus* 54

3.3. Eduard Steinberg, *Composition November–December* (1979) 71

4.1. Pärt and Alexei Lubimov during setup for an RPI festival performance held at the Latvian Academy of Art, April 1976 84

4.2. Alexei Lubimov and Tatiana Grindenko at the RPI festival, April 1976 85

4.3. Lubimov at the RPI festival, April 1976 86

4.4. Lubimov at the RPI festival, April 1976 87

4.5. Program for the Festival of Contemporary Music at the Riga Polytechnic Institute, October 1977 94–95

5.1. Pärt and Alfred Schlee at the Festival of Early and Contemporary Music in Tallinn, November 1978 113

5.2. Celebrating at the Festival of Early and Contemporary Music, November 1978: Grindenko, Kremer, Lubimov held by Mustonen, and Pärt 116

5.3. Pärt receiving his Award of the Year from the Ministry of Culture of the Estonian SSR, May 1978 119

6.1. Lediņš walking to Bolderāja, June 14, 1981 129

6.2. Juris Boiko and Hardijs Lediņš, *Empty/Alone* (walking to Bolderāja, June 14, 1981) 131

6.3. Juris Boiko walking to Bolderāja, January 16, 1982 132

6.4. Cassette preserved in the Pärt estate 138

ONE

SPACES BEYOND

————————

An Introduction

"We live in the gaps between the gears," the pianist Alexei Lubimov told the violinist Boriss Avramecs of the spaces he'd found for creative work in the 1970s USSR. Lubimov, in turn, recalls the composer Valentin Silvestrov telling him something similar. "We could do anything," Silvestrov remarked, "because we lived in the holes in the system."[1] Whoever it was who first said these words, they capture something essential about an artistic scene that thrived beneath the radar in Brezhnev's Soviet Union, when countless gaps seemed to open between the cogs of the Soviet bureaucratic machinery. Some were so large that an artist could feel as though they virtually lived within them. In such spaces, one could create and compose, even perform and exhibit all kinds of novel and potentially provocative works of art, as if unseen by the Ministry of Culture, unpoliced by uncomprehending officials, seemingly beyond the care of authorities disinclined to look beyond their formal charges. As the painter Vladimir Yankilevsky recalled of his own relationship to Soviet officialdom in the 1970s, it felt as though "*we*, for *them*, simply did not exist. We were invisible, transparent."[2]

While Yankilevsky and his friends were busy painting, sculpting, and composing, others committed considerable energies to organizing the events at which such presentations took place. Lubimov was one, and he has lately written of the "surprising ability" he seems to have had "to realize everything" he could dream up at the time, even

"things that seemed completely fantastical at first."[3] Helping to organize the underground premiere of *Sarah Was Ninety Years Old*, one of
the very first works Arvo Pärt composed in what has since become
known as his signature "tintinnabuli" style—broadly modal music,
unfolding slowly, which listeners often describe in terms of stillness,
quiet, even healing—was just one of Lubimov's fantastical achievements, accomplished in a decommissioned Riga church that was home
to a vital disco scene. That took place in April 1976.[4] More surprising
still was a follow-up project of October 1977, when Lubimov helped
stage the premiere performance of Pärt's very first openly liturgical
composition, the *Missa syllabica*, a complete Latin mass, its sacred text
clearly declaimed by the choir. This latter concert was part of a festival
of new music organized by a group of Riga students, billed as marking no less hallowed an occasion than the sixtieth anniversary of the
Bolshevik Revolution (fig. 1.1). It was a remarkable event, an incred-
ible juxtaposition of sacred repertoire and Soviet celebration. But it
went off without a hitch. We have the recording to prove it, preserved
on reel-to-reel tape.[5]

  Just how such an event could ever have been staged in the centrally
planned, officially atheistic, pre-perestroika USSR is the animating
question of this book. My answer, in part, is that the composer accomplished it with a great deal of help from others—in fact, from a largely
forgotten community of individuals, of which Pärt and Lubimov were
both a part. Their group consisted of a multinational, evolving bunch
of musicians, students, audio engineers, sympathetic administrators,
star performers, and one aspiring DJ, who worked together for a handful of years to open and maintain a shared space for musical experimentation, largely unhindered by bureaucratic strictures or Soviet
cultural norms. Other writers have lately revealed the key roles played
by communities and networks in the experimentalist projects of John
Cage, Karlheinz Stockhausen, Morton Feldman, and other composers from the Euro-American West.[6] Yet the landscape of experimental
music in the USSR remains terra incognita for the most part, and Pärt
himself is still widely regarded as an isolated, solitary figure, who appeared out of nowhere in 1980s Berlin, his crystalline musical language
already fully formed. One of my goals in this book is to shed light on
the collective origins of his project in these years, to understand Pärt's

RPI STUDENTU KLUBS

21. oktobris — 30. oktobris 1977. g.

MŪSDIENU
MŪZIKAS DEKĀDE

VELTĪTA

Lielās Oktobra sociālistiskās revolūcijas
60. gadadienai

Senās mūzikas ansamblis «Hortus musicus» (Tallina)
Viļņas stīgu kvartets
Sitamo instrumentu ansamblis. M. Pekarskis (Maskava)
Saksofonu kvartets. L. Mihailovs (Maskava)
Elektroniskās mūzikas studija (Maskava)
Vokālais ansamblis «Tonika» (Ļeņingrada)

Programmā padomju komponistu skaņdarbi

Biļetes RPI studentu klubā, Bibliotēkas ielā 2a

FIGURE 1.1 Flyer for the Festival of Contemporary Music at the Student Club of the Riga Polytechnic Institute, where Pärt's first openly religious tintinnabuli-style works were premiered in October 1977. The festival was "dedicated to the 60th anniversary of the Great October Socialist Revolution." Collection of the Latvian Centre for Contemporary Art.

work as one of many expressions of commitments shared, nurtured, and celebrated by others in the Soviet spaces in which he began.

And yet, I will also suggest that Pärt, and especially his tintinnabuli-style compositions, focused the efforts and cemented the bonds that sustained this particular group of artists. Its members were drawn to the sound of Pärt's music, which they heard as an intoxicatingly principled rejection of an esoteric avant-garde on the one hand and the ubiquitous pablum of Socialist realism on the other. (The Latin moniker, "little bells," Pärt chose in order to highlight the transparently triadic foundations of his new musical language.) But they were also drawn to Pärt and his work for the ways in which they seemed to embody an uncompromising sort of spiritual practice—in his case, the practice of Orthodox Christianity, to which he had recently converted. In the mid-1970s, Pärt was already a star of the Soviet classical music world. His early works, none of them sacred, were sometimes censured but also widely celebrated, and his new tintinnabuli style of composing was officially unveiled in a suite of ideologically neutral works in a series of Estonian SSR Philharmonic concerts in autumn 1976.[7] Yet, drawing upon a first-ever look at Pärt's composing diaries, I will suggest that nearly the entirety of his creative project of the period was, covertly, a sacred one: a search for means of sounding musically his newfound Christian faith. Such music should never have been publicly performable in the USSR. But it was: at the Riga discotheque festivals of 1976–77, in venues not so much hidden as unnoticed by officials charged with caring. Writing in the early 1980s, the Russian painter Ilya Kabakov observed that religious proclamation was a defining feature of a culture of "underground art" (*podpol'noe iskusstvo*) that thrived beneath the surface of Brezhnev's Soviet Union.[8] The festivals organized by the Riga/Tallinn collective constituted just such an underground scene, built and maintained by a community of musicians who sought nothing more or less than the freedom to engage in artistic experiment, wherever it might lead. In that space, in declaring his faith, Pärt was not alone.

In six chapters, this book charts the coalescence of this group of artists between 1974 and 1976; its heyday organizing festivals of new music in Riga and Tallinn between 1976 and 1978; and its dissolution by early 1980. It documents its origins at the Riga Polytechnic Institute, where the disco dreams of an architecture student gave rise to an underground new music scene that drew participants from as far away as Moscow and Yerevan. It mines Pärt's compositional diaries for evidence of the religious project that underlay his creative work of the decade. It draws on archival documents and oral history to recon-struct the festival events of 1976–78, which seemed for a time to ac-complish the impossible, attracting top talent from across the USSR to this corner of the empire's northwest, all while remaining largely un-noticed—or at least unpoliced—by the Ministry of Culture and other officials. Finally, it traces the dissolution of the collective in the wake of personal decisions made by key members: religious conversion, shifts of focus, and emigration. This first chapter charts preliminary histories and theoretical terrain, mapping the landscape of gaps and holes in the system about which Avramecs, Lubimov, and Silvestrov all spoke; surveying the field of experimental art and performance in the 1970s USSR; extending into musical domains Kabakov's linking of religious practice to a culture of underground art; and exploring some of the distinctive features of artistic communities in late Soviet spaces.

In the end, what I hope emerges is not just a new picture of Pärt and his work but a renewed appreciation for the deeply searching, stunningly fertile, often audacious musical culture—*alternative* mu-sical culture—of the 1970s USSR.[9] Long maligned as a fallow period in Soviet cultural life, a time of stagnation (the Russian poet Gennady Aygi dismissed the 1970s in hindsight as "desolate" or "deaf years" for music), it is important to recall, as the anthropologist Alexei Yurchak points out, that "stagnation" (in Russian, *zastoi*) was a label applied to the decade only in retrospect, in the time of perestroika.[10] Recently, the period has been reconsidered, foremost by Yurchak himself, and also by artists like Lubimov, whose recollections and artworks of the decade have lately filled volumes.[11] Pärt is understandably reluctant to revisit the period himself, overshadowed as it was in hindsight by his family's heartrending decision to emigrate to the West in 1980, fol-lowing a decisive break with the regime that we will chart in the final chapters of this book. But for many artists who stayed behind, mem-ories of the decade are different. For Lubimov, the 1970s were a time of "tremendous" or "stunning openings" (*potriasaiushchie otkrytiia*) in the cultural life of his country, when things formerly believed to be impossible were somehow made a reality. For the Russian composer Vladimir Martynov, another key member of Pärt's circle, the period seemed in hindsight to be a "a white-hot time" for Soviet art. For the Latvian DJ and musician Hardijs Lediņš, the principal organizer of the Riga festivals that hosted the premieres of Pärt's sacred music in 1976–77, the decade was "a period rich with ideas, more ideas than one could possibly realize."[12]

For Yurchak and others, the gaps and holes Lubimov described were not bugs in the system at all. They *were* the system, at least in part, and a person attuned to the ideological tides could feel as though they were free do almost whatever they wanted to in life, so long as they performed a certain kind of conspicuous "upstandingness" where and when it mattered.[13] But as the story unfolded in this book makes clear, the stunning openings the decade provided were unevenly distributed geographically, and they were not accessible to all. Artists and historians have lately noted remarkable regional disparities in artists' abilities to engage in alternative forms of cultural practice across the Soviet bloc, with one describing the region as a whole as a "geography of differences" with respect to opportunity.[14] As we will see, it was no coincidence that the Baltic capitals of Riga and Tallinn gave rise to the particular experimental scene that nurtured the underground performance of Pärt's sacred music, a thing that would have been impossible in many other Soviet locales. We will also see how some individuals—Lediņš, foremost, in this story—were, by virtue of family or professional ties, able to tap into possibilities that most contemporaries could never have imagined, and were able in turn to provide opportunities for colleagues that they would otherwise never have experienced.

To recount this history of spaces, relations, and the sound world in which Pärt's tintinnabuli project took shape, I rely not only on written documents but on a wide-ranging project of listening: to the sounds of archival recordings, preserved on reels of magnetic tape recorded by those present at events, and to the words of artists and others who experienced those events firsthand and who shared their recollections with me. Time and again while writing this book, I've been struck by the delicate, ephemeral, contingent nature of the stories I am trying to fathom and tell. Memories fail, and they're always shifting. Much of what I have read and heard is filtered through languages I've come to know but which are not my own. Sometimes my conversations with participants have been vexed by what the musicologist Benjamin Piekut calls "the problem of relative importance": people simply don't always share my obsession with distant, fleeting moments of their own histories.[15] I've sometimes felt that every other sentence I write must be hedged by "*x* remembers," or "*y* doesn't recall," or "we just don't know how *z* happened." In my own reiterative acts of listening, writing, asking questions, recounting stories, and trying to make sense of it all, I have tried to heed the counsel of the art historian Matthew Jesse Jackson, to whose words I'll add my own emphasis. "Works of unofficial art," he writes, "must be understood within the broader field of late Soviet culture *but also* as indices of the constraints and possibilities encoded in the 'real spaces' of their production."[16] In the pages that follow, I hope to do justice to those spaces, and to the individuals who made them come alive.

CHANGES ALL AROUND

The formal unveiling of Pärt's tintinnabuli-style music took place in an Estonian SSR Philharmonic concert of October 27, 1976, an event whose arresting sounds I'll try to recount in chapter 3. Staged in the Estonia Concert Hall, the republic's most prestigious, it was performed by the Tallinn Chamber Choir and the wildly popular early music ensemble Hortus Musicus. In short, it was as official an event as any concert in the Estonian SSR could be. The program featured seven works arranged in what Pärt called his *Tintinnabuli* suite. Four of those works were instrumental, along with three others scored for wordless singing: *Calix, Modus,* and *In spe* (fig. 1.2).[17]

The high-profile billing was unsurprising for one of the leading Soviet composers of his generation, who had made a name for himself by pushing the boundaries of the Soviet avant-garde in the 1950s and 1960s, employing such compositional devices as dodecaphony and collage. Still, by some accounts, the public's response to Pärt's latest stylistic turn was mixed. Even Andres Mustonen, the conductor of Hortus Musicus, remembers having doubts. "It was not yet clear if anything would come of this," he later remarked.[18] Such doubts were

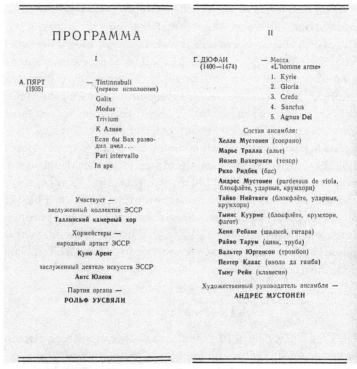

FIGURE 1.2 Concert program for the official Tallinn premiere of Pärt's *Tintinnabuli* suite, October 27, 1976, with Hortus Musicus under the direction of Andres Mustonen, the Tallinn Chamber Choir, and others. The Russian titles on the program are *Für Alina* and *If Bach Had Kept Bees*. The second half of the concert featured the *L'homme armé* mass by Guillaume Dufay. Estonian Theatre and Music Museum. Courtesy of the Estonian Theatre and Music Museum and the Arvo Pärt Centre.

eased the following September with the sensational premiere of *Tabula rasa*, Pärt's double concerto in the tintinnabuli style composed for the virtuoso Soviet violinists Gidon Kremer and Tatiana Grindenko. A few weeks later, Grindenko and Kremer took *Tabula rasa* on tour through Austria and West Germany, where the sparkling sounds of Pärt's new music captured the imagination of audiences larger than any of which he had dreamed.[19] (A list of key premieres and early performances of Pärt's tintinnabuli-style works is given in the appendix.)

These public triumphs were preceded, however, by years of private travail, marked by nagging self-doubt, attacks by officials, and a retreat from the concert stage that lasted, with a handful of interruptions, from the end of 1968 all the way until 1976. Two days before the Tallinn unveiling, Pärt arranged a dry run of the *Tintinnabuli* suite at Tartu University in eastern Estonia. Six months before that, in April 1976, the first piece to which he had appended the label—calling it, in manuscript, "Tintinnabulum 1"—was played in the Soviet Republic of Latvia at a discotheque in the Student Club of the Riga Polytechnic Institute, which made its home in a disused Anglican church. The title of that composition, *Sarah Was Ninety Years Old*, alluded to the book of Genesis, but it would be changed for its official premiere in Tallinn to *Modus*, Latin for *method*, a word without religious connotations.[20] As it happened, Pärt had good reason for keeping the titles and origins of his tintinnabuli experiments under wraps. For they all had emerged as part of a distinctly sacred project for the composer: his search for a musical language capable of expressing his Orthodox Christian faith, of accommodating his vision of the divine.

Pärt was not the only artist to experience a breakthrough in these years. In fact, variants of his artistic turn were appearing all across the landscape of Soviet alternative art. As the photographer and performance artist Georgy Kiesewalter recalls of his own experience of the Moscow art scene of the period, an almost hyperactive kind of creative searching pervaded his creative community, with ideas emerging "one after another as if in queue, drowning in their abundance." Lubimov concurs, recounting an "an element of sports-like excitement in the search for new possibilities" in those years.[21] For Martynov, who described his own first experience of Pärt's tintinnabuli-style music at the Riga festival of 1977 as something "volcanic, tectonic," its effect was prepared by the sights and sounds of changes occurring all around him.[22]

As Martynov recalled in later decades, the Ukrainian composer Valentin Silvestrov, a leading figure in the Soviet avant-garde of the 1960s, surprised his contemporaries in 1974 with the first of his *Quiet Songs* (*Tikhie pesni*), whose bracingly simple, quasi-tonal language seemed to bid adieu to musical modernism, pointing toward . . . no one yet knew. (Listen, for instance, to the final song, "Farewell, world, farewell, earth" [*Proshchai, svite, proshchai, zemle*], from his 1974 collection.)[23] Soon, together with the composer Eduard Artemyev and the audio engineer Yurii Bogdanov, Martynov dove into pathbreaking work at the electronic music studio of Moscow's Skriabin Museum, just as a momentous shift, at once technological and generational, was overtaking the institution. Since the 1960s, the museum's basement had been home to the legendary ANS synthesizer developed by the engineer Yevgeny Murzin, on which Alfred Schnittke, Sofia Gubaidulina, and Edison Denisov had all composed their first electronic works: Denisov's *Singing of the Birds* (*Penie ptits*, 1968), Gubaidulina's *Vivendi non vivendi* (1971). But shortly after Murzin's death in 1970, the ANS was traded for a British-built Synthi-100, an instrument "with practically unlimited capacities," Martynov recalled, which was a perfect match for the interests of the young composer and his friends, who generally preferred the sounds of British and West German progressive rock to the avant-garde experiments of their elders. (King Crimson and Tangerine Dream were favorites.) For this junior group, the use of synthesized sound as a resource seemed not novel but second nature. Soon, Martynov recalled, he and his friends "changed the face of the studio" entirely, "squeezing out" the older generation by mid-decade. (In truth, their elders had already moved on.)[24]

The generational shift Martynov describes was not absolute, however, and he counted Silvestrov and Pärt among his fellow travelers on the creative paths he trod (fig. 1.3). Indeed, just about all the members of Martynov's circle considered Pärt and Silvestrov inspirations, for they seemed to anticipate, with works like *Sarah Was Ninety Years Old* and *Quiet Songs*, the same sort of turn from avant-garde modernism that Martynov and his friends were then making.[25]

For Martynov, the crux of the aesthetic shift he sensed consisted in composers striving to direct their listeners' attention beyond musical structures, however cleverly designed, and also beyond what he described as the modernist fetishizing of the musical score as testament to the genius of the composer. All around him, he saw evidence of what he described as the "collapse of the idea of the ego" as the raison d'être of artistic work: in the Orthodox faith that informed the highly disciplined language of Pärt's early tintinnabuli-style music, in the Cage-inspired Zen and yogic practice that animated his own contemporary experiments, in the communally articulated repetitive

FIGURE 1.3 Vladimir Martynov and Arvo Pärt in Tallinn, November 1978. Photographer unknown, possibly Hardijs Lediņš. Collection of the Latvian Centre for Contemporary Art. Courtesy of Pēteris Lediņš.

gestures of Terry Riley's *In C*, even in the literary theory of Roland Barthes ("The Death of the Author") and Jacques Derrida (the idea of *mise en abyme*). All of these projects, Martynov held, contributed to "discrediting the principle of self-expression" as the principal goal of artistic practice—an outmoded principle, as he saw it, that was rooted in nineteenth-century Romanticism and still guided the post-war avant-garde.[26]

Thinking back to Gennady Aygi's remarks on the 1970s as "desolate" or "deaf years" for music, it is clear that the aesthetic and generational changes Martynov diagnosed must also have signaled, for many of Aygi's generation, the end of a vital, even heroic way of living and working as artists in the Soviet Union. Indeed, Martynov described these shifts in dramatic, even traumatic terms: as the "death of the avant-garde" (*smert' avangarda*).[27] The artistic culture whose passing Aygi mourned had been deeply courageous in the Khrushchev years, when to create or practice in unofficial domains entailed an existential commitment, one that could preclude a person from enjoying any vestige of a normal life. And yet, to Martynov and his friends in the 1970s, to close the door on that postwar culture seemed desirable, necessary, even inevitable. Times had changed, and a new generation had come of age without ever having experienced Stalinism as a living force.[28] In declaring through their musical work their decisive turn beyond the concerns of the generation of the 1960s, Martynov and his colleagues believed they were laying foundations for a wholesale renewal of Soviet music and art—and, with that, to usher in a vital, communally and spiritually engaged future for Soviet society as a whole.

EXPERIMENT/EXPERIMENTALISM

Accounting for his concerns of the decade in this way, Martynov retrospectively aligned his activities of the 1970s with the concerns of many other artists simultaneously engaged in experimental projects around the world. While sounds and approaches varied widely, a common denominator among far-flung scenes was the conviction that "in experimental music, real change occurs in the realm of human thought and experience," as Jennie Gottschalk writes. "The experimentalist is not trying to change the musical world," she continues, "but to change the thinking of one or more listeners during—and possibly after—the performance." In the words of Piekut, what nearly all experimentalist circles had in common was a "restless desire to be elsewhere, [a] searching for an otherwise."[29] As we will see, this searching for an "elsewhere" or an "otherwise," this striving to change one's experience of the world, animated just about all the creative projects considered in this book. To be sure, the location or outlines of that longed-for state or locale varied widely from artist to artist and from one project to the next. It often coincided with images of the West, but it could also be an imagined "East," or even an ideal socialist society undelivered by the Soviet state itself. Still, if there is any single idea that might be said to distill the essence of Soviet experimentalism of the 1970s, this longing to be *somewhere else* might well be it.

To understand the particular variety of experimentalist longing that united the efforts of the group to which Pärt, Lubimov, and Martynov all contributed, which encouraged and fostered spiritual searching while distancing itself from the aesthetic claims of the postwar avant-

garde, we might do well to begin in another realm of creativity altogether: the visual arts, which were simultaneously undergoing a generational shift of their own. As in music, Stalin's death in 1953 ushered in a
period of new creative freedoms in painting, sculpture, and the graphic
arts. But in those fields, that openness came to an abrupt and early end
with the so-called Manezh Exhibition of 1962, held in Moscow. There,
a number of the city's leading artists exhibited some deeply provocative paintings and sculptures, attracting the attention and provoking
the ire of Nikita Khrushchev himself.[30] The fallout was swift. Con-
tributing artists were harassed, censorship of discourse on the arts
ramped up, and the public exhibition of "nonconforming" works—
those deemed not to adhere to the tenets of Socialist realism—was so
tightly controlled that it became virtually impossible to display them
in the years immediately following. But gradually, as the years went
by and nothing harsher befell nonconforming artists than occasional
hounding by authorities, there coalesced, as Kiesewalter writes, a critical mass of creative individuals no longer willing to conceal the fact
that "different forms of culture" still existed on the margins of Soviet
society, along with the "different means of self-expression" to which
those forms gave rise.[31]

   Led by the painter Oscar Rabin, a group of nonconforming artists
(often called the Lianozovo Group) organized their own, unofficial exhibition in September 1974, in a space beyond the ostensible control
of the Soviet bureaucracy: namely, outdoors, on an undeveloped plot
of land in the Moscow suburbs. Sensing trouble (or perhaps attempt-
ing to capitalize on its inevitable arrival), Rabin made sure to attract
the attention of foreign journalists beforehand. Just after the opening of their unauthorized showing, the expected crackdown came in
the form of a band of civic workers who descended on the lot and destroyed many of the artworks displayed, thus endowing the event with
the enduring moniker of the Bulldozer Exhibition. Despite the loss
of work, Rabin's ploy was successful. The startling violence of the encounter was widely covered in the Western press, and authorities, ea-
ger to undo the damage to their image, agreed to a follow-up open-air
exhibition two weeks later in Moscow's Izmailovsky Park. The latter
event, sometimes called the Soviet Woodstock, was open to everyone
who had anything to exhibit, regardless of the character of their work

and whether or not they were members of a creative union. The Iz-mailovsky exhibition attracted thousands of visitors, a number wholly unexpected by the regime.

Ilya Kabakov did not participate in the Bulldozer Exhibition. He was afraid, he recalls, and also felt that Rabin's political maneuvering was beneath the concerns of "art in itself." But he later acknowledged the exhibition as "the most important event, socially speaking, in the art world" of the decade.[32] In the wake of authorities' capitulation after the Bulldozer fiasco, "the extent and nature of fear" lately felt by non-conforming artists began to diminish. With this, he reflected, many artists' "hopes for living a normal creative life" gradually began to grow. A graphic artist by vocation, Kabakov summarized his impressions in his *Graph of Hope and Fear* (fig. 1.4).[33]

The bottom line, the "line of hope" (*liniia "nadezhdy"*) shows a sharp fall after Manezh, after which it slowly begins to rise. Above that, the "line of fear" (*liniia "strakha"*) indicates a substantial decline between the years 1974 and 1976. Kabakov concedes that even after Izmailovsky, official stances could shift unpredictably, and individuals were some-times harassed. Still, after autumn 1974, nonconforming artists were

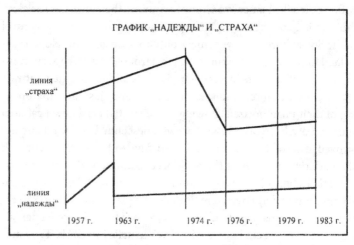

FIGURE 1.4 Ilya Kabakov, *Graph of Hope and Fear* (1983). Copyright Ilya & Emilia Kabakov. Ilya Kabakov © 2020 Artists Rights Society (ARS), New York / VG Bild-Kunst, Bonn.

effectively able to think of themselves as "no longer 'underground'"—
with one key exception, considered below—"but rather 'unofficial,' a
designation that was much easier to bear," in the words of the art historian Octavian Eşanu. "No longer was there any reason to hide. Instead, one had only to accept that one would remain unacceptable."[34]

Born in 1933, Kabakov was two years older than Pärt. Like him, his
work and personality inspired a community of mostly younger artists,
many of whom, like Martynov, sensed a profound aesthetic shift taking place around them. The principal group Kabakov inspired would
identify as the Moscow Conceptualists. Cutting across artistic media
and forms, core concerns of the group included (to follow the critic
Margarita Tupitsyn) "an orientation toward the visualization of verbal
concepts"—an engagement with texts, often literally so—and "a will-
ingness to appropriate aspects of popular culture" in creative projects.
Together, these tendencies had the effect of "redirect[ing] alternative
art away from Western sources and closer to local ones."[35] A landmark
work of Moscow conceptualism is Eric Bulatov's painting *Dangerous*
(*Opasno*, 1972–73; fig. 1.5). There, an idyllic scene of a countryside
picnic is superimposed with red block text in the manner of a Socialist Realist print.

Not only is the text in Bulatov's painting—DANGEROUS—oddly
incongruous with the scene depicted, but the words also seem to be
advancing toward (or away from) the viewer along all four sides of
the painting at once, as if in cinematographic motion. (An American
observer might recall the opening frames of *Star Wars* from 1977.) In
Dangerous, we find brought together all the tendencies Tupitsyn describes. Its textual engagement is literal, its allusion to popular media is immediate, and its rootedness in postwar Soviet artistic tradition (here Socialist realism) is both evident and perplexing, and thus
obliquely critical.[36]

As Martynov understood, the Moscow Conceptualists looked
beyond the modernist ideal of the self-expressing artwork to focus
instead on the creation of broadly accessible works of art that invite
questioning, discussion, and open-ended wondering by those en-
countering them.[37] And, much as Martynov would write of Pärt's
tintinnabuli-style compositions, so too would Tupitsyn describe
Moscow conceptualism as a critical response to—even a broadly

FIGURE 1.5 Erik Bulatov, *Dangerous* (1972–73). Collection Zimmerli Art Museum at Rutgers University, Norton and Nancy Dodge Collection of Nonconformist Art from the Soviet Union, 2000.0868. Photo of image by Peter Jacobs. Erik Boulatov © 2020 Artist Rights Society (ARS), New York / ADAGP, Paris.

generational rejection of—Khrushchev-era modernism. Modernism in the visual arts, she writes, had sought "to create an aesthetic counter to the steady diet of Socialist realism, mass culture, and stultifying verbal propaganda," by "resurrect[ing] such disreputable concepts as pure form and abstract uses of color." In contrast, the Conceptualists strove to "undermine" that modernist project, rejecting abstraction and engaging directly with the iconography of Socialist realism and other forms of popular culture.[38] In this way, the advent of conceptualism can be seen as broadly paralleling what the musicologist Peter J. Schmelz describes as a generalized evolution of unofficial music from abstraction to mimesis in the Soviet 1960s and 1970s, from the formal, theoretical concerns of serialism and other varieties of avant-garde modernism to such "representational styles" as aleatoric composition and polystylistic collage.[39]

One of Kabakov's younger colleagues took the concerns of the Conceptualists in a more radically experimental direction, the spiritual overtones of which might help us understand the broad receptivity to Pärt's openly devotional music in alternative circles. In March 1976, the poet Andrei Monastyrsky and a handful of friends staged the first of what would become a series of "actions" (*deistviia*) in forests and fields beyond the Moscow suburbs. The group, which would call itself Collective Actions, focused on organizing activities in which the very concept of the autonomous artwork all but disappeared. Their projects consisted in "journeys beyond the city" (*poezdki za gorod*), in which guests would be invited to some unfamiliar, uninhabited place. There, they would witness a deliberately ambiguous action performed by members of the group. The first such event, titled *Appearance (Poiavlenie)*, consisted solely of artists crossing a field (located in Izmailovsky Park, as it happened) and handing certificates to visitors providing "documentary confirmation" of their attendance. Sometimes, following written instructions, guests would participate in the action themselves, as in *Ten Appearances* (1981), where they were instructed to cross a snowy field unspooling threads as they went, and then to reel in their threads to find piece of paper attached to its end, documenting the time and location of the action as well as the participants' names (fig. 1.6). Whenever an action was completed, participants were asked to reflect and record their impressions of what had taken place.[40]

Deeply moved by his encounters with the Zen-inflected writings of John Cage, Monastyrsky described his group's actions as spiritual events or rituals. Their goal, he explained, was to effect a change in perception and self-reflection on the part of participant-observers, "to make extraordinary the perception of ordinary appearances, disappearances, absences, colors, sounds, and so on," he wrote in 1980.[41] In a letter to Tupitsyn in 1981, he elaborated: "Our activities are spiritual practice, but not art in any commercial sense. . . . If it is indeed possible to consider our work as art, then only as a 'tuning fork' for direct-

FIGURE 1.6 Collective Actions Group, *Action 16: Ten Appearances*, February 1, 1981. Photo by Igor Makarevich. Collection Zimmerli Art Museum at Rutgers University, Norton and Nancy Dodge Collection of Nonconformist Art from the Soviet Union, 2013.016.023. Photo of image by Peter Jacobs. Courtesy of Igor Makarevich.

ing the consciousness outside the boundaries of intellect."[42] Surveying the responses of participant-observers to Collective Actions' work
of the 1970s, Eşanu notes that the performance itself was, for many, not
the most memorable part of the experience at all. Rather, it was the
waiting—sitting aboard the train as it made its way into the countryside, standing around in snowy fields in anticipation of whatever might
take place. Members of the group, Eşanu writes, "deliberately used actions and gestures of a very low degree of 'artistry' . . . in order to suggest that what was really taking place in front of [the observer] was not
as important as that which was emerging 'inside' them. They were expected to 'turn their eyes inward' and observe their own state of waiting, looking, listening, or any other state that might emerge in the emotional space of their own perception." What Collective Actions strove
for, he summarizes, was "achieving an almost mystical experience."[43]

    With respect to this, the work of Collective Actions exemplifies a tendency that Kabakov (who often attended their performances) described as ubiquitous in alternative artistic circles of the period. Namely, the group's work embodied a kind of generalized religious sensibility, however typically unconnected to any formal religious practice. As Kabakov put it, their artworks strove to answer the question of "how one could be a religious artist without being an artisan in a churchly sense." Or: "whether one can be a religious artist who posits religious problems at the center and foundation of one's art, without being engaged in church-focused work."[44] In 1978, Kabakov's question was answered with a resounding *yes* by the principal philosophical interlocutor of Moscow conceptualism as a whole, Boris Groys. In a 1978 issue of the Leningrad samizdat journal *Thirty-Seven: A Journal of Artistic and Religious Life*, Groys posited a kind of informal religious searching at the very core of the Conceptualists' project.[45] "Russian art," Groys suggested, "from the age of icons to our time, seeks to speak of another world." He continued:

Culture emerges as the guardian of primordial revelation and also as the mediator for new revelations. The language of art differs from everyday language not because it speaks of the world in a more elegant and beautiful way or discloses the "internal world of the artist." What makes it different is the message it has to convey about the other world—something only art can say.[46]

"What is that other world?" Groys continued. "It is the world opened up to us by religion. It is the world that opens itself to us only through the medium of art." Of the Conceptualists, he concluded: "Art, as they see it, involves impingement of that other world upon our own.... The artists whose works have been discussed here are not religious persons, yet they are able to comprehend art in terms of belief."[47]

This sense of artistic creativity verging on religious practice was so widely shared in alternative circles that nearly every artist to have penned reflections on the 1970s has acknowledged it with respect to their own work. To Lubimov, who was drawn especially to Hinduism and Zen, it seemed in hindsight as if "Eastern philosophy and religion [had been] the principal basis for all the changes" in his creative life of the time, "since the search for spiritual sustenance and meaning in life was never disconnected from performance."[48] Pärt, too, has described his musical experiments as reflections or even by-products of a deeper, spiritual searching—in his case, of a distinctly Christian variety. "I believe that this music was so attractive to me," he has said of his study of medieval musics in the 1970s, "not because of music but rather because of religion. For me, religion was the principal problem, and in Gregorian chant I found what I was thirsting for."[49]

Lubimov was not the only artist to find spiritual sustenance and creative inspiration by looking eastward—or at least to an imaginary "East," typically mediated through the work of other artists and writers. For ages, Russia and the Soviet Union have been objects of Western artists' orientalist fantasies. But the brand of orientalism that coursed through alternative Soviet artistic circles was wholly of a piece with contemporary Euro-American trends, with connections forged via books, recordings, and even personal contacts established through artistic exchanges.[50] After meeting the composer Karlheinz Stockhausen in 1968, Lubimov received from his West German colleague a copy of a book by the Hindu philosopher Sri Aurobindo. Soon he began compiling a samizdat library of kindred titles: by the German mystic Meister Eckhart, by the Zen philosopher Daisetz Suzuki.[51] Lediņš's creative searching was not tied to religion in a structured way, but he too was drawn to imaginary Asian locales. Recording his piano composition *Kuncendorf's China Notes* (he titled the work in English) on reel-to-reel tape in February 1978, he proclaimed what would become a lifelong fascination with an idea of China, a place "understood not as a concrete geographical or political entity, but as a kind of ideal state that everyone strives to attain in their life."[52] A samizdat translation of R. H. Blyth's *Zen and Zen Classics* (1960–73) is said to have circulated widely in Riga.[53] But it was Cage's work—in the USSR as in the West—that provided many with their first taste of Zen.

Copies of Cage's breakout book, *Silence* (1961), could be hard to come by in the USSR. But Lubimov had begun performing Cage's music already in the 1960s, and he quickly became, as William Quillen notes, one of the most important mediators of Cage's ideas in the Soviet world. In an encyclopedia entry he authored on the composer in 1974, Lubimov described not only Cage's music but also his Zen commitments. Anticipating Martynov's much later remarks on "discrediting the principle of self-expression" in art, Lubimov observed that "Cage strives to separate form and sound from every sort of imported content, whether rational or emotional."[54] Cage's ideas also received coverage in a book by a Russian literary scholar that attained iconic status in alternative circles. As the journalist Andrew Solomon reports, "everyone" in the Moscow art scene seemed to be reading Yevgeniya Zavadskaya's *The East in the West* (1970) for years and even decades after its publication, all the way into the time of perestroika. The Lithuanian musicologist Rūta Stanevičiūtė recalls that she read it, too, as a teenager in Vilnius.[55]

Touching briefly on Cage's philosophies in *The East in the West* (whose title was likely taken from an essay by Cage in the journal *Asian Music*), Zavadskaya delved more deeply into his ideas in her follow-up book of 1977, *The Culture of the East in the Contemporary Western World*.[56] There she elaborated a distinctly Soviet reading of Cage's aesthetic theory, one that emphasized communal experience as the core of its spiritual import. Through his work, Zavadskaya wrote, Cage sought to inspire a sense of personal connectedness to the "deep unity of the human spirit [*dukh*], which is disclosed everywhere and in every moment, and which music is called upon to express—bringing into balance self and other, the present moment and eternity."[57] Alexei Yurchak writes of a pervasive searching for "deep truths" in artistic projects of the 1970s, a wrestling with "problems and concerns that transcended any given social world or historic period."[58] In Zavadskaya's Cage, in Groys's writings, in the music of Pärt and Martynov's friends, we find innumerable examples of such searching for transcendent truths. As the painter Vladimir Yankilevsky writes of his own experiments of these years, he sought in his art to capture something of "the image of a person against the background of eternity."[59]

The pervasiveness, even the ubiquitous nature of such broadly spiritual searching can go a long way toward helping us understand why so many artists were so powerfully attracted to Pärt and his music in these years. Not only did the resonant harmony of his new tintinnabuli style comport with the distinctly postmodernist, often pop-inflected aesthetics that many young artists were exploring on their own, but the spiritual commitments for which he was already famous intersected with theirs, at least in a general way. The fact that Pärt's latest stylistic

turn was inspired by his religious awakening only deepened the sense
of identification some felt with him. In at least one important respect,
however, Pärt's religious engagements were different from those of his
mostly younger peers. For his tintinnabuli style of composing was, for
him, an expression of specifically Christian devotion. As if to make the
point crystal clear, among his works performed at the Riga festival of
1977 was a choral setting of the Latin mass, a text that stands at the very
heart of the Catholic liturgical rite. Even after Izmailovsky, when Kabakov's "line of fear" had begun its descent, the performance of *that* kind
of music remained impossible, unimaginable within the confines of acceptable, mainstream Soviet society. To arrange such a performance,
one would need to find a location somewhere off the radar, unnoticed
or unmonitored by authorities charged with policing ideologically dubious behavior. To find such a space, one needed to go underground.

UNDERGROUND SPACES

What cemented Pärt's reputation as an artist on a spiritual quest was
one of the most notorious events in the history of alternative music
in the USSR, the Tallinn premiere of his *Credo* for chorus and orchestra in November 1968. Conducted by the celebrated Neeme Järvi and
broadcast live on Estonian Radio, *Credo* opens with this line: "I believe
in Jesus Christ." To this day, we do not know how the work came to be
performed. Stories vary. Some say that the performance fell in a period
when key figures in the Estonian SSR Philharmonic (the state organization charged with planning and producing concerts) and the Ministry of Culture were traveling or otherwise distracted by other projects.
Pärt recounts that members of the Estonian SSR Composers' Union
charged with previewing the piece "felt good about" its musical quotations from works by J. S. Bach and "thought the text was completely
harmless, presumably because it was in Latin."[60] In any case, the performance went ahead. For the Estonian musicologist Toomas Siitan,
the most remarkable thing about the *Credo* premiere was that "in the
Soviet Union of that period, such an unambiguous proclamation of
[Pärt's] way of thinking signaled a deliberate parting with official ideology."[61] Shortly afterward, Pärt was harassed and interrogated by a
parade of officials. But as the Russian scholar Svetlana Savenko recalls,

the officials' response backfired: it helped make Pärt into an international star, stoking fascination with his music at home and abroad.[62]

Pärt joined the Orthodox Church in 1972—a move, we will see, without which his discovery of the tintinnabuli style would have been unthinkable.[63] But he began studying Western medieval repertoires—largely sacred repertoires, including Gregorian chant—several years before that. Later he came to understand those studies as reflections of a spiritual search of which he himself was only dimly aware at the time. To study Gregorian chant was one thing, however. To compose and perform a work like *Credo* was something else entirely, and the fallout from its premiere contributed to the great creative crisis of his life. While he continued to compose, following the *Credo* scandal the vast majority of his work was for film.[64] He would not come forward with another openly devotional work until *Sarah* in 1976. All the while, his private engagement with Christian texts and practice, and ultimately with Orthodox practice, was becoming more and more intense. Between 1968 and 1976, he effectively led a double life.

To be clear, Christian devotional music never completely disappeared from Soviet concert halls. Even at the height of the Stalinist terror, the country's premiere orchestras and choirs performed sacred music by Bach, Mozart, Handel and other Western classics.[65] Much later, in 1964, the New York early music ensemble Pro Musica visited Moscow and inspired a flurry of interest in pre-Baroque musics, including Christian musics, performed on period instruments and often in period-inspired costumes. That year, the composer and keyboardist Andrei Volkonsky founded the early music ensemble Madrigal in Moscow. In 1972, Andres Mustonen founded a similar group in Tallinn, Hortus Musicus.[66] From the start, the audience for early music overlapped substantially with the audience for experimental music, as did many of the performers—as audience members widely noticed and still recall today. (Volkonsky, for instance, was also a leading composer in the 1960s avant-garde, and Lubimov played in Madrigal.) Many heard early and new music alike as exciting alternatives to the usual Socialist Realist fare.[67] Much of the music played by Soviet early music groups was sacred. When Hortus Musicus gave the official premiere of Pärt's *Tintinnabuli* suite in October 1976, it was paired with Guillaume Dufay's fifteenth-century *L'homme armé* mass (see fig. 1.2).

But, significantly, all of the sacred music performed was centuries old and Western. Like Orthodox music generally, sacred works that were newly composed or set to Russian texts were avoided, either out of caution or because of outright prohibitions.[68]

This does not mean that Soviet artists did not write sacred music or participate in private religious study, as Pärt did. But to engage in such practices publicly was, as Yurchak observes, substantially outside the bounds of what constituted "normal" behavior for a Soviet citizen. "Religion was tolerated by the state but disconnected from state institutions (education, media, industry, public associations, army, bureaucracy, etc.)." Its practice was "tolerated but viewed with suspicion and hostility."[69] Like Pärt, the violinist Tatiana Grindenko, one of the dedicatees of *Tabula rasa*, also led a double life in the early 1970s. While a standout student at the Moscow Conservatory, she sang in the choir of an Orthodox church, unbeknownst to teachers and friends. "Since I was in a scarf," she recalls, "nobody would recognize me."[70] In his memoirs, Kabakov links this kind of quiet religious practice to a subculture of "underground art," which persisted throughout the Brezhnev years and all the way into the time of perestroika, with openly religious content being one of the few things that still compelled artists to hide or disguise the nature of their work.[71] Among painters, a handful of artists engaged in projects that verged upon Pärt's in terms of religious commitment (we'll visit one in chapter 3). Among composers, no one really matched him in terms of the explicit nature of his liturgical engagements or the public nature of his pronouncements in this time. Schnittke, perhaps, came closest, along with Gubaidulina. As it happened, Schnittke's journey intersected directly with Pärt's at what would prove to be a decisive moment in the Estonian composer's career.

Although he wasn't baptized until much later (in Vienna, in 1982), Schnittke hazarded, in 1966, a boldly devotional project with his Second Violin Concerto, in which he sought to follow "unerringly" a Biblical Passion narrative of Christ's death and resurrection. As a concerto, the work had no text, so the link between its sounds and any such narrative was ambiguous and deniable. Even the violinist Mark Lubotsky, who gave the premiere, did not discover until years afterward what Schnittke had intended.[72] A more overt statement came a decade later, when Schnittke composed a requiem mass for choir, vocal soloists, and an eclectic ensemble of instruments (percussion-heavy, with electric guitar and bass). For his text, Schnittke followed closely the portions of the Latin requiem famously set by Mozart and Franz Xavier Süssmayr, with the key addition of the Nicene Creed, *Credo in unum Deum*: "I believe in one God." Significantly, Schnittke's Requiem was officially acceptable in its original form, for he had composed it not as a stand-alone piece but as incidental music for a production of Friedrich Schiller's *Don Carlos*, to be staged by Moscow's prestigious Mossovet Theater. In that context, the sacred content was justified by the dramatic requirements of the play. Three years later, Schnittke revised his requiem for concert use, but it seems to have been performed only once as such prior to the 1980s: in Tallinn in February 1976, with Tõnu Kaljuste on the podium.[73] After that concert, Schnittke reportedly traveled to Riga to attend a meeting with the Composers' Union of the Latvian SSR. While in town, Lediņš is said to have persuaded him to visit his disco in the city's former Anglican Church, to lecture on his requiem and play a recording from the Tallinn concert.[74] Two months later, in that very church, Pärt's *Sarah* would have its premiere.

Pärt and Schnittke met in Tallinn while rehearsals for the requiem's concert performance were underway. Looking back, Pärt recalls the encounter as crucial for having given him the courage to bring his first tintinnabuli-style compositions before the public. Pärt acknowledged the debt at the time by dedicating *Calix* (1976) to his friend from Moscow, explaining that Schnittke's Requiem had inspired his choice of instrumentation.[75] But the courage Pärt received from Schnittke surely extended to the domain of religious engagement as well, for *Calix* was composed as a setting of the *Dies irae* hymn, a portion of the requiem mass that Schnittke had also set. Pärt's work was performed just three times before he withdrew it from public circulation, and each time the choir sang solfege syllables in place of the sacred text.[76] In sharp contrast, Pärt made no effort to disguise his *Missa syllabica* when it was premiered at the Riga festival in 1977. There, the text of the Latin mass was openly sung by the choir. And significantly, unlike Schnittke's Requiem, the *Missa syllabica* did not originate as incidental music (although, as we'll see, a dubious connection to a film would later be claimed). Put simply, the *Missa syllabica* was liturgical music, nothing more and nothing less. As if to sharpen the point, it was preceded on the Riga festival program by the premiere of *Summa*, Pärt's choral setting of the Nicene Creed. To arrange for the public performance of such ideologically unacceptable music as this, care had to be taken to assure that it wouldn't attract the attention of Soviet officialdom, and that required the help of a carefully orchestrated team of individuals. First and foremost, it required an organizer able to find and exploit some useful gaps in the bureaucratic machinery. That figure, in this case, was Hardijs Lediņš.

FINDING THE GAPS

In their accounts of the 1968 premiere of *Credo*, Pärt and others point to a classic way in which potentially fertile gaps could be found in the facade of Soviet bureaucracy. Those individuals involved in organizing the project simply waited for potentially antagonistic officials to leave town. Recalling preparations for the concert, Pärt remembers that his nemesis in the Composers' Union was absent from the organization's meeting on the very day when *Credo* was considered for performance. Others recall that a number of key officials were away on cultural exchanges to Uzbekistan or the GDR.[77] Sometimes, even when officials were present, their oversight was marginal at best. The violinist Donatus Katkus of the Vilnius String Quartet, which played at the 1977 Riga festival, recalls that concert programs approved in advance could often be changed by performers at the last minute. When sitting down to present a program of music by Tchaikovsky and Myaskovsky, say, he or his colleagues would simply announce from the stage, "Oh, Myaskovsky won't be played tonight," and then they would play Pärt instead. To officials, Katkus explains, it often made no difference. "They didn't know Myaskovsky, and they didn't know Pärt." Moreover, he adds, the officials were often drunk. Echoing a refrain that Schmelz has heard from Lubimov, Grindenko, and the percussionist Mark Pekarsky, Katkus summarized: "We were crazy. We played whatever we wanted."[78]

Another way in which opportunities to engage in unsanctioned activity could be found consisted in taking advantage of the sometimes ambiguous overlap of authority granted to the various administrative units charged with overseeing different spheres of cultural life. In Riga, the Latvian Ministry of Culture supervised the activities of the Latvian SSR Philharmonic Chamber Orchestra more or less directly. But the city's *other* professional orchestra—the Latvian Symphony, officially called the Latvian SSR Radio and Television Symphony Orchestra—was overseen by a different body, the State Committee for Radio and Television, and it seems to have operated at least somewhat independently of direct oversight by the Ministry of Culture. During planning for the Riga Polytechnic festival of 1976, Avramecs recalls, ministry officials prohibited musicians from the Philharmonic Chamber Orchestra (including Avramecs) from taking part. In response, festival organizers turned to musicians employed by the Latvian Symphony instead, thereby sidestepping (apparently) notice by the Ministry of Culture.[79] These sorts of ambiguous overlaps in bureaucratic authority could be leveraged in all kinds of ways. For instance, in Riga as elsewhere in the USSR, performances of work by professional composers were coordinated by local composers' unions. But Lediņš, who composed a great deal of music, was an architecture student (and later theorist) by profession, and thus his musical activities seem to have gone completely unnoticed by Composers' Union officials.

Other factors that made possible the concerts at which Pärt's sacred music was performed include the political, social, and economic climates in the Baltic capitals themselves, where state institutions were often staffed and sometimes led by figures who asserted a remarkable degree of autonomy with respect to higher-level bureaucracies in Moscow. Both Latvia and Estonia had been independent republics prior to their annexation by the USSR in World War II, and a culture of self-conscious difference vis-à-vis Soviet Russia could be felt in many aspects of daily and institutional life—as Russian visitors to the region sometimes noted.[80] The busy ports of Riga and Tallinn provided access to LPs, technologies, and foreign tourists, and Tallinn's residents could tune into radio and even television broadcast from Helsinki (many Estonian speakers can understand Finnish). In Estonia, the University of Tartu was home to a thriving hippie culture. Riga was home to a black market for pirated copies of Western recordings that drew buyers from as far away as Smolensk.[81] Both cities were renowned as hotbeds of Soviet rock and roll in the 1960s and as points of origin for the disco craze that would sweep across the union in the later 1970s.[82] All of these things made the cities magnets for creative individuals from throughout the USSR. As Grindenko recalls of her own impressions of Tallinn in these years, it "was known as a city where the impossible was always just a little bit more possible."[83]

Blurring or transgressing the boundaries between musical idioms was another way to open spaces for experimental work. While the performance of classical music by professional musicians was overseen by composers' unions and regional philharmonics, rock concerts were typically coordinated through the Communist youth league, Komsomol. While highly professionalized in its upper, centralized tiers, Komsomol authority was usually delegated at local levels—at the level of the Riga Polytechnic, for instance—to "unprofessional" figures, as Yurchak calls them, individuals (unsalaried, typically students) who were appointed "not necessarily because they displayed some extraordinary ideological activism and loyalty but because they enjoyed organizing people and orchestrating social activities, they were seen by teachers and peers as responsible people, or they simply were unlikely to turn down requests."[84] To participate in the polytechnic festivals of 1976–77, Martynov traveled to Riga not as a representative of the Composers' Union but as a member of the rock band Boomerang (*Bumerang*), which operated out of the Skriabin Studio. He attended the Tallinn festival of 1978 as a member of another rock band, Outpost (*Forpost*). At the time, the Komsomol office at the Riga Polytechnic was renowned for its support of student musicians and activists, organizing such events as an annual DJ competition that drew contestants from Moscow and Tashkent.[85] As we will see, Lediņš was adept at working productively with Komsomol representatives, gaining not only their acquiescence but their enthusiastic support for his disco and music festival projects.

Of course, genre boundaries were transgressed for aesthetic reasons as well, and to some extent just about every figure in this book considered the sounds of rock a resource to be mined in their own creative projects. In this way, their work again crossed paths with experimental musicians in Western spaces, some of whom, like Laurie Anderson in New York and the band Henry Cow in the UK (both followed by Lediņš), were simultaneously exploring cross-pollinations of classical and popular idioms.[86] Picking up on the model of Schnittke's

Requiem, Pärt scored *Calix* for electric guitar and bass, and the Tallinn premiere of *Modus* featured an extended electric-guitar break at its climactic moment.[87] Avramecs remembers attending a concert at the Skriabin Museum where a rock band, probably Outpost, performed Martynov's arrangement of Renaissance works by the English composer William Byrd, attesting again to the crossing of genres and also of audiences for early and avant-garde music.[88]

To some, British progressive rock in particular appealed not only for its complex forms, novel arrangements, and blending of acoustic and electronic sounds, but also for its practitioners' ambitions to inspire self-awareness, social engagement, and even spiritual enlightenment through collaborative, improvisatory performance. Martynov, Grindenko, and Lediņš shared a love—bordering on obsession—with King Crimson and their guitarist Robert Fripp in particular. "I was certain that rock was connected not only to a fundamental renewal of music," Martynov recalls, "but to a revitalization of life itself."[89] Others simply considered the erecting of fences between rock and classical music to be arbitrary or old-fashioned. As the composer Georgs Pelēcis, a regular at the Skriabin Museum's nighttime listening sessions, recounts of his friends' preoccupation with progressive rock, "For us, that *was* new music."[90] Lediņš, we will see, began his compositional journey trying to imitate the avant-garde sounds of Cage, Stockhausen, and early Silvestrov. But soon his work came to evince a distinctly rock-inflected sensibility, ranging from the repetitive melodic gestures of *Kuncendorf's China Notes* (1978) to the polished, synth-pop stylings of his magnitizdat album *Medicine and Art* (1985).[91] With typical absurdist humor, he described his view of the boundary between classical and popular music in an imaginary newspaper article he penned as a student in the mid-1970s, reporting on the opinions of a fictitious elder composer:

> Our correspondent recently interviewed our city's distinguished composer B. Vienpadsmitštoku [roughly, "B. Elevenfloors"]. In frank conversation, the artist shared his thoughts about light and serious music. He said: "Light music is and always will be light music, and serious music is and always will be serious. Just like eleven times eleven is and always will be a hundred twenty-one. But if we

take the square root of a hundred twenty-one, we come back again to eleven. And that is very important, regardless of whether the music is light or serious."[92]

The distinction, for Lediņš, was as absurd as it was incomprehensible—*and irrelevant.*

COMMUNITIES

"The regime seemed eternal," the painter Ivan Chuikov recalled of his life in 1970s Moscow. "No one had any illusions that it would ever be brought down. But we had our own fenced-off domain of freedom, of relations with friends, of understanding." He continued:

> An artist involved with official structures always had to be concerned with what was permissible and what was not permissible. But for us, those problems did not exist. We lived outside of that system, untroubled by those problems. . . . We had personal freedom as artists, and also freedom within the community. Within our circle or community of artists, you lived as if in a normal, free society. Socially, you were free.[93]

In this passage, Chuikov describes an instance of what Yurchak calls an "ideology of everyday existence vis-à-vis the political sphere of the state," where people lived life in such a way that they "simply did not notice" the political apparatus operating behind the scenes. In turn, that apparatus (ideally, at least) took no notice of them.[94] Theoretically, an individual might have lived in such a manner while not identifying as a member of any particular group. But in nearly every firsthand account of alternative art scenes of the 1970s, living this "ideology of everyday existence" was something undertaken within a community. In hindsight, the communal nature of artistic activity can even seem to have been more important than any artworks produced in themselves. As Avramecs has described the Riga festivals of 1976–77, they were spaces in which "people sought to make connections with like-minded individuals, to feel that they were not alone."[95]

The importance accorded to communal activity in the late Soviet art world has been explored at length by the critic Victor Tupitsyn, who invokes the metaphor of the commune to link this collective sensibility to a line of Russian social theory extending back through postwar Stalinism to the religious and political polemics of a range of nineteenth-century writers. For Tupitsyn, the "great experiment" of Stalinism consisted foremost in the project of "mass communalization." The goal was "'de-individualizing' the consciousness and daily life of the Soviet people," with the principal vehicle employed to that end being the collectivization of living space in the urban environment. (The collectivization of agriculture was its counterpart beyond the city.)[96] A building boom in the Khrushchev years alleviated much of the postwar housing shortage, with massive housing blocks rising in suburbs from Tallinn to Vladivostok. But Tupitsyn suggests that communally oriented habits of thinking endured: while artists and their families moved to private flats, they simultaneously clustered in shared studios, which "became the incubators for developing new forms of relations in the art world." With the weakening of institutionally imposed "communality" during the Thaw, a "contractual" or intellectual form of the same took root, as artists and others united together around shared concerns, desires, or antagonisms. This "principle of *optional* communalization," Tupitsyn suggests, "became the ecological niche for Muscovite alternative art over the course of three decades— right up to perestroika."[97]

Just what these "optional" communities coalesced around is the subject of much of Yurchak's anthropological work, and what he finds are some of the very things that united the group of musicians considered in this book. Namely, Yurchak writes of individuals who, even in the 1970s and 1980s, were inspired by and remained deeply committed to ideals that had animated the Soviet socialist project since its earliest, revolutionary days. "For great numbers of Soviet citizens," he observes,

> many of the fundamental values, ideals, and realities of socialist life (such as equality, community, selflessness, altruism, friendship, ethical relations, safety, education, work, creativity and concern for the future) were of genuine importance. . . . For many, "socialism" as a system of human values and as an everyday reality of "normal

life" was not necessarily equivalent to "the state" or "ideology"; indeed, living socialism to them often meant something quite different from the official interpretations provided by state rhetoric.[98]

It was this sense of dissonance, this yawning chasm between the enlightening promise of Soviet socialism and the reality of what the system had actually delivered that inspired and animated countless artistic works and the formation of creative collectives in the 1970s, including the discotheques, festivals, and other events in which Pärt's sacred tintinnabuli project began. Yurchak makes a similar point about the Leningrad performance artists on whom his recent research has focused:

> While the Soviet bureaucratic system in its late period employed many ideological slogans of revolutionary times, that system had already lost the original ethos of experimentation, sincerity and genuine commitment to the future that existed during the early period. However, that ethos survived in various forms in mundane Soviet life even during late socialism *in spite* of the stagnant bureaucratic party system. One place where it survived was informal Soviet art.[99]

Chuikov's recollections are a case in point. Neither the painter nor his friends desired or even thought about working to undermine the Soviet system. And, despite their attraction to such Western artists as King Crimson and John Cage, they were decidedly *not* seeking simply to emulate the sounds, art forms, or social structures of the West in their work. Rather, they were trying, through their collective projects, to invest in the Soviet world itself: to make their lives together richer, more beautiful, more fulfilling. In an interview with a West German art historian in 1988, this point was made plainly by the Latvian poet and musician Juris Boiko, Lediņš's lifelong collaborator whom we'll meet in chapter 2. "What, then, is socialism?" Boiko asked rhetorically. "It is social life. It is active contacts between individuals."[100]

Of course, just as Stalin's collectivization campaigns were attempts to realize, however inhumanely, one particular vision of postwar utopia, so too is there a heady dose of utopianism in the nostalgic recollections of Chuikov and others.[101] But as Solomon observes of a number of alternative Soviet artists on the brink of the empire's collapse in 1991, they still, even then, forthrightly evinced a "serious engagement with the idea of utopia, shimmeringly bright."[102] Reflecting on his collaborations with Lediņš, Boiko described their creative projects as so deeply rooted in a vision of communality that their individual contributions simply seemed to disappear. And he was unabashed in describing their work as paving the way toward a brighter future. Referring to their partnership as a metaphorical "workshop," Boiko observed:

> In this case, to speak about the members of the "workshop" separately is meaningless, because the "workshop" cannot be divided into separate components. At the same time, it cannot be called a simple collaboration. What the "workshop" reveals in its daily activities is the individual and the intimate, not within ourselves but between us and around us.[103]

Asked about his work in the broadest sense, he continued: "You could say that it is the artist's mission to prepare for the future. And preparing for the future means bringing a utopian element [*utopisches Element*] into the here and now."[104] As we will see, Pärt's music provided a focal point and soundtrack around which a community of musicians coalesced in an avowedly utopian, experimental effort to make their world a better place. In the expansive sounds of its musical textures and the resonance of its quasi-modal harmonies, many heard echoes of an "elsewhere" or an "otherwise," of a deeply longed-for *beyond*. The spaces and places they imagined varied widely across members of the group, but they all had things in common. Together, they listened beyond the discomfiting noise of contemporary urban life, beyond the esoteric sounds of the postwar avant-garde, beyond the overly familiar tropes of much official Soviet music—even, in the arc of its sonic prayer, beyond the sounds of the world itself. In doing so, they found themselves in an open space, in an underground space, of communion.

TWO

A BEGINNING

The Riga Polytechnic Disco, 1974–76

"Like mushrooms after the rain, like rain after a hot day: that's how discotheques are springing up today." With metaphors of inevitability and the satisfaction of pent-up desire, Hardijs Lediņš (1955–2004) described the rise of disco culture in the journal of the Latvian Komsomol, a culture he did more to shape than anyone else in the republic, maybe the empire.[1] In the winter of 1975, while a second-year student of architecture at the Riga Polytechnic Institute (RPI), Lediņš made his debut as DJ at a disco held in the school's Student Club. Within a year, his discotheques were drawing students from throughout the city and beyond, tickets selling out within minutes, a line snaking out the door (fig. 2.1).

Arvo Pärt's *Sarah Was Ninety Years Old*, a wordless work with an Old Testament title and the first to which the composer appended the label "tintinnabuli," had its first public performance in April 1976 under the auspices of Lediņš's Riga discotheque. Eighteen months later, at a festival of new music produced by Lediņš and hosted by his disco, Pärt's *Missa syllabica*, a plainly liturgical composition, was unveiled. In a book focused largely on these and other works by Pärt, one might expect to start with something the composer himself attempted. In this chapter I take another path, exploring another beginning: the coalescence of an alternative music scene without which Pärt's tintinnabuli project—a self-consciously devotional project—might well have never gotten a hearing. At least not in the USSR.

FIGURE 2.1 Hardijs Lediņš behind the turntable at an RPI discotheque, mid-1970s. Photographer unknown. Collection of the Latvian Centre for Contemporary Art. Courtesy of Pēteris Lediņš.

The Soviet disco craze of the 1970s did not start with Lediņš, and it was not unique to the Latvian capital. By the early 1980s, it would sweep the whole of the Soviet Union, with its possibly dangerous music—and also its potential for cultivating a population of morally and politically upstanding youth—vigorously debated in homes, the press, and even halls of government.[2] The historian Sergei Zhuk, who both studied and lived the Soviet disco phenomenon, reports that 187 discotheques had been registered with the Moscow Komsomol by the end of 1978 in that city alone, and there were known to be over 300 discos active in Latvia at that time.[3] In New York, London, and other Western locales, the disco experience was focused almost exclusively on dancing. But many Soviet discos were different, featuring dancing only in their second half, after an opening portion in which seated attendees would listen together to live or recorded music, and often to lectures by the DJ or guests about what they were hearing. The Russian journalist Artemy Troitsky claims to have pioneered this kind of "stationary" disco, as Lediņš called it, in Moscow in 1972, where it did not immediately catch on. But Lediņš was a master of the form, which quickly took root in Latvia and Estonia and spread from there across the USSR in the second half of the decade.[4]

Much of the music played and discussed at Lediņš's discotheque was British and West German progressive rock, but it also included jazz, classical, and avant-garde music. Whatever his topic, Lediņš took seriously the project of educating his audience, preparing and reading lectures from manuscript that required days or even weeks of research, often making use of materials exceedingly hard to come by in the USSR. Writing of youth rock culture in the final years of the Soviet Union, the anthropologist Thomas Cushman catalogs among its hallmarks "a comprehensive and sophisticated knowledge of Western culture, the creative and often ingenious deployment of that culture as a means of crafting an alternative identity within the space of Soviet society, [and] a commitment to a sense of individual calling as the source of creative inspiration."[5] As a DJ, Lediņš exhibited all of these traits and more. Without his organizational talents, social network, family ties, and the loosely monitored spaces afforded by his discotheque, it is hard to imagine how Pärt's sacred music would ever have received its first performances in Soviet spaces. Before turning to Pärt's achievement directly, we should, I think, consider that of Lediņš: his discos, and the open spaces for experiment, expression, and communion they provided.

ENTER THE DJ

Lediņš's path to the polytechnic was both natural and miraculous, for his creative gifts were as apparent in high school as was his disregard for social norms. Together with his lifelong collaborator, the poet and musician Juris Boiko (1954–2002), he made his public debut as an artist by creating and distributing to classmates a series of homemade journals under the title *Zirkahbols*—Latvian for "horse shit," rendered in their personalized, esoteric orthography. To judge from the single extant issue—labeled "Nº 11" in the run, the rest (reportedly) having been confiscated and presumably destroyed by the KGB—*Zirkahbols* consisted of collages of clippings from historical publications interspersed with hand-drawn illustrations and absurdist statements. Once discovered, these things struck school officials as highly suspect: "satire for or against something," as they explained in disciplinary actions taken against the duo in February 1973.[6] For what was deemed the subversive political work of compiling their journal, Boiko was sentenced to military service upon graduation. Lediņš, whose mother had ministerial ties that would profoundly shape the range of opportunities afforded to her son, was spared the fate of his friend. At the end of their senior year, Boiko shipped out to the Kazakh border. Lediņš moved across town to the prestigious Riga Polytechnic Institute to study architectural theory.

Despite the physical distance between them, Lediņš and Boiko kept up their production of homemade journals over the course of the 1973–74 academic year, sending issues of various successors to *Zirkahbols* back and forth through the mail between Riga and Rubtsovsk.[7] In a new journal they called *WCZLS*—an acronym, again using an eccentric orthography, for *My, What a Green Umbrella!*—their passion for music became clear. An early issue of *WCZLS* included a column headed "Pop Music News" (*popmuhsikas jaunumi*), which referenced the British magazine *Melody Maker* and reported on cancelations of imaginary Riga concerts by Pink Floyd, Roxy Music, and the band Chicago.[8] The journal's fifth volume, from 1974, advertised a fictitious upcoming concert by one "A. Lichtenberg & seine Gruppe," supposedly to be held in the fish pavilion of Riga's central market.[9] Later that year, in yet another homemade journal, *The Riesling Brothers on Tour in Latgalia!* (its title was penned in English), Lediņš and Boiko compiled a "Top-74" list of fictitious bands and songs in the "Mestnij" category ("local," in Russian: *mestnyi*), along with a list of their actual favorites under the English heading "International." The latter included Peter Gabriel, Greg Lake, and Jon Anderson of Yes. Two of their top five albums were by King Crimson: *Starless and Bible Black* (#1) and *Red* (#3). Best of all, they loved Robert Fripp, King Crimson's founder and lead guitar player, who took the top spot on both their "guitar" and "komposer" lists.[10]

For the historian Ivars Ījabs, these ads and lists produced by the duo made ironic "play" of the "chasm between the provincial culture of the USSR and the global 'normality' of the West, smuggled in from abroad."[11] They also made clear the remarkable breadth of their knowledge of, even fluency with, Western rock. They seemed, at this time, to have had no genuine interest in popular musics produced locally, either in Latvia or in the greater Soviet Union. The pathways through which they acquired their knowledge of Western music are complex and partly obscure. Years before a broadly resonant rock journalism took root in the Soviet Union (in the form of the widely distributed samizdat journal *Roksi*, produced in Leningrad under the direction of Boris Grebenshchikov of the band Akvarium starting in 1977), Lediņš began mining the record and magazine collections of the Latvian Conservatory and National Library. His reading is documented in a handwritten alphabetical index he compiled of *Melody Maker* going back to 1970.[12] (The high school he and Boiko attended offered instruction in German; and, as Boiko's brother Martin explains, many in their circle taught themselves to read English.)[13] He might also have frequented Riga's famous black market for pirated cassettes, which Yurchak and others recall as drawing young people from hundreds of miles away.[14]

Some suggest that Lediņš's mother, Rute Lediņa, was a source of recordings and information. A journalist and translator, she worked as host of a radio program called *Amber Coast* (*Dzintarkrasts*), which broadcast Soviet propaganda to Latvian émigrés in Scandinavia. The show was a project of an office called the Committee for Cultural Relations with Compatriots Abroad. Ostensibly a nongovernmental organization, her office, as the Latvian historian Ieva Zake documents, was "in reality . . . part of the Latvian KGB."[15] Officially, the organization employed only about a dozen individuals, but its staff was augmented significantly by artists and academics who volunteered their time and efforts in exchange for the opportunities for foreign travel that work for the office provided. Rute's ties to state security likely accounted for the starkly different fates experienced by Hardijs and Juris in the wake of the high school fiasco surrounding their production of the *Zirkah-bols* journals. (Protocols from their hearing indicate that they were tried as a pair.) Her foreign travels and the elite, cosmopolitan circles she traveled in would also have provided ready-made avenues for acquiring records, publications, and technologies from the West. In turn, the protections afforded by her employment might later have offered a degree of protection not only to her son but to the community of musicians drawn to Lediņš's disco (Pärt among them), and to the sometimes provocative creative projects they undertook in that space.[16]

School notebooks from the 1975–76 academic year at RPI testify to Lediņš's reading and listening, and to the degree to which his musical interests had already eclipsed his architectural studies by that time. Amid notes he took while attending lectures on structures, acoustics, and other technical subjects, his doodling and marginal notations inscribe his mind's wanderings: various listings of bands and acts, a definition of John Cage-inspired Happenings. A reference to the British experimental band Henry Cow. In the midst of a lecture on thermodynamics, in stylized, all-caps lettering: *JAM SESSION*. In a lecture on principles of architectural lighting: *J. S. BACH*.[17]

Although he never articulated things in quite this way, the bands and acts that spoke to Lediņš most directly seem to have had some things in common: complex arrangements, often featuring extended passages of improvisation; instrumental tracks or extended instrumental intros or interludes, often combining electronic sounds with orchestral instruments; and lyrics that were both occasional and oblique. Henry Cow's album *Unrest* (1974), for instance, is impossible to pin down, occupying some inarticulable space on the rock/free-jazz/avant-garde spectrum (a "vernacular avant-garde," Benjamin Piekut calls their music).[18] One of Lediņš's favorite albums, Robert Wyatt's *Rock Bottom* (1974), is anchored by the epic "Little Red Riding Hood Hit the Road," where a choir of trumpets plays loosely coordinated riffs for minutes before an impossibly stilted speaking voice comes in with remarks about how he'll "give it to you back [*what?*] when I finish the manuscript [*what??*]." The title track on King Crimson's *Red* is an aggressive display of Fripp's solo guitar work, the meter shifting from five to six to four beats per measure from bar to bar. As Zhuk would describe it, Lediņš's taste in music planted him firmly on the "intellectual" side of Soviet listening culture of the period, with a clear majority of young people preferring more accessible, danceable Western pop by such mainstream bands as Queen and Slade.[19] In contrast, one can imagine Lediņš's attraction to the complex, largely instrumental work of Henry Cow and King Crimson as paving the way for his emergent interest in contemporary classical music, already evinced in fleeting references to Cage in his school notebooks.

At the start of the 1974–75 school year, Aina Bērziņa, president of the RPI Student Club, used her column in the student paper to announce a new initiative, the polytechnic discotheque:

This year, the Student Club is organizing something new: the discotheque. It will be a new kind of recreational evening for students, distinguished from typical events by virtue of the fact that a significant portion of our attention will be on the educational part of evening. We'll strive to acquaint ourselves with the newest jazz, estrada [a variety of mainstream Soviet popular music], and pop. We'll organize meetings with experts and discuss subjects of vital interest today. In this way, the events will constitute something new at our institution.[20]

The idea behind an "educational" RPI disco did not come from Lediņš. Another student, Edmunds Štreihfelds, had experienced such events while visiting East Germany and approached the management of the Student Club about the possibility of starting something similar at home. Although Bērziņa announced a launch in the fall, the project she and Štreihfelds envisioned took months to get off the ground, with the first event being scheduled only in February 1975. Štreihfelds was the official convener, but Lediņš was DJ from the start. Held once or twice a month thereafter, the polytechnic disco was soon identified with the architecture student himself.[21]

An early, undated program for one of Lediņš's discotheque presentations gives a sense of the ambitious—maybe impossibly ambitious—scope of the events as he initially imagined them. His plan for the "stationary" or "educational" first half of the evening included no fewer than eleven topics to be addressed, which he gave as follows:

1. A look at history / Development of music to the 20th century
2. Musical experiments at the start of the century / "The New Viennese School" / A. Schoenberg
3. A. Berg / A. Webern
4. Hindemith / C. Ives
5. O. Messiaen
6. J. Cage / P. Boulez
7. Electronic music / K. Stockhausen
8. "New music" by Polish composers / K. Penderecki / Lutosławski
9. Recent experiments in music

10. The return to early music
11. Music of the East[22]

Marginal jottings on the page include references (again) to Henry Cow and also to the Latvian composer Juris Karlsons. Another discotheque program, from November 1978, might be more representative of the kinds of presentations he typically made:

Part I: Educational
Electronic musical instruments and their use in rock music
  1. Survey of the history of electronic music
  2. K. Stockhausen: one of the founders of electronic music
  3. The group Tangerine Dream, and their electronic rock music
  4. Electronic musical instruments: a new resource in rock music

Part II: Dance music
  The best examples of Soviet and foreign disco music
  Information about recent disco music
  The crisis of punk rock, its reflection in music and society[23]

In both of these programs, his interest in probing the history of contemporary musical developments is clear, as is his resistance to any suggestion that learning about classical music was conceptually distinct from learning to appreciate rock.

Further information about the RPI discos can be gleaned from more detailed notes for two of Lediņš's discotheque lectures, where he interrogated histories of Western music through the prism of Marxist-Leninist critique.[24] He opened one, entitled "Revolution in Music," with this: "Contrary to the widely held view that music is universal, it has always been connected to its specific time, political formation, and social environment. For example, the madrigal as a genre was invented by intellectuals and dilettantes of the Renaissance. And the genre died out as soon as social circumstances changed, which in turn gave rise to opera." In another lecture, called "Culture: Synthetic Ferment of Our Environment," he anticipated some of Vladimir Martynov's statements about the social hierarchies reflected in discourse about Romantic and modernist music. Identifying "three stages in the development" of music as an art form, Lediņš described the earliest stage as one in which "listeners and creators could take pleasure in making music together." In the second, which extended from the eighteenth century through the 1930s, "listeners and creators became separate from each other." With this, he explained, "there coalesced a cult or religion of music." His notes for the lecture cut off at that point, leaving the third stage unknown.

Other lecture scripts preserved from these years focus on individual artists or albums, often mixing biography with observations about genre and social or cultural criticism. Preserved among his papers are a four-page manuscript on Gentle Giant, seven pages on Miles Davis, and a seven-page lecture on Wyatt's *Rock Bottom*.[25] His most expansive set of discotheque notes is a seven-part lecture series on King Crimson, comprising nearly a hundred manuscript pages. In the first installment of the series, he began by observing that contemporary rock and classical music have a great deal in common, including the emergence of "spontaneous improvisation" as an element of both. (Alongside his emerging fascination with Cage, he was drawn to Karlheinz Stockhausen's improvisatory "intuitive music," especially *Aus den sieben Tagen*.) But, he continued, classical music and rock are often distinct with respect to their social or aesthetic "function." Whereas one can regard the principal function of music by popular acts like the Who or Deep Purple as "creat[ing] impressions of strength and elation" in their listeners, the function of Stockhausen's work, in contrast, "is to educate and challenge a thoughtful individual. Roughly speaking, the distinction is one between the body and the mind." And yet, he continued, "there are some [artists] whose function touches on both of these spheres." The prime example, he held, was King Crimson. "King Crimson's music," Lediņš wrote, "could be called the classical-rock music of our age. If Wagner still lived, he would be partnering together with King Crimson."[26]

The outsized presence of King Crimson in the creative imagination of many in Lediņš's circle is clear: as we have seen, his fascination was shared by Martynov and the violinist Tatiana Grindenko, to name just two. As Yurchak documents, King Crimson's music, along with that of some other progressive bands—the electronically manipulated sounds of their instruments and their novel, sometimes unabashedly experimental song forms—"resonated unusually well" in Soviet spaces "with something of which these bands were probably unaware—the futuristic, avant-garde, experimental aesthetics that remained an important part of the ethos of socialism even during the late Soviet period."[27] To Boriss Avramecs, who sometimes provided musical illustrations on his violin for Lediņš's discotheque lectures, his colleagues' obsession with progressive rock signaled something else as well. He explains:

> Art rock, early music, the avant-garde. What was it that united them? First of all, the foundations of all three, whether speaking in terms of construction, meaning, or performance, differed radically from what underlay the music of the Romantic era. And in the context of Soviet culture, which constituted, in large part, an artificially created preserve for nineteenth-century culture and ways of thinking, this anti-Romantic tendency was highly significant.[28]

For Avramecs, a big part of the attraction of King Crimson, no less than Stockhausen or Hortus Musicus, owed to the fact that their music was heard as a radical alternative to the typical Socialist Realist fare pedaled on the radio and at the conservatory. The Estonian musicologist Toomas Siitan concurs, recalling his own experience of "listening discos" at the Tallinn Polytechnic. There, Siitan recalls, he and his friends were just as excited to hear Hortus Musicus as they were to hear the latest Peter Gabriel LP. They "didn't think of it as ideological at all," Siitan says. "It was just rare new music, something real, something fresh."[29]

Lediņš's first season at the helm of the RPI discotheque ran through the end of spring semester 1975. He took a break during the summer. When he returned in the fall, he found that his following had grown substantially in his absence. On September 25, the student paper recounted the excitement that surrounded his first disco of the new year:

> The other night, the hall of the Student Club was completely packed, with a healthy crowd of "unfortunates" gathered outside the doors because it was impossible to fit anyone else inside. Was this some kind of meeting, or a concert? No, it was a discotheque! . . . The evening was opened by the current head of the disco-

theques, Edmunds Štreihfelds, but then the microphone was passed
to the person in charge—the "disc jockey," the architecture student
Hardijs Lediņš. His lecture was accompanied by passages of music and novel lighting effects. . . . Whatever a person's knowledge of
music, it was tested in a little contest afterwards, where questions
were posed about classical and popular music alike. Fans of dance
music were treated to all kinds of recordings. There was nowhere
for boredom to set in this evening. During the brief lulls, students
from various areas of study exchanged words, and there was a lot
to discuss, compare, and assess. Indeed, the assessment was always
high, especially among visitors from the Latvian State University,
who attended our first disco of the year in great numbers. Everyone
wanted to know: What's coming next?[30]

To this question, posed directly by the student journalist, Lediņš
replied in a way that reads as if he had prepared for it in advance. "We
haven't changed the structure of our discotheques at all," he said, comparing the events of the previous year to what he planned for the upcoming season.

> In their first part, we'll acquaint ourselves with musical selections
> by local and foreign bands alike. We'll have dance music in the sec-
> ond half, and we'll also schedule contests. In this way, we'll con-
> tinue to pursue our primary objective, musical education. In Oc-
> tober, we'll dedicate several evenings to classical music. We'll have
> a number of discotheques where we become acquainted with pro-
> gressive avant-garde jazz, as well as with the newest recordings from
> [the Soviet label] Melodiya.[31]

In this passage, we glimpse Lediņš's talent for keeping his audience on
their toes—and also something every bit as crucial to the success of
his disco project and the festivals of new music he would organize in
the coming months. In stressing that his "primary objective" was the
"musical education" of his fellow students, he aligned his endeavor
squarely with the official charge of the RPI Student Club, and also
with the Komsomol, the organization of Soviet youth charged with
overseeing the club's activities. With these words, he signaled that he

understood clearly the boundary between acceptable and unacceptable spheres of cultural activity. And he made clear that he knew exactly what was needed to maintain the good graces of officialdom.[32]

KEEPING THINGS OFFICIAL

Asja Visocka, who succeeded Aina Bērziņa as head of the RPI Student Club in 1978, recalled for me the tremendous support that the club and its activities, including its disco, received from the RPI administration in these years. (Bērziņa has since passed away.) Such high-level institutional support, she suggests, was crucial to establishing and maintaining the favorable reputation of the club all the way to Moscow. The Student Club, Visocka recounts, was the "most progressive" youth organization in Riga, its members taking "a leading role" in organizing cultural activities at the polytechnic. The club's hall, which housed the RPI disco, had been renovated only in 1974, in a feat that attested to student initiative and also to the considerable backing they had from the university itself.[33] Located in Riga's historic Anglican Church, a structure badly damaged in World War II, the renovation of the club's premises was the brainchild of an architecture student, Anda Liepiņa. After some lobbying, RPI administrators lent their support to Liepiņa's vision for rebuilding and repurposing the church—and, according to Visocka, a significant amount of funding as well. Lacking the financial means to complete the project with professional workers, a virtual army of students—a "renovation brigade"—mobilized to replace the church's burned-out flooring, rebuild the balcony, fix windows, and shore up a collapsing roof. In September 1974, the church's doors were reopened as the new home of the Student Club. With this achievement, the club became the only student organization in the city—surely one of the only such groups in the USSR—with a full-size, acoustically vibrant concert hall at its disposal (fig. 2.2).[34] That same month, in the student paper, Bērziņa announced the launch of Lediņš's disco.

Visocka describes Lediņš and other members of the club as "very, very active" in shaping cultural life at their institution. And, she stresses, "all of them were upstanding."[35] As a group, the club operated under the umbrella of the Komsomol's Commission for Cultural Work, which answered directly to the organization's Division of Ideol-

FIGURE 2.2
Lediņš's disco-
theque at the RPI
Student Club
(formerly An-
glican Church),
mid-1970s. Lediņš
is seated on
the left behind
the desk with
audio-playback
equipment.
Photographer
unknown. Col-
lection of the Lat-
vian Centre for
Contemporary
Art. Courtesy of
Pēteris Lediņš.

ogy.[36] Lediņš's disco was just one part—one small part, Visocka emphasizes—of the substantial array of musical programming organized and sponsored by the club. The organization coordinated the activities of men's and women's student choirs; it sponsored a "festival of political song" in spring 1976; it hosted a concert by the Tartu-based rock band Fix the following winter; and it arranged a concert and lecture by the celebrated Latvian estrada composer Raimonds Pauls in April 1977.[37] None of this work overlapped thematically with Lediņš's discotheque, which provided the club's only lecture series on music as well as the only place on its slate of activities to feature the performance of avant-garde music. In a Komsomol meeting of December 16, 1974, the organization's Commission for Cultural Work reported on all of the musical events that were planned for the remainder of the academic year. Among those projects anticipated in the spring was the launch of Lediņš's discotheque. Noting that his proposal had garnered support not only from members of the commission but also from editors of the student paper, the governing board of the Komsomol lent its unqualified blessing to Lediņš's plans, without any further recorded deliberation.[38]

If anyone doubted that Lediņš would stick to officially sanctionable programming and activities, their concerns would likely have been dispelled by the very first of his discos, where the lecture portion of the evening was given over to the composer Ģederts Ramans, chair of the Latvian SSR Composers' Union. Probably unbeknownst to Lediņš, the governing committee of the Composers' Union was engaged just then in conversation about how to advance "the aesthetic education of children and youth," as a memo on their plans for 1976 indicated. The following year, the union's top priorities included "regular presentations by composers in professional and technical schools," and its board identified Ramans as the most important of the union's ambassadors to that end.[39] At the inaugural evening of Lediņš's discotheque on February 22, 1975, Ramans appeared before an "enormous crowd" (the student paper reported) of students in the Anglican Church, where he spoke about the recent All-Union Congress of Composers' Unions in Kyiv and about a jazz festival he recently attended in Yugoslavia. After his presentation, a student reporter recounted, "we were given the opportunity to listen to passages of music in which composers from abroad are exploring new directions in form and content." The second half of the evening featured dancing, as would become the rule. The report concluded: "We appreciate the fact that discotheques at our institution . . . emphasize the educational half especially, the project of musical education."[40]

Time and again in contemporary accounts of the Riga Polytechnic discos, attendees emphasized the latter point: Lediņš's events were, first and foremost, educational activities. If they happened to be a lot of fun as well, that only made them more effective vehicles for achieving their principal goal. "We're heartened by the fact that the crowd of listeners is full of 'thoughtful individuals,'" one student wrote of the events. "Those who don't wish to engage with the true essence or substance of the discos, who only come to dance, are gradually 'dropping out.'"[41] The promise of Lediņš's discos to cultivate and nurture a population of thoughtful, civic-minded, even ideologically clear-headed students was widely recognized by officials, too, as attested in the RPI Komsomol's plans for sponsored activities in spring semester 1976. Under the heading "Mass Cultural Work," the second of five key projects listed was "to assist in organizing discotheques." That same project was identified as the Komsomol's second-most important cultural undertaking in its plan for 1977.[42] As Zhuk reports, Komsomol authorities across the USSR were, at that moment, promoting discos as one of "the most progressive and ideologically safe venues for Communist entertainment for Soviet youth." In their discussions, the Riga disco scene was often held up as a model. In Zhuk's hometown of Dniepropetrovsk, Ukraine, the Komsomol even brought in a delegation of DJs from Riga to coach local activists on how to run a successful disco in their city. (It is not known if Lediņš participated in that project.)[43]

Perhaps because of the institutional confidence widely invested in Lediņš and his discotheque, his activities seem to have been allowed to unfold without any direct, day-to-day oversight. Detailed protocols of Komsomol meetings and reports on the organization's activities preserve hardly a trace of discussion of Lediņš's programs beyond repeated affirmations of support—despite the fact that other student projects, such as those organized by the International Club or undertaken by the student paper, were regularly subjected to detailed scrutiny and discussion. In an interview of September 1975, Lediņš reported that he planned to "expand cooperation" with the Latvian Composers' Union and its chair Ramans in the upcoming year. But to judge from extant records of conversations among members of the Composers' Union itself, that group, too, was paying no attention to what Lediņš was actually doing.[44] This lack of documented institutional concern seems to comport with Visocka's characterization of the Student Club as a whole. The individuals involved, Lediņš prominently among them, were among the most upstanding members of the polytechnic community. Their activities gave absolutely no one pause. They were entrusted to do as they pleased.

As we will see, this lack of oversight had the unintended effect, as far as university or state officials were concerned, of making Lediņš's discotheque an *open* space, a space where activities that should have been deeply unsettling to authorities could be organized—an underground space, as it were. Nevertheless, reviews and reports on the Student Club's activities remind us of just how deeply ingrained Lediņš's discotheque was in the official culture of the institution. On April 2, 1976, some 350 "friends of music" gathered in the Anglican Church for what was advertised as a "Diskoabend mit Solisten." There, in partnership with the polytechnic's Department of Foreign Languages and its highly scrutinized International Club, Lediņš organized an elaborate disco to showcase German language and music.[45] After kicking things off by playing LP selections from organ works by J. S. Bach, Lediņš lectured on Viennese classicism, and a string quartet of conservatory students played selections by Mozart and Haydn. Then the DJ expounded on Schubert. "In his works," he reportedly explained, "there was achieved a unity of words and music that has never since been attained in German song. With his cycles, he elevated song to a form that is intimate and yet national or communal." His words were followed by a conservatory singer performing selections from Schubert's *Die schöne Müllerin*. After that, the mic was passed to another speaker, who lectured on Richard Wagner, and to yet another, who played selections of recent estrada music from East Germany. Following these lectures and performances, a contest was held to test attendees' learning. Prizes were awarded, records and toy instruments. Then more listening, this time to recent releases by "the most popular groups in the GDR"—Oktoberklub, the Klaus Renft Combo, Brot & Salz, Wir.

Finally, the evening concluded in the way that all of Lediņš's discos did: with "dancing, of course."

———————

That very same month saw Lediņš's first disco-sponsored new music festival, the one at which Pärt's biblically titled *Sarah Was Ninety Years Old* was premiered. There is nothing in the documentary record to suggest that Lediņš had any subversive intent when he organized the latter event, or the second festival of new music he'd arrange under the auspices of his disco in October 1977. But, as we will see, he clearly regarded the festivals as pivotal moments in his life and in the life of his institution. And, as had been the case with the scandal surrounding *Zirkahbols* in his high school days, he seemed—perhaps owing to prior experience, perhaps on account of his mother's status and work—to feel as if no overly onerous punishment would befall him even if something were to go awry. While he busied himself arranging travel for musicians and negotiating for support with the Komsomol, it is unclear whether he knew or cared what, exactly, the festival musicians would perform once they arrived. We do not know if he knew in advance that Pärt would use the opportunity to stage the premieres of openly religious works of music, or whether he knew that Martynov would use the occasion of the 1977 event to unveil his *Passionslieder*, a vocal setting of a Lutheran chorale. When those composers did those things and it was finally discovered that some deeply troubling activity was indeed taking place at the RPI disco, the hammer of officialdom came down upon the DJ and his Student Club colleagues. But even then, it is unclear whether Lediņš was truly bothered by the turn of events. He simply dove headlong into his next project, as he'd always done before. In his life as an artist, Lediņš was nothing if not constantly on the move. But his travels as a DJ in the 1970s had a momentous, career-defining impact upon Pärt, and also upon the community of musicians to which they both belonged.

THREE

TINTINNABULI
AND THE SACRED

DISCOVERIES

On September 14, 1976, Arvo Pärt presented the first two works of
what he was calling his *Tintinnabuli* suite to the Estonian SSR Composers' Union for obligatory preconcert vetting. One was *Aliinale*,
later published and recorded under its German title *Für Alina*.[1] Initially scored for organ (though never, it seems, performed on that instrument), it consists of a lyrical, freely composed melody in the keyboardist's right hand: slow and measured, rising and falling in the key
of B minor, a study in lonesome melancholy that would, much later,
make it a staple in feature film. Below that melody, the left hand plays
a single line of counterpoint, always sounding the nearest pitch of the
B-minor triad to whatever note the keyboardist's right hand plays. This
two-voice structure, with melodic upper and triadic lower voices moving note against note (often called M- and T-voices), would eventually become synonymous with the term "tintinnabuli" itself.[2] As the
musicologist Saale Kareda first pointed out, the sound and structure
of *Für Alina* came to Pärt suddenly, as if out of the blue. In an entry in
his compositional diaries from February 7, 1976, its score appears fully
sketched, like a spontaneous utterance after years of searching for a
musical language capable of accommodating his vision of the divine.[3]

The genesis of *Für Alina* comports with what would become a popular mythology surrounding Pärt's discovery of his tintinnabuli style
in 1976: a retreat into silence broken by sudden inspiration and a sub-

sequent outpouring of musical works, with the structure and sound of those works largely unconnected to what he had composed before.[4] But the *other* one of those first two *Tintinnabuli* pieces he presented to the Composers' Union on September 14, *Modus*, tells a different story, albeit one that is just as important for understanding Pärt's music and concerns of the time. The genesis of *Modus* was far from spontaneous, and the work was not even wholly new. Months before the union's meeting, it had already been premiered, unofficially, at a festival of contemporary music organized by Hardijs Lediņš under the auspices of his Riga Polytechnic disco, under the biblical title *Sarah Was Ninety Years Old*. That concert took place the prior April.[5] But some of the music in *Modus* had originated earlier still, in Pärt's work on an Estonian film from 1974 called *Colorful Dreams*. That hour-long movie, largely devoid of dialogue, follows a deeply imaginative young girl through the end of her summertime stay on the seashore and her tearful, even mournful return to the city. At the point of her arrival back in Tallinn, about halfway through the film, a harpsichord plays the passage transcribed in example 3.1. In Pärt's manuscript score for

EXAMPLE 3.1 Pärt, funeral (*matus*) music from the film *Colorful Dreams* (1974). Transcribed by the author (ETMM, M238:2/38).

this part of the film, the passage is headed *matus*, meaning "funeral" or "burial" in Estonian.[6]

Also preserved in the archives is a sketch that shows something of the process by which Pärt transformed this *matus* music into *Modus*. If the genesis of *Für Alina* suggests a spontaneous, intuitive approach to composition, that of *Modus* reveals a work arising from a considerable amount of carefully deliberating, even quasi-mathematical labor. The relevant passage from *Modus* is shown in figure 3.1, given in Pärt's manuscript fair copy. Figure 3.2 reproduces a sketch that connects the concert work to the film. (To read the score of *Modus*, start with the cell in the upper left, then read the cell in the upper right, then proceed to the left-hand cell in the second row, and so on.)[7]

In *Modus* and *Matus*, the pitch material is the same: the eight-note arcing series of pitches B–C–D–E–A–E–D–C. In both works, Pärt superimposed that series of eight pitches onto a repeating pattern of twelve note lengths: basically, *long-short-short / long-short-short / long-short-short / long-long-long*. In the first two systems of the film score, shown in example 3.1 (mm. 1–10), Pärt paired three run-throughs of the

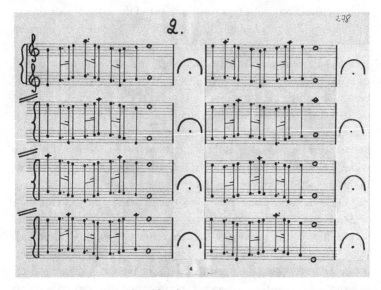

FIGURE 3.1 Pärt, page from *Modus* (1976), manuscript fair copy. Estonian Theatre and Music Museum. Courtesy of the Estonian Theatre and Music Museum and the Arvo Pärt Centre.

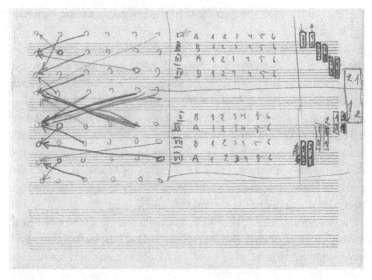

FIGURE 3.2 Pärt, compositional sketch for *Modus*. Estonian Theatre and Music Museum. Courtesy of the Estonian Theatre and Music Museum and the Arvo Pärt Centre.

eight-note melody with two run-throughs of the twelve-note rhythmic pattern. The melody and the rhythmic pattern conclude together in measure 10, after which they start over, in sync, at the start of measure 11. (Three iterations of an eight-note melody yield twenty-four notes; two iterations of a twelve-note rhythmic pattern likewise make twenty-four notes.)

To rework the film music in example 3.1 into the *Modus* score of figure 3.1, Pärt made one simple but highly significant change to the earlier arrangement. He altered the second system of example 3.1 so as to make the melody in measure 6 start not on whichever note comes next in the eight-note series but on the *same* pitch on which measure 5 had just finished. Comparing the second system of example 3.1 to the second cell (upper right) of figure 3.1, we see that instead of beginning the second iteration of the twelve-note rhythmic pattern on A as he had done in *Matus*, in *Modus* he started that second iteration on E—that is, on the note where the previous rhythmic pattern had just ended. In figure 3.2, we see the composer experimenting with various ways of permuting reiteratively an abstract series of pitches. One possibility he hit upon is what he ultimately used to make *Modus* out of *Matus*; in figure 3.2, this is seen most clearly between lines six and seven, where an arrow (Pärt drew it with a green pen) connects the final pitch of the sixth line to the first pitch of line seven—the same delayed continuation of the pitch series we see in the *Modus* score. Modifying the score of *Matus* in this way with each successive iteration of its underlying series of pitches enabled Pärt to expand the two distinct pairings of rhythm and melody shown in example 3.1 into eight distinct pairings, yielding the passage from *Modus* given in figure 3.1. What the music theorist Thomas Robinson has observed of the pairing of pitch and rhythm in the now-canonical version of *Sarah* (1990) applies perfectly here as well. Pärt's arrangement of his material in *Modus* exhausts all "combinational and permutational possibilities" inherent in mapping an eight-note melody onto a twelve-note durational pattern. "With minimal materials," Robinson writes, "Pärt forges maximal variety."[8]

In *Für Alina*, Pärt employed a freely composed melody to highlight the strict interplay of M- and T-voices in counterpoint. In doing so, he showcased a structural arrangement he would revisit repeatedly in his tintinnabuli-style works. In *Modus*, he indulged a different concern that would likewise characterize many of the works to which he has appended the Latin moniker: the generation of melodic material algorithmically, subjecting an initial idea to a reiterative process of manipulation according to a predetermined rule.[9] Taken together, these first two pieces of the *Tintinnabuli* suite reveal something important about Pärt's project of the 1970s. They remind us that the word "tintinnabuli" did not, at the time, stand for a single technique or method at all. Rather, it comprised a number of different ways of creating music— and a number of ways of *experiencing* music—that together enabled him to find a way out of the creative crisis into which he had plunged with the premiere of *Credo* nearly a decade before.

As we'll see, these technical concerns point to more than an obsession with musical structure. In fact, Pärt's experimenting with various means of imposing order on his working method was itself a product of his search for ways of expressing musically his newfound Orthodox Christian faith. To unfold this history, this chapter will survey the diversity of sounds and aesthetic possibilities that attended the first official concerts of Pärt's tintinnabuli-style compositions in and just after 1976, when he and his wife Nora provided their audiences with printed explanations of his ideas, albeit without reference to Pärt's officially unacceptable religious concerns. Then, diving into his unpublished compositional diaries, we will see how his creative project of these years was, nonetheless, a deeply devotional one. It consisted first and foremost in his search for a sounding expression of the Orthodox faith to which he had recently converted. Elaborating a suggestion made by the art historian Ekaterina Degot', I will continue by considering some ways in which Pärt's approach to creating a devotional music intersected with the work of other members of alternative artistic circles in the Soviet 1970s, especially the Russian painter Eduard Steinberg (1937–2012). Finally, looking ahead to the RPI discotheque festivals of 1976 and 1977, I will point to some of the means by which Pärt and his performers disguised the devotional nature of his project for officially sanctioned concerts, even as it was being openly proclaimed and celebrated underground.

"TINTINNABULI," 1976

Not everything about Pärt's tintinnabuli-style music, officially unveiled in an Estonian SSR Philharmonic program on October 27, 1976, struck listeners as radically different from what they had heard before. Tellingly, some who attended the concert did not consider it to mark a stylistic turning point for Pärt at all. At a meeting of the Estonian SSR Composers' Union held some three weeks before the event, the composer and musicologist Uno Soomere admitted that he would need to hear Pärt's new works repeatedly before he could issue a firm judgment about them. But in an appreciative essay published in a multiauthored book on Soviet composers in 1977, he described Pärt's *Tintinnabuli* suite as "continuing along the lines" of such earlier compositions as his Third Symphony of 1971, especially with respect to the "considerable weight" Pärt gives to "every sound, line, and coloring."[10] In a review of the October concert that appeared in the paper of the combined creative unions of the Estonian SSR, the musicologist Merike Vaitmaa described its sounds as melding Pärt's recent, quasi-medievalist concerns with those of his earlier avant-garde years. Lately, she wrote, Pärt seemed to have traded his serialist's fixation on formal structures for a

new, animating concern for the expressive or "intonational" side of his
thematic materials, which she had heard in the chant-like melodies of
his Third Symphony and the poetic imagery of his *Song to the Beloved*
(*Laul Armastatule*, 1973). Now, in the *Tintinnabuli* suite, Vaitmaa heard
not a new departure but a "synthesis" (*süntees*) of Pärt's recent, expressive concerns with his earlier modernist preoccupations. "Pärt's new
approach to composition," she wrote, "reminds us partly of the strict
counterpoint of early music, partly of the strict serial techniques of the
twentieth century."[11] Later, Vaitmaa would acknowledge the year 1976
as an important one for Pärt. But even then, she maintained that its
significance was more biographical than stylistic. Prior to his discovery of his tintinnabuli style, she explained, his creative path had been
marked by sudden shifts and changes of direction. But once he'd found
his tintinnabuli idiom, she observed, he ceased his searching and entered into a period of relative stability. "It is as if the composer found
value in standing still amid the onrushing times."[12]

The opening number of the *Tintinnabuli* suite heard on October
27, 1976, was hardly a musical portrait of poise, however. Indeed, that
number, *Calix*, inhabits a sound world not far removed from that of
Credo or *Song to the Beloved*.[13] (The program for the concert is given
in fig. 1.2.) With a quick timpani roll, *Calix* begins: a four-part choir
singing loudly above the organ, which plays along with a noisy ensemble of trumpet, trombone, electric guitar and bass, gong, and bells.[14]
For the next three minutes, the ensemble is divided, with half of its
members singing and playing a series of modal scales descending at
different speeds simultaneously (a structure Pärt would soon revisit
in *Arbos* and *Cantus in Memory of Benjamin Britten*, both from 1977),
and the others playing a repeating three-note figure identified in a
draft with the requiem text "Tuba mirum." In sketches for the work,
transcribed in example 3.2, Pärt set the descending lines of the opening to the Latin *Dies irae* sequence, also from the requiem mass: "Day
of wrath."[15]

Just over three minutes into the performance, the ensemble fell
momentarily silent, before its musicians let loose an unprepared di-
minished chord on E♭, everyone playing and singing full volume and
the percussion loudly crashing. Another pause, and then the process
reversed: the gong and electric instruments rested while modal scales

EXAMPLE 3.2 Pärt, sketch for the opening of *Calix* (vocal lines only). Transcribed by the author (ETMM, M238:2/61).

ascended into the heavens, the organ playing and the choir singing lines originally set to the Latin "Rex tremendae": "King of terrible majesty, who bestows salvation freely, save me, fount of mercy." The audience at the philharmonic premiere concert did not hear these sacred words, because nonsemantic solfege syllables (*fa, sol, la . . .*) were substituted for the Latin text; the copy of the score prepared for the performance did not include any text at all.[16] Nonetheless, the choral declamation in *Calix*, its aggressive scoring, and its easily understood dramatic trajectory—God's wrath leading to a dissonant crisis, which ultimately resolves into a vision of transcendent salvation—were all of a piece with *Credo*, where Pärt had been before.

With the second piece on the program, however, the diversity of styles brought together under the heading "tintinnabuli" became apparent. At that point in the concert, at the start of *Modus*, a single drummer played a measured, meditative, ascetic pattern lasting over two minutes in performance, before a harpsichordist picked up the contrapuntal passage shown in figure 3.1. For the next fifteen minutes, individuals alternated: the lone percussionist, the solitary harpsichordist. But then, a surprise. Just before the end, at the climactic moment of the piece, an electric guitar and bass took highly amplified solos, the guitar distorted and the bassist adding glissando-like descending slides to the part. For forty-three seconds near the end of the work, the sounds of progressive rock—King Crimson, say—burst out suddenly from Hortus Musicus, Andres Mustonen's early music ensemble.[17]

After *Modus*, another shift: Pärt's *Trivium* was played by a solo organist, Rolf Uusväli, after which a pair of Baroque viols delivered a distinctly unsentimental *Für Alina*, the choir intoning a drone underneath and chimes tinkling up above. As the Estonian musicologist Urve Lippus later recalled, this latter music struck her as so shockingly simple, so fleeting and transparent, as to make her wonder at first whether Pärt had gone "completely mad."[18] After the melodic transparency and textural repose of *Für Alina*, the *Tintinnabuli* suite made another arresting turn, into the machine-like pulsations, dissonant clusters, and historical quotations of *If Bach Had Kept Bees*, a work that Vaitmaa heard as yet another sign of continuity with Pärt's earlier, avant-garde (here, polystylistic) concerns.[19] With this back and forth between modernist complexity, early music instruments, rock intrusions, and extended passages of breathtaking simplicity, all performed without a single sung text to help guide the audience's understanding, what *were* listeners to make of "tintinnabuli" in 1976?

Anticipating the question, the composer and his wife provided listeners with an explanatory program note at the premiere, versions of which would be distributed at concerts over the next two years. Their note opened with Nora Pärt explaining that, after *Song to the Beloved*, "it became clear to the composer that he needed to develop a more harmonious form of self-expression." She explained that the title of the suite, *Tintinnabuli* (Latin for "little bells": *kolokol'chiki* in Russian, *kellukesed* in Estonian), alluded to the "balance, harmony, and purity" of the sounds Pärt sought to conjure with his prominent use of triadic pitch structures. From there, she moved through a number of compositional, aesthetic, and metaphysical concerns, unsurprisingly making no reference to the spiritual travels that propelled Pärt's latest musical discoveries. "The constructive simplicity and strictness" of his new works "are easily 'read' by the mind," she wrote. "The logic of the process is fully exposed, as it were (*Modus*). This perceptibility is an important part of the overall aesthetic effect. The listener is invited to become a co-creator."[20] And then:

Never before have number and mathematical calculation appeared in the work of a composer in such a naked way, as if underlining the beauty of their essence. Number has informed the melodic line, form, polyphonic structure, and rhythm, and it has excluded the possibility of anything happening by chance. This is what allows one to call these seven compositions *strict*.[21]

Elsewhere I have suggested that the Pärts' emphasis on "number and mathematical calculation" as a means of "exclud[ing] the possibility of anything happening by chance" in his music aligned the composer's concerns with those of many in the postwar Euro-American avant-garde. As the musicologist Richard Taruskin points out, numerical obsessions undergirded statements by composers from Cage to Pierre Boulez and György Ligeti, all of whom sought, in varying ways, to bring themselves and their work "in touch with something less vulnerable than personal wishes or tastes, or subjective standards of beauty." In "number," Taruskin writes, they believed they had connected with an "ultimate and imperishable reality"—a connection freighted with existential gravity in an era still haunted by the experience of global war.[22] Ceding part of the compositional process to the dictates of his algorithmic designs, the program notes implied, Pärt distanced the genesis and sound of his music from his drive to express himself *in* his music. In the coming years, he would repeatedly emphasize the mathematical "essence" of his work in this way. In notes distributed at the premiere performance of *Tabula rasa* in September 1977, he invited attendees to strive to follow the "strictness of the mathematical structure" as they listened.[23]

Such words, however, also point to concerns shared locally, in the community of experimenting musicians of which Pärt was a member. For Vladimir Martynov, the "strictness" of Pärt's algorithmic designs made his music a model for the heralded "collapse of the idea of the ego" in postmodernist art. And, with their invitation to audience members to trace the "logic of the process" as they listened, and with their identification of that mental exercise with "becom[ing] a co-creator" in the event, the Pärts aligned the composer's project with another aesthetic shift Martynov described: a turn toward thinking about the concert experience as an occasion for sharing between a composer and the audience, toward regarding the composer not as the author of a text but as the "initiator of a project."[24] Alexei Lubimov recalled such a moment of reorientation at one of his performances of Cage's so-called silent piece, 4′33″, in Moscow. He described the organizer of the concert, held in a private club, growing frustrated as Lubimov sat unmoving on the piano bench. Finally, the organizer shouted: "Play! Play! Do something, whatever you want! Don't just sit there silently!" Thus, Lubimov observed, the flustered man became more than just a listener. With the sound of his voice, he had contributed to shaping the performance itself.[25]

The official premiere of the *Tintinnabuli* suite in Tallinn was repeated in Leningrad the following January, with a nearly identical program note distributed to the audience.[26] The Pärts revised their note more thoroughly for the performance of a new version of the suite at Tallinn's Festival of Early and Contemporary Music, held in November 1978. In her notes for the latter, Nora Pärt divided the composer's creative output into two stylistic periods. The first, running through 1968, saw him experimenting with serialism, aleatoric writing, and other avant-garde techniques. In his second, into which he'd entered after the premiere of *Credo* in November of that year, he worked to expand "the boundaries of simplicity and clarity of musical language." Once again, she described the composer's fixation on the triad as the foundation of his new harmonic vocabulary, and also his attempts to create music that embodies "mathematical order" in an immediately perceptible way.[27] Then she turned to something new:

> In tintinnabuli, Pärt discovered a new principle by which music relates to a text. The word is articulated in a manner determined by a unique and dynamic feature of the system, and numerical parameters of construction contribute to the creation of form. In this way, the semantic aspect of the word is partly infused into the musical fabric.[28]

None of Pärt's works on the 1978 festival program set vocal texts. But Nora Pärt's words were not out of place. For as soon as the official premiere of his *Tintinnabuli* suite had been given in autumn 1976—indeed, just two weeks after the Tallinn concert—Pärt dove into a project that would occupy him until and beyond his emigration to the West. He embarked on a search for means of adapting the still-nebulous principles of tintinnabuli-style composition to the setting of sacred texts. This fact is important, because what united the disparate styles, techniques, and aesthetic positions under the umbrella of the Latin word was Pärt's unabating search for means of embodying and expressing his faith in his music. In the words of the scriptures, the liturgy, and the writings of the Orthodox fathers and saints, he found his daily spiritual sustenance. Now, with the premiere of the *Tintinnabuli* suite behind him, he realized that he had to make those words the generative center of his work.

WHEN THINGS HAPPENED, AND WHAT THEY WERE

A month before the Tallinn premiere of October 27, 1976, Pärt had finished composing all but one of the works of the *Tintinnabuli* suite. Only *If Bach Had Kept Bees* remained, and, as his composing sketchbooks (*muusikapäevikud*, "musical diaries") reveal, he spent the first two weeks of September working to complete it. At the same time, he was searching for titles of the suite's movements, compiling lists of Latin words and their Estonian translations that would figure in the official unveiling. *Pari intervallo* and *trivium* appeared on his sketchbook lists on the third of September; *modus* and *tintinnabulum* on the thirteenth.[29] Every piece on the October program was either instrumental or planned for wordless singing, yet his musical diaries show that he was clearly thinking of the suite as a whole as a sacred work leading up to the premiere, albeit one whose outlines were still flexible and to some extent unclear. *Calix*, as noted, he had initially conceived as a setting of the *Dies irae* hymn, and in his diaries he was still referring to it as "Dies Irae Calix" in mid-September. During this period, he referred to the second movement of the suite variously as *Modus* (Latin for *method*) and *Saara* (Estonian *Sarah*), but he sometimes also called it *Ortus*, Latin for *birth* or *origin*—likely a reference to Genesis 21, where Sarah gives birth to Isaac at the start of her tenth decade on earth. The final piece in the suite, *In spe*—a wordless, algorithmically generated choral work later published as *An den Wassern zu Babel saßen wir und weinten*—he alternately identified with the

Kyrie from the mass ("Lord, have mercy") and with the Latin phrase *Beatus est* ("He is blessed"), which figures in the Gospel of Luke and a number of parascriptural texts. On October 19, eight days before the Tallinn premiere, a note: "*Calix* rehearsal failed" (*Calixi proov luhtus*). Around that time, Pärt took a break from daily composing until after the concert. Then, on the first of November, five days after the official unveiling of his new style of composing, he returned to a project with which he had already filled hundreds of manuscript notebook pages: composing free, monodic melodies in the manner of Gregorian chant, sometimes setting psalms or Russian devotional texts. For the next ten days, he produced nothing but page after page of chant-like melodies, dozens of exemplars daily.[30] A more immediate statement of Christian devotion, musically expressed, is hard to imagine.

What brought Pärt back to his tintinnabuli project was the Nicene Creed, the *Credo* of the Latin mass: "I believe in one God." On November 11 or 12, 1976, he began searching for a melodic line to set the text, and it was through this round of work that his experiments acquired a different cast.[31] From that point until the end of the following year, Pärt's principal, abiding concern became the adapting of various tintinnabuli principles to the setting of undisguised sacred texts. He took occasional breaks from this project to produce instrumental pieces he'd promised to others. But those he either dispatched quickly, returning as soon as possible to his more explicitly devotional work (as in the case of *Fratres*), or else he executed them in bits and pieces, around the edges of his text-setting project (as with *Tabula rasa*). In the Soviet 1970s, Pärt's laser-like focus on setting sacred texts was wildly impractical, even "unnormal," in Yurchak's terms.[32] There was literally no place in the Soviet Union where a new setting of a *Credo*, a Passion, or a mass could be performed in the open. But practicality is not what drove him. His project was as idiosyncratic as it was deeply felt and obsessively pursued.

Between the eleventh and the thirteenth of November 1976, Pärt experimented with several possibilities for setting the *Credo*, soon arriving at the freely composed melody that would eventually serve as the opening of *Summa*. At the same time, he worked out the reiterative algorithmic process that would enable him to elaborate that melody into a structure capable of accommodating the entire lengthy text.[33] (The complex algorithm, the details of which Pärt cannot recall and which have resisted attempts at complete reconstruction, entails excising pitches from the middle of one melodic iteration and moving them to the end of the next, with an overlapping process of melodic augmentation and diminution.)[34] Then, temporarily putting his work on the *Credo* to the side, he turned on November 14 to work on another text from the Latin mass, the *Gloria*. Six days later, he explored yet another approach to setting the Nicene Creed.[35] On December 13, he turned to another mass text, the *Benedictus*. In January 1977, he came back to his initial setting of the *Credo*. On the twenty-second or twenty-third of that month, he wrote out the full score of what he would eventually call *Summa*, giving it the title "Credo XI 76—I 77."[36]

He followed the completion of *Summa* with days of composing chant-like melodies, ceasing this work on the twelfth of February, when he had a breakthrough. He began that day as he sometimes did, inscribing the Orthodox "Jesus Prayer" in the form of the Russian acronym **Г И Х С Б п м г**: *Gospodi Iisuse Khriste, Syne Bozhii, pomilui moiu greshuiu,* "Lord Jesus Christ, Son of God, have mercy on me, a sinner."[37] Then he wrote out, as if spontaneously, a melodic setting of a prayer attributed to the fourth-century Orthodox saint Macarius the Great, by means of a procedure that would later become known as his "syllabic" method of composing: a way of deriving a melodic line directly from the structure of the text itself.[38] Immediately after setting the saint's prayer to music in this way, he returned to the Latin *Gloria* and applied the same syllabic technique to it, generating from its textual structure a melodic line for tenor. Five days later, he paired that tenor with a countermelody for alto, composed using the same syllabic method. Example 3.3 shows how this compositional principle works at the start of the two-voice setting he produced.[39]

In the tenor line, every word of the *Gloria* text begins on the same pitch, D. From that D, the melodic line descends one diatonic step with the articulation of each successive syllable of a word. Since the first word of the text, *gloria*, has three syllables, its melodic line descends from D through C to B♭. The second word, *in*, has only one syllable, so the melody it inscribes consists of just a single D. After that comes *excelsis*, whose three syllables determine a melodic line identical with

EXAMPLE 3.3 Pärt, opening measures of the *Gloria* from the *Missa syllabica*. Transcribed by the author from the musical diaries (APK 2-1.21).

that of the word *gloria*. Then, a two-syllable word, *Deo*, whose line descends from D to C. The melody of the alto voice is formed in the same way as the tenor's, only in its case the *final* syllable of each word is always sung on the pitch A, and the melodic motion is always ascending from below, rather than descending from above. The three-syllable word *gloria* is therefore sung F–G–A; the word *Deo* inscribes the two-note ascent G–A.

This is the procedure—the so-called syllabic method—to which Nora Pärt referred when she wrote her program notes of November 1978, explaining that "Pärt [had] discovered a new principle by which music relates to a text." What he'd discovered, in fact, on February 12, 1977, was a method of setting sacred texts that he finally deemed sufficient for the task of expressing musically his devotion to them. Once he found that method, it was as though the creative floodgates opened. Between the twelfth and the fifteenth of February, he used the technique to sketch melodic lines not just for the *Gloria* but also for the *Kyrie, Agnus Dei, Sanctus,* and *Credo* of the mass. He spent the next three days filling out secondary contrapuntal lines (like the alto voice in example 3.3) and also adding triadic voices in the manner of *Für Alina.* By the eighteenth, he had finished a complete Latin mass, which he would later call his *Missa syllabica.* After that, he did not stop. On the single day of February 21, he composed an early version of *De Profundis* using the same syllabic principle.[40] Three days later, he dove into work on a syllabic setting of the St. John Passion. He sketched out Biblical characters and their distinctive scoring as well as the melodic lines prescribed by the text at key moments. From time to time, he paused in this work to compose chant-like melodies. In the first week of March, he produced hundreds of pages of material for his Passion setting, which would eventually become the *Passio Domini nostri Jesu Christi secundum Joannem*—among the longest of his syllabically conceived compositions, which he would finish only five years later, after emigrating to the West.[41]

To my knowledge, Pärt has never remarked on his discovery of his syllabic method, though he has spoken a great deal about the relation between text and music in his works. But Nora Pärt, in her program notes for the 1978 festival, provided some clues about why this method seemed exactly the solution to the problem of setting texts with which Pärt had begun to wrestle immediately after unveiling his tintinnabuli style. There she observed that "the word" in the composer's syllabic music (*slovo* in Russian, *sōna* in Estonian) "is articulated in a manner determined by a unique and dynamic feature of the system," according to which "the semantic aspect of the word is partly infused into the musical fabric." Given that she had already noted Pärt's attraction to "number" (*tsifra, arv*) for its capacity to generate musical structures in a way that "excludes the possibility of anything happening by chance" in the compositional process, it seems only natural that Pärt would latch onto an algorithmic method of autonomously generating pitches directly from the structures of the texts he wished to set. If his first round of tintinnabuli experimentation, as in *Modus*, consisted in ceding aspects of his compositional decision-making to mathematically determined algorithmic processes, he now simply shifted, in this latest round of work, to a new form of input into the algorithm. Numbers were replaced by words.

With respect to this issue, Toomas Siitan has pointed to something crucial and still deeper. For Siitan, the syllabic method constitutes, in itself, an expression of Pärt's Orthodox faith. "In his relationship with the Word," Siitan writes, "Arvo Pärt is close to the original Christian way of thinking, which has been preserved more purely in the Orthodox Church." He continues:

> He is not a "construer" of the texts in his works; he does not highlight a personal aspect in them, but rather presumes that the text comprises the entire message perfectly. The texts likewise possess their own music, which must merely be brought forth. As such, the composer does not have all that much to add to the texts on his own part—the music only serves and carries out the text, giving it a sound-based existence.[42]

In this passage, Siitan is referring to a way of thinking musically about—and also within—ritual practice in the Orthodox Church. There, as the ethnomusicologist Jeffers Engelhardt documents, the singer, in her act of devotion, does not seek to give voice to sacred texts in an individuating, personally expressive way. Rather, the singer submits to various melodic "prototypes" of the Orthodox modal system. It is through such singing—through such "disciplining, emptying, and effacing a desirous, individuated self," so that the spirit itself can be heard—that the Orthodox singer strives to know or become closer to God.[43] With respect to Pärt, Engelhardt suggests that the syllabic "formula derived from a sacred text" is akin to "the prototype that Pärt renders in sound, attenuating or effacing his own subjectivity to make manifest the beauty and truth of the prototype, similar to the prayerful ascetic discipline of creating an icon according to a sacred prototype."[44] For Pärt, the word of the scriptures, the liturgy, and the saints is where all meaning resides, and the word is therefore what must sound—clearly, directly, and without personalizing inflection. In the syllabic method, he believed he had found a way of reducing his creative intervention in the setting of texts to the point where he merely attended to their words, setting them free, as it were, to determine their own melodic course. In this respect, Martynov was right when he described Pärt's tintinnabuli-style music as a powerful testament to the "collapse of the idea of the ego" in contemporary experimental art.[45] For Pärt, devotion to the word was everything. The sound of his own music was secondary. It was nothing more—and nothing less—than a vehicle for sounding his devotion to sacred texts.

In spring 1977, life intervened into Pärt's text-setting project, as he was compelled to turn his attention to a list of instrumental works he had promised to others. On March 14, he broke off work on *Passio* to revisit the opening of *Calix*, whose descending series of modal scales he subjected to various modifications that would yield several new compositions. In one variant, he let the descending arc of the melodic line unfold in piecemeal fashion: first A, then A–G, then A–G–F. In the midst of this experiment, in bold red pencil, he added the word *Cantus* to his notes.[46] (His *Cantus in Memory of Benjamin Britten*, which follows this basic design, would be premiered on April 7, 1977 by the Estonian SSR Philharmonic Orchestra.)[47] In another variant on the *Calix* idea, he let the polyphonic voices fall silent one by one as their lines descended into the depths, eventually leaving only the lowest voice to complete its modal descent. By the third or fourth of April, this latter experiment had clearly evolved into the ending of *Silentium*, the second movement of *Tabula rasa*, which Tatiana Grindenko and Gidon Kremer had commissioned as a companion to Schnittke's First Concerto Grosso.[48]

The next two months were largely consumed by work on *Tabula rasa*, though Pärt took several, often days-long breaks from that project, during which he returned to filling page after page with chant-like melodies.[49] On June 5–6, he hit upon the modal scale and generative algorithm used in *Fratres*, a work he had promised to Mustonen.[50] On the seventh, however, his attention shifted back to sacred texts, and he paused his work on *Fratres* to sketch a syllabic setting of the Latin *Te Deum*. More chant-like writing, and then it was back to *Tabula rasa* on June 18. Two days later, another break: On June 20, he composed the entire syllabic setting of *Cantate Domino*.[51] In July, he delivered the score of *Tabula rasa* to Kremer and Grindenko, and he spent the remainder of the summer making final preparations for the discotheque-festival concert with Hortus Musicus at the Riga Polytechnic Institute, scheduled for October.[52] He started on *Arbos* on September 12 and completed *Fratres* on October 3.[53] Then, while Mustonen's ensemble rehearsed, he turned back to the project of setting devotional texts. On October 8, he began work on a syllabic setting of the Marian antiphon *Salve Regina*. On the fifteenth, he sketched a syllabic setting of Psalm 120 ("I call upon the Lord in my distress"). Five days later, he produced a syllabic setting of Psalm 102 ("Hear my prayer, Lord").[54] Then he took a break.

On the last weekend in October, Pärt traveled to Riga to attend the festival organized by Lediņš, Lubimov, and their friends. It was there, on the twenty-eighth, that much of Pärt's music from 1977, some overtly sacred, had its first public performance: *Arbos* and *Fratres*, *Cantate Domino* and *Summa*, even the *Missa syllabica*. We'll visit that concert in chapter 4. Three days later, back in Tallinn, Pärt returned to work in his compositional diaries. He started by inscribing a passage of text, as if to remind himself of his devotional project and his role as an artist in relation to it. Copying in Russian script the words of the nineteenth-century Orthodox saint Theophan the Recluse, he wrote the following on the cover of a new manuscript notebook, underlining some of Theophan's words for emphasis:

> Why are we sad after a lengthy conversation with someone? Because during the conversation you turn away from the Lord. *This is unpleasant for the Lord, and he lets you know this through your sadness.*[55]

Pärt's transcription ends there, but Theophan's text continues:

> Whatever one is doing, you should strive never to turn away from the Lord, and you should endeavor to do everything for Him, to think according to His commandments. If you do this, you will never be sad, for you will understand that you have done His work.[56]

As we will see, the Riga festival was a massive success for Pärt, with the impact made by his devotional works resounding for decades in the minds of attendees. But immediately after what must have registered as one of his greatest public triumphs to date, Pärt recalled the words of Theophan, recentering his compositional work in relation to God and His word. Immediately, he dove back into work, experimenting first with permutations of simple melodic lines, and then, beginning on November 10, sketching further syllabic settings of the psalms.

APOPHATIC SPACES

Siitan's remarks on the syllabic method point to an aspect of Orthodox practice, *hesychasm*, that has been widely associated with Pärt and his music in Western commentary since the 1990s, when the conductor Paul Hillier, an early collaborator, first began writing on Pärt's work.[57] Typically linked to the trope of silence that frequently attends conversations about Pärt's tintinnabuli-style music (the term derives from the Greek word *hesychia*, for *silence* or *stillness*), the Orthodox notion of hesychasm might more accurately be described as "the practice of prayer in inner silence, in the renunciation of thoughts, passions, and images," as the theologian Peter C. Bouteneff writes.[58] The silence inherent to Orthodox hesychasm is neither exclusively nor even specifically aural. Rather, it is also metaphorical, signaling one's abandoning the will to interpret or engage as interlocutor with sacred words received. It constitutes an effacing of the self and the creative, interpreting, expressive ego. "Stone-silence is precisely the appropriate posture before the divine," Bouteneff writes. "Intelligent, word-bearing creatures must therefore mimic the dumb stones. . . . Renunciation and silence [are] understood as indispensable to the discipline of apprehension of truth, of self, of the divine."[59]

For Engelhardt, this notion of prayerful silence is inseparably tied to that of the Orthodox principle of *apophatic* (or "negative") knowledge of God. Since "God's nature [is] beyond the capacities of human knowledge to express," he writes, only "negative statements about divinity"—about what God seems *not* to be, about when and where His presence does *not* seem to be felt—can constitute "true reflections of individual experiences" of the divine. By silencing the subject within, "prayer and participation in the life of God (*theosis*) become possible through lived faith and the grace and mystery of God rather than through the accomplishments of human reason."[60] With the syllabic method, as Siitan understands it, Pärt accomplished something akin to this. Pärt's input into the algorithmic system was the word of God, the prophets, or the church fathers. Inscribing in his notebooks the autonomously generated musical output of that system, he ceded his urge to interpret, reflect, or express his own ideas about the meaning of their words, about what God might be said positively to *be*. "The music only serves and carries out the text," Siitan writes, "giving it a sound-based existence."[61]

Similar statements are widely made about the art of a nearly exact contemporary of Pärt, the Russian painter Eduard Steinberg (Shteinberg, in strict transliteration from the Cyrillic). Born in 1937, Steinberg spent his formative years in internal exile from Moscow with his father Arkady, also a painter. During that time, living in the village of Tarusa over 100 kilometers south of the capital, Eduard acquired through his father an enduring fascination for the art and literature of the Russian and Soviet avant-garde of the 1910s and 1920s.[62] Rehabilitated and returned to Moscow in 1961, the junior Steinberg found work as a graphic artist, while on the side he emerged as an important if eccentric member of the group of 1960s modernists against whom the even

FIGURE 3.3 Eduard Steinberg, *Composition November–December* (1979). Photo courtesy József Rosta/Ludwig Museum—MoCA, Budapest (Long-term loan from Ludwig Stiftung, Aachen). With permission of Galina Manewitsch.

younger Moscow Conceptualists would soon position their endeavors. But sometime in the late 1960s, in unknowing parallel with Pärt, Steinberg's thinking began to shift. He found himself drawn ever more deeply into Orthodox theology and eventually into practice. Converting from Judaism to Orthodox Christianity around 1970, his paintings, always sparse, became increasingly abstract, with birds and seashells evolving into triangles and spirals against a sky-blue horizon.[63] Soon he eschewed figural representation altogether and entered into an abstract creative realm he called "metageometry." His *Composition November–December* (*Kompozitsiia noiabr'–dekabr'*, 1979) is typical of his work from this period (fig. 3.3): a meeting of two planes, triangles, circles, and lines. And, as we often see in Steinberg's paintings of the decade, two of those lines intersect at right angles close to the center of the canvas, inscribing the unmistakable shape of a Christian cross.

In an open letter of 1981, Steinberg connected his leap into geometrical abstraction directly to his practice of his Orthodox faith. Addressing his missive to the long-dead Russian avant-gardist Kazimir Malevich (1879–1935), he asked what had become of the life of the spirit over the course of Russia's twentieth century. Thanking a theologian friend for awakening him to the importance of a Neoplatonic "language of geometry" in early Christian thought, he went on to describe contemporary Russia as "a nation that has become cut off from beauty, which has gradually become mute, where the connection with the eternal word has frayed."[64] Turning to Malevich, whose own starkly geometrical paintings of the 1910s had inspired some of his own, Steinberg continued:

> It is clear that you were born to remind the world of the language of geometry ... the language of Pythagoras, of Plato, of Plotinus, of the ancient Christian catacombs. For me that language is not universal, but within it one finds a longing for truth and transcendence, and a certain affinity to apophatic theology. Just as you set the observer free, so does the language of geometry compel the artist to renounce the ego.[65]

The painter Ilya Kabakov, whom we met in chapter 1, did not share Steinberg's Orthodox faith. He looked upon his colleague's stance in relation to his painterly project somewhat pityingly, and he even produced a "gentle parody" of Steinberg's canvases in his so-called white board paintings of 1969–70.[66] "The artist in this case feels subjectively that he is a conduit rather than someone actively creating," Kabakov wrote of his friend. "In essence, he is nobody. Humble and subdued, he is thankful that he had a part to play [in his art], that his work passed 'through him.'"[67] Despite Kabakov's assessment, Steinberg stood by his vision. "Is the artist free?" he asked rhetorically in 1983. "Yes, but his freedom is a gift. For this reason, the sincerest gesture the artist can make is to say that 'I' do not exist."[68]

For Ekaterina Degot', such statements by the painter suggest a link between aspects of Orthodox theology and the imagery of Steinberg's work itself, with the open spaces of Steinberg's paintings inviting or enabling the observer to connect with something of the apophatic tradition.[69] I would extend and complicate her view by shifting our attention away from the blank spaces of Steinberg's canvases and toward his words about geometry, expression, and the creative self, in ways that might help us understand something further about Pärt's project in turn. For the painter, restricting one's visual resources to flat, featureless geometrical shapes was a means of silencing the expressive and interpreting subject within oneself, of disciplining and effacing the creative ego. Importantly, I think, it is in the abstraction of those shapes, rather than in the blank spaces between them, that apophatic knowledge takes hold. The line, the square, and the triangle are emphatically *not* representations of God. And precisely for that reason, their beholding discloses for the viewer a kind of silent, hesychastic space, a space in which the believer might feel closer to His unknowable mystery. With Pärt's syllabic method, the situation is much the same. The apophatic spaces disclosed by his music do not derive from the transparency of its textures or the ostensible purity of its harmonies. Rather, in a kind of aural analogy to a metageometrical painting by Steinberg, those spaces are disclosed by the radical, even stunning abstraction of Pärt's musical structures.

If we think back for a moment to Pärt's earliest, nonsyllabic tintinnabuli-style works, we can see that a great deal of that music unfolds according to an audible logic. For example, *Für Alina* inscribes a freely composed melody that, by its midpoint, has risen two octaves from its opening pitch. Then, by the time its final measure arrives, it has descended all the way back to the register of its first note, audibly ending at a point close to where its journey began. Or take the ending of *Tabula rasa*, which attains its famously powerful effect precisely because the melodic process unfolding at its close leads the listener to expect the work to end on the pitch D—when, in fact, it fades off into silence just before that longed-for note arrives, leaving us hanging in suspense. In contrast to these examples, Pärt's syllabic compositions offer nothing to the listener in the way of a musical syntax that might help us make sense of the pitch structures we're hearing as they unfold in real time, nothing that enables us to follow aurally the progress of a work in terms of musical logic, or even to hear a clearly audible beginning, middle, and end. True, works like the *Gloria* in example 3.3 might hover around a focal pitch, which functions like the unmoving horizontal line in many of Steinberg's paintings. But around that pitch, each and every individual word inscribes a musical gesture unto itself. The words of the text connect to each other through the logic of Latin grammar and the semantic content of the liturgy. That is, they cohere as *verbal* statements. But the melodic gestures generated by those words do not move from one to another according to any kind of *musical* logic whatsoever. Mapped through Pärt's syllabic algorithm onto the pitch-space of his notebook pages, the words give rise to a music that is utterly abstract—to compositions that are completely incomprehensible, *as musical constructions*, without the words they set.

Listening through a broad swath of unofficial Soviet music from the 1950s through the 1970s, Peter Schmelz posits a general move from what he calls "abstraction to mimesis" in the work of many, from an emphasis on simply arranging notes on pages to exploring such "representational" approaches to composition as polystylism and aleatoric writing. Schmelz notes that this "aesthetic shift" is "no more than a general observation," but the idea captures something important about Pärt's journey as a composer—up to a point.[70] Pärt first made his name as an artist with such "abstract" serial works as *Nekrokog* (1960) and *Perpetuum mobile* (1963). Soon, however, his interest in serialism dovetailed with his first polystylistic experiments, notably *Collage über B-A-C-H* (1964) and *Credo* (1968), which eventually gave rise to the mimetic sounds of the Third Symphony of 1971, with its echoes of Gregorian chant and medieval polyphony. For many early listeners (Vaitmaa, Soomere, Nora Pärt), that symphony was stylistically of a piece with much of what they heard in the *Tintinnabuli* suite, at least when they first heard it.

But as we have seen, shortly after the premiere of that suite in October 1976, Pärt discovered his syllabic method. And with that discovery, he veered sharply back toward musical abstraction. Indeed, for the musicologist Svetlana Savenko, the rationalistic basis of Pärt's tintinnabuli-style music represented nothing less than his "transferring the idea of serialism onto modal material, [with] the totally diatonic style of tintinnabuli turn[ing] out to be the flip side of the total chromaticism of serialism."[71] Not since his serial experiments of the 1960s had Pärt produced music as abstract as his syllabic compositions. And as with the parallel journey undertaken by Steinberg in these years, so too was Pärt's dive into abstraction attendant upon his spiritual search. For the painter as for the composer, in abstraction lay a path toward quieting the mind, to overcoming the ego. In attending to abstraction, so they believed, one might position oneself in an apophatic space, a space in which a person might feel just a little bit closer to the divine.

HIDING YET NOT HIDING

On October 28, 1977, the *Missa syllabica* had its first performance, at a disco-festival of new music organized by Hardijs Lediņš at the RPI Student Club. There the musicians of Hortus Musicus played period instruments and sang the full text of the Latin mass in the sanctuary of Riga's recently repurposed Anglican Church. No program for the concert is known to survive, but Lediņš recorded the performance on reel-to-reel tape. I'll try to reconstruct the events and sounds of that evening in chapter 4. But here, in a chapter devoted to written texts, I'll close with another: a title. Inscribing the names of the works he heard in felt-tip pen on the cardboard box housing the tape, Lediņš recorded the title of the work as *Mass (in 6 parts) (Test)*—in Latvian, *Mesa (6 daļās) (Tests)*.[72] Why "test"? I wondered, when I first saw the tape. What was being tested? In Latvian, "test" is *izmēģinājums* or *pārbaude*, but Lediņš gave the word *test* in English (or in Estonian, where it is a perfect cognate), only adding the final *-s* that marks gender and case in Latvian. The concert that night featured several other works by Pärt that were likewise having their first-ever performances: *Fratres, Cantate Domino, Arbos, Summa*. None of those he identified as a "test." In the case of the mass, it seemed that Lediņš was recording an alternate title for the work, rather than indicating that the performance itself was somehow provisional, a test.

The following spring, a work called *Test* began appearing on printed programs and official worklists. On May 15, 1978, *Test* was performed by Hortus Musicus as part of a new version of the *Tintinnabuli* suite, in an Estonian SSR Philharmonic concert at Tartu University. On December 19, Hortus Musicus played *Test* at the Leningrad House of Composers.[73] Back in February, Pärt had included *Test* on a form he filed with the Estonian SSR Composers' Union, listing all the works he had completed in 1977. There, he described it as "'Test' music for a

Poland-USSR film" (*"Test" muzyka k kinofil'mu Pol'sha-SSSR*).[74] As the musicologist Christopher J. May has documented, Nora Pärt brought the score of the *Missa syllabica* to the Composers' Union for discussion on May 23, 1978, where she explained that her husband was calling it *Test* because it originated in his soundtrack for an upcoming film, *The Test of Pilot Pirx* (*Test Pilota Pirxa* in Polish, *Navigaator Pirx* in Estonian).[75] Her account would seem to explain the English/Estonian (or Polish!) title that Lediņš recorded, but the connection between the mass and the film is far from clear. As we have seen, Pärt composed the *Missa syllabica* in February 1977, amid the flurry of compositional activity that attended his discovery of the syllabic method. At that time, there was no material related to a film project anywhere nearby in the compositional diaries. So what, then, was this film about a pilot? And what was its putative connection to Pärt's mass?

The film to which these references point was produced in 1978–79, adapting work by the Polish science fiction writer Stanisław Lem. It follows the journey into space of an eponymous astronaut and his crew, comprising a mix of humans and potentially untrustworthy androids that Pirx struggles to distinguish from each other. Pärt's hint at a link between the film and the mass, which appears to have originated at the Riga festival, would seem to signal that he was already thinking about his commission for the soundtrack at that point, even though all surviving manuscript materials related to his work on *Pirx*—everything from rudimentary sketches to fair copies of large sections of music—are dated much later, between August and October 1978.[76] The soundtrack he eventually produced makes use of material from *If Bach Had Kept Bees*, but it contains nothing related to the *Missa syllabica* and no music composed with the syllabic method, and no such music is anywhere found in archival sources related to the project.[77] Delving into the archives and the film, the mystery of the connection only seems to deepen.

Church scene or no, *Pilot Pirx* includes a fair amount of talk about religion, as Pirx, in his attempt to differentiate the androids among his crew, identifies faith in God as a distinctly human trait.[78] May suggests that this fact might provide an important clue about what the Pärts were after when they claimed a connection between the movie and the mass. Namely, the soundtrack commission, whenever it came, might

have seemed to provide the composer with "helpful institutional leverage" when he first dared take his openly religious tintinnabuli-style
music before the public. It may have afforded him opportunities to
discuss or even schedule performances of "items of sacred music that
had [already] been written," but which would, absent plausible filmic
origins, have been deemed too risky to perform in public—much as
the connection to Schiller's *Don Carlos* had been used to render performances of Schnittke's Requiem at least occasionally permissible.[79]
At that same Composers' Union meeting in May 1978, Nora Pärt further asserted that *Summa* and *Cantate Domino* had likewise originated
in Pärt's score for *Pilot Pirx*, even though his composing diaries make
clear that they too were written well before he started work on the film.
In this light, the discussion that ensued among the union's members
during the meeting seems revealing. Apparently responding to the abstract nature of these pieces, the first Pärt composed with his syllabic
method, one meeting attendee remarked, "as stand-alone works they
would be boring." Another wondered aloud: "There are no Catholic
churches here. I don't know, where will this music be performed?"[80]

When Pärt embarked on the devotional project that led to his discovery of the syllabic method, he knew very well that a Latin mass had
no place within the official, "normal" confines of Soviet musical life.
But he was already familiar with a number of ways of navigating an alternative path within the gaps and holes of the Soviet bureaucracy, and
he soon connected with a community of musicians—Lediņš and his
friends—who knew how to make the most of the possibilities they afforded. In October 1976, when his *Tintinnabuli* suite was unveiled in a
philharmonic concert in Tallinn, he understood that the official status
of the concert required adjustments to his works as he conceived them.
He swapped the sacred text of *Calix* for nonsemantic solfege syllables,
he traded the Biblical reference of the title *Sarah* for the neutral moniker *Modus*, and he let *In spe* simply be *In spe* (Latin for "in hope") rather
than *Kyrie* or *Beatus est*, as he had called it in his musical diaries. But
by the middle of 1978, a great deal had changed in his world. By then,
he had the wildly popular success of *Tabula rasa* behind him. And, as
we'll see, he had recently been honored by the Estonian Ministry of
Culture. These laurels afforded him leverage and creative freedoms he
had not enjoyed before, and he hazarded performances of the *Missa*

syllabica at Hortus Musicus concerts in Tartu and Leningrad. But even then, when the mass was performed, he continued to cover his bases, identifying the work on programs as *Test* and linking it explicitly to *Pirx* in official documents. In 1976, Pärt was still hiding, but by 1978 he had begun to take a different approach. By then, he was *hiding yet not hiding*, hiding just enough to avoid a repeat of the *Credo* fiasco of a decade earlier, taking care to lay a foundation of plausible deniability if a concerned official should ask too many questions, listen too closely, or approach too near.[81] A critical, ritual moment of transition between hiding underground and coming out into the open was the Riga festival premiere of all three sacred works that Pärt would soon identify with *Pirx*. For it was there, in October 1977, that a major revelation took place. It was there, in the largely unmonitored space of the Riga Polytechnic discotheque, that he finally revealed his tintinnabuli project as the devotional one it had been from the start.

FOUR

RITUAL MOMENTS

The RPI Festivals, 1976–77

When the audience filed into the Student Club of the Riga Polytechnic Institute (RPI) around ten in the evening on October 28, 1977, few of its members would have heard the music that Pärt had been calling "tintinnabuli" for a year. But everyone would have heard of Pärt, whose fame had been cemented in Soviet classical music circles more than a decade earlier. Arranging for Pärt's attendance at the festival was clearly something of a coup, and Hardijs Lediņš made a big deal of it in promotional copy aimed at drawing young people to the event. "If you want to find out what kind of work the Estonian composer Arvo Pärt is doing now," he wrote in the newspaper of the Latvian Komsomol, "we invite you to the festival of Soviet music at the RPI Student Club."[1] Befitting his fame, Pärt's music had appeared regularly on Latvian SSR Philharmonic programs in the 1960s and early 1970s. But with his partial retreat from the concert stage following the *Credo* scandal of 1968, performances of his music had dried up, and his last mention in the Riga press had appeared back in 1973. At the time of the festival, none of his tintinnabuli-style works had been performed beyond the empire's northwest. Between October 1976 and autumn 1977, versions of his *Tintinnabuli* suite were played in Tallinn, Tartu, and Leningrad. But his first unambiguous success with his new style came just weeks before the Riga festival, with the Tallinn premiere of *Tabula rasa* on September 30, 1977. A repeat performance of that momentous concert was given in Leningrad on October 27, the night before Pärt's festival appearance at RPI. It would not be until 1979 that any of Pärt's tintinnabuli-style music would be performed in Moscow.[2]

Riga was a different kind of place for Pärt than Tallinn, Tartu, or Leningrad, however. For despite the lack of official performances in the Latvian capital, Lediņš's polytechnic disco had already hosted, in April 1976, that very first, *unofficial* performance of the first work Pärt identified with the word "tintinnabuli." There and then, *Modus* had its underground premiere under the Biblical title *Sarah Was Ninety Years Old*.[3] That concert was part of Lediņš's first attempt at organizing a festival of new music at his discotheque. Now, some eighteen months later, the follow-up festival of October 1977 presented Pärt with another key opening. While the official unveiling of the *Tintinnabuli* suite featured works scored either for instruments or for wordless singing, among the premieres at the 1977 festival were *Summa*, a setting of the Nicene Creed, *Cantate Domino*, setting Psalm 96, and the *Missa syllabica*, all performed with their Latin texts clearly declaimed by the choir. If the underground premiere of *Sarah* provided a hint of where Pärt was going in 1976, the festival of 1977 was a kind of public unmasking. It was there that he revealed his tintinnabuli project to be a sacred one, and it was at that festival that he publicly declared his previously guarded identity as a composer of sacred Christian music.

Documentation of the festival events of 1976 and 1977 is sparse. They received little coverage in the official press, and what attention they did garner was sometimes ambiguous, contradictory, or erroneous. Nevertheless, archival materials, interviews with participants, and scattered published sources reveal glimpses of events and snippets of sounds, and also something of the institutional affordances, personal relationships, and social networks that enabled Lediņš and his friends to cultivate, from the roots of his disco, a remarkable annual phenomenon. By 1977, the RPI festival was drawing celebrated musicians from across the USSR, including Tatiana Grindenko, the soprano Lydia Davydova, and the Vilnius String Quartet. At the same time, it remained sufficiently under the radar as to enable the performance of the most ideologically questionable music Pärt would ever compose in the Soviet Union. This chapter aims to recover something of these festival events: the atmosphere of uninhibited experimentation in which Pärt's sacred tintinnabuli project took hold, and the alternative forms of sociality they nurtured among participants in turn. For the violinist Donatas Katkus, a member of the Vilnius String Quartet, the community-cementing, utopian quality of the events seemed in hindsight to be their most important legacy. "We were all together," he told me, recalling his participation in the 1977 festival, and "felt as [if] underground." Afterward, he remembers feeling a rush of optimism about cultural life in the Soviet Union, a place that many in his generation believed they would soon inherit and change for the better. As he put it to me directly, "We were creating a new future."[4]

APRIL 1976

When Lediņš recounted the history of the festivals from the vantage of the 1980s, he described their origins amid a season of encounter and disappointment: in his life-changing experience of hearing the pianist Alexei Lubimov performing new and experimental music in Riga, marred by the abrupt cancelation of Lubimov's concert series after official upset at his choice of repertoire.[5] A resident of Moscow, Lubimov was a regular presence in the Latvian capital, where he had acquired a substantial following by mixing avant-garde compositions into his programs of Russian and Western classics. "The overflowing hall," read a review of a 1975 recital at which he played works by Mozart, Debussy, Schoenberg, and Cage, "attests to the topicality of the event."[6] At the end of that year, the Latvian SSR Philharmonic invited Lubimov to present a series of concerts under the title "Old and New Works," or "Works of the Past and the Present" (*Pagātnes un tagadnes skaņdarbi*).

The first performance of the series, on December 10, 1975, was widely advertised in the Riga press and featured works (unspecified in published ads) by Machaut, Edgard Varèse, Cage, Sofia Gubaidulina, and Vladimir Martynov, as well as "everyday music of the 13th and 14th centuries" (*13.-14. gadsimta sadzīves mūzika*).[7] Lubimov brought along an ensemble of talents from his regular roster of Moscow collaborators, including Grindenko and her brother, the bassist Anatoly Grindenko, the soprano (and musicologist) Svetlana Savenko, and the percussionist Mark Pekarsky. A review indicated that the cellist Natalia Gutman made an unadvertised appearance as well.[8] The second concert of the series, on February 28, 1976, received little notice in the daily papers, but its impact upon the Riga Polytechnic DJ was profound. Here is Lediņš's account:

I went to my first-ever concert of avant-garde music: Alexei Lubimov and Tatiana Grindenko were appearing in Riga. They played
Cage and Stockhausen, and the audience laughed the whole time.
Those days it was funny to see a violinist hitting the piano strings
with her bow rather than playing. But the prepared piano is an important component of avant-garde music. I went home and decided
that I, too, needed to try my hand at preparing a piano. I stuck in
pieces of paper, erasers, pins, and scissors, and it sounded just like
Lubimov. So, why shouldn't I try making a recording? Some friends
came over. I put on the tape and asked them: "What's this?" They
said, "It's probably something by Stockhausen. . . ." And that's how
[I] got started.[9]

It was around this time, in the 1975–76 academic year, that Lediņš
began filling his school notebooks with reflections on Cage, Bach, and
other classical composers, as we have seen. And it was then that he
started assembling discotheque programs on which progressive rock
and avant-garde music were played and discussed side by side. Soon,
he would also begin to compose, producing the first of his "Seque"
tapes shortly after Lubimov's recital.[10]

As it happened, the falloff in official coverage of Lubimov's series in
early 1976 was not incidental. As Lediņš's friend and frequent collaborator Boriss Avramecs recounts, a minor scandal unfolded immediately after the pianist's first concert of the series, when "some listener"
reportedly wrote a letter complaining about the repertoire performed,
addressing her missive "not to the philharmonic but to the Central Committee of the [Latvian Communist] Party"—a high-handed
move that was, Avramecs adds, "wholly characteristic of the mentality
of Soviet citizens of the time." Evidently, the second concert of Lubimov's series was allowed to proceed, albeit without the publicity that
had accompanied the first. Once again, however, after the show, someone reportedly filed a complaint, this time (another attendee suggests)
about a performance of Valentin Silvestrov's *Drama* (1971), in which
the violinist sometimes bows the piano strings, as Lediņš described.
After that, the series was canceled.[11] Lediņš was incensed, Avramecs
remembers, especially when he learned that Lubimov had been planning to perform Terry Riley's *In C* in an upcoming series recital.[12] To-

gether, Lediņš and Avramecs, who first bonded in the listening room of the Latvian National Library, determined to find a way to stage the scuttled concert after all.

The venue they envisioned was the RPI Student Club, the event to be one of the wildly popular discotheques Lediņš had been running there since 1975. Through his day job working for the state, another friend, a local artist, enjoyed unmonitored access to a long-distance phone line, which Avramecs and Lediņš used at night to place calls to Lubimov in Moscow.[13] (It was a classic example of what Daniel Muzyczuk identifies as a key way in which underground events were sometimes organized across the Socialist bloc: "opportunities offered by the state, whether in terms of infrastructure or other, were eagerly exploited" by clever, knowing actors.[14]) Lubimov's interest in the disco-festival project was piqued, and he recruited his friends at the electronic music studio of the Skriabin Museum to join him for the trip: members of the rock band Boomerang, including Grindenko and Martynov, along with the audio engineer Yurii Bogdanov. Their plans for a concert quickly expanding into an outline for a multiday festival of new music, Lediņš reportedly approached the RPI Komsomol for their approval, without being asked (according to Avramecs) for details about what exactly they had planned. Protocols of the Komsomol's meetings make no mention of preparations for the festival, but Avramecs's contention seems plausible, given the organization's consistent support of Lediņš's discotheque without questions or substantial oversight.[15] On April 28, 1976, Lubimov was scheduled to return to Riga for a Philharmonic Chamber Orchestra concert of music by Bach and the Latvian composer Romualds Kalsons.[16] That official visit provided an opening. Lubimov would arrive a couple days earlier. The date of the festival was set.

In his musical diaries, Pärt recorded traveling to Riga on the twenty-sixth of April and attending the premiere of *Sarah* at the Anglican Church, home of the Student Club, the following day.[17] Beyond these facts, we can pin down few details about the festival or its events, which Avramecs remembers lasting between three and five days.[18] Memories of participants are fragmentary and sometimes contradictory in their details, and little documentation is known to survive, if it was ever produced at all. In a letter to Silvestrov of July 1977, Lubimov described performing at the Student Club in April of the previous year, along with "our ensemble," presumably Boomerang.[19] More recently, he recalled playing the festival premiere of *Sarah* on the harpsichord (more likely the piano, given the venue?), and he claimed that the celebrated Lydia Davydova sang the vocal part.[20] But Avramecs insists that Davydova attended only the 1977 festival, not the event of 1976, and Pärt recalls that the singer on the premiere was pregnant, whereas Davydova, born in 1932, was not at the time.[21] (In a recent conversation, the Pärts could not recall the name of the singer who performed the premiere, but they confirmed that it was not Davydova.)[22] Avramecs has told me that Pärt, too, did not attend the festival of 1976, and Pärt remembers only the single concert where *Sarah* was performed, not an entire festival.[23] But a photograph of festival preparations taken by the artist Kirils Šmeļkovs (fig. 4.1) shows Pärt together with Lubimov

FIGURE 4.1 Pärt (*left*) and Alexei Lubimov (*second from right*) during setup for an RPI festival performance held at the Latvian Academy of Art, April 1976. Photo by Kirils Šmeļkovs. Collection of the Latvian Centre for Contemporary Art. Courtesy of Kirils Šmeļkovs.

FIGURE 4.2 Alexei Lubimov and Tatiana Grindenko at the RPI festival, April 1976. Photo by Kirils Šmeļkovs. Collection of the Latvian Centre for Contemporary Art. Courtesy of Kirils Šmeļkovs.

and others, standing not in the Anglican Church but in the great hall of the Latvian Academy of Art, where Šmeļkovs was studying graphic arts, and where a wholly different festival event from the *Sarah* premiere was being staged. When I shared this photo with the composer through an interlocutor, he still did not remember any events beyond the performance of *Sarah*.[24]

Other photos taken by Šmeļkovs offer glimpses of further preparations for the concert: Lubimov and Grindenko consulting in rehearsal, a drum kit in the background (fig. 4.2). Lubimov arranging music on stands, a giant T-shaped stack of speakers and electronic equipment to his left (fig. 4.3). Lubimov crouched in study (fig. 4.4).[25]

Avramecs describes some of the repertoire.[26] Riley's *In C* was performed, and Pekarsky played a percussion piece by Martynov that had him loudly reciting a poem by the Russian futurist Velimir Khlebnikov—probably an early version of a work that Pekarsky would later record as *Ierarkhiia razumnykh tsennostei* (1977–90). In the final

FIGURE 4.3 Lubimov at the RPI festival, April 1976. Note the bank of electronics to his left. Photo by Kirils Šmeļkovs. Collection of the Latvian Centre for Contemporary Art. Courtesy of Kirils Šmeļkovs.

concert, at the Latvian Academy of Art, Boomerang performed *Setz die Segel zur Sonne* from Stockhausen's *Aus den sieben Tagen*, a landmark work of the composer's freely improvisational "intuitive music" from 1968. Then, Bogdanov read Cage's *Lecture on the Weather*—composed that very year—in Russian translation. The event closed with a Happening, spontaneously created by Avramecs and Lubimov with assistance from members of a local experimental theater troupe. These latter performances, as the work of the Russian musicologist Tat'iana Cherednichenko suggests, would likely have been regarded as deeply significant, even programmatic statements at the time. She notes that an earlier, kindred work by Cage, *45' for a Speaker* (1954), attained emblematic status among young musicians of the 1970s looking for alternatives to the "very-very-very deep talk about music" that still prevailed in Soviet conservatory and classical music culture. In a similar spirit, she notes, Martynov organized some of the first Cage-inspired

FIGURE 4.4   Lubimov at the RPI festival, April 1976. Photo by Kirils Šmeļkovs. Collection of the Latvian Centre for Contemporary Art. Courtesy of Kirils Šmeļkovs.

Happenings in the USSR in 1972–74. In fact, Pärt had participated in such events in Tallinn as early as 1968.[27]

Despite the stature of the participating artists, the Biblical reference in the title of Pärt's contribution, and the minor scandal that engulfed Lubimov's concert series at the start of the year, the RPI festival of April 1976 seems to have passed entirely beneath the radar of Soviet bureaucracy, which either did not notice or did not care about Lediņš's latest musical undertaking. It did receive at least one report in the local press, a cursory recap in the polytechnic's student paper about a week after the event. As the review makes clear, the festival was enthusiastically attended by a broad swath of Riga's listening public, who came from well beyond the halls of the polytechnic to see and hear what Lediņš had arranged. "There was, once again, a great flood of listeners coming to the latest discotheque," the paper reported. "The reason was simple: visitors from Moscow. The director of the ensemble was the famous avant-garde composer [*sic*] and international laureate, A. Lubimov. Not in vain did one search the audience for a number of musicians and music critics!" The paper's summary assessment was bland: "This discotheque provided an opportunity to become better acquainted with progressive, avant-garde music."[28] Yet, surveying attendees' recollections some twenty years after the event, another journalist recounted different impressions of the final concert in particular. "We can only defer to the statements of witnesses and participants about the hypnotic effect that all this apparent chaos had upon the public," she wrote, "about [feelings of] lasting catharsis and spiritual cleansing, after which one couldn't help but look at the world with new eyes."[29]

OCTOBER 1977

If the festival of 1976 was a ghostlike affair, a milestone in Pärt's life that left little trace in the documentary record, the follow-up festival of 1977 was more widely noticed. Nevertheless, its organizers still managed to avoid the sort of official scrutiny that would have made the public performance of Pärt's sacred music impossible. For Lubimov, in hindsight the second RPI discotheque festival seemed to number among his greatest organizational triumphs of the decade—a span of years, he recalled, that had been full of artistic and organizational triumphs. For Martynov, it was an event in which "we—Pärt, Silvestrov, and myself—came out as if in a united front," to declare "a new compositional truth."[30] That truth, for Martynov, was a postmodernist truth, the collective sounding or sonic intimation of a harmonious future for Soviet culture and society. It was also a moment of spiritual truth, the event at which Pärt, and Martynov as well, first appeared publicly as Christian artists, as composers of openly, explicitly devotional music.

According to Avramecs, plans for this second festival began almost immediately after the conclusion of the first. Buoyed by the success of the latter project, which they'd pulled off without any hint of official concern, he and Lediņš resolved to make their next event even bigger and better than the last. To this end, they hit upon what turned out to be a brilliant plan: to tie their festival project to the numerous events being held throughout the USSR to celebrate the sixtieth anniversary of the October Revolution of 1917.[31] Already in April 1977, Augusts Voss, secretary of the Latvian SSR Central Committee, had invited organizations and individuals across the republic to dedicate their efforts in the upcoming months to commemorating this foundational moment in Soviet history. On April 22, the text of Voss's address was published in the weekly paper of the combined Latvian artists' unions.[32] At a meeting of their governing committee in June, the Composers' Union of the Latvian SSR confirmed that concerts marking the anniversary would be a priority for its upcoming season. The Latvian SSR Philharmonic dedicated all of its programming in the month of October to the commemoration, and the Riga Polytechnic Institute marked the occasion by staging an October festival called "Science Week."[33] As Avramecs recounts, he and his friends in Moscow and Riga divided up the organizing work. Lubimov would enlist the participation of performers and composers, and Avramecs would handle the logistics. Meanwhile, Lediņš would work to assure that the festival would once again unfold without interference from authorities.[34] In fact, Lediņš sought something more than that: material support from government entities, yet without the official oversight that such support might be expected to entail.

Key to gaining official sanction, it seems, was the help of a pair of young Latvian musicologists with ties to the leadership of the Composers' Union. One year earlier, the union's governing committee had resolved to "take an active role in the production of events dedicated to the sixtieth anniversary of the October Revolution," and the union's secretary had identified the republic's technical schools as particularly ripe for such engagement.[35] Avramecs has published the organizers' formal description of their goals for the festival, the contents of which were reportedly conveyed by the musicologists to the Composers' Union along with a request for sponsorship:

Festival of Contemporary Music in the USSR, Dedicated to the Sixtieth Anniversary of the Great October Revolution. Description:

The festival of music is organized by the Riga Polytechnic Student Club, with contributions from the Composers' Union of the Latvian SSR and the Latvian Conservatory. Festival concerts will take place on October 21–30 in the Student Club (Anglican Church), in the railroad workers' cultural center, and at the Latvian Conservatory.

Musical events and goals:

1. To popularize recent achievements in the music of Soviet peoples. Almost all of the festival concerts will feature works performed for the first time in our republic.
2. To promote exchanges of ideas and contacts between creative youth of the brotherly republics. This will foster the inclusion of new Soviet music in our republic's concert life.[36]

While his colleagues were lobbying the Composers' Union for their support, Lediņš worked his Komsomol connections. Nothing relating to the festival plans is preserved in the organization's protocols or reports from the period, but a document produced for its governing committee meeting of May 30, 1977, enumerates fifteen ways in which the Komsomol intended to work in support of events marking the anniversary of the revolution. Several of these seem directly relevant to Lediņš's plans, including:

8. Foster meaningful contemplation in student circles of the decrees of the C[ommunist] P[arty] of the USSR "regarding the 60th anniversary of the Great October Socialist Revolution."

And:

13. Organize festivals for various groups.[37]

In a letter to Silvestrov of July 1977, written just after his return from a visit to Riga, Lubimov described Lediņš's strategy of enlisting Komsomol support as a way to head off more careful scrutiny by the Ministry of Culture. "The festival taking shape," Lubimov wrote to Silvestrov, "is being supported by people from the Komsomol. In particular, it's being organized under the banner of the 60th [anniversary], because if you're already [operating, as the Komsomol was] within the sphere of the Ministry of Culture, the censor will leave you alone."[38]

In the end, Avramecs remembers, the Composers' Union declined to sponsor the event, reportedly having found the proposed programs to be mostly unworthy of their support.[39] Nevertheless, in October, flyers for the festival went up on campus (see fig. 1.1). The "Ten-Day Festival of Contemporary Music, Dedicated to the Sixtieth Anniversary of the Great October Socialist Revolution" would take place at the end of the month. Its organizers had managed to secure and retain the backing of the Student Club, and, through their networking, they had booked some of the leading performers of new music from throughout the USSR, including Pekarsky from Moscow, the Vilnius String Quartet, and Hortus Musicus from Tallinn. (When I showed a photograph of the flyer to Katkus, the Vilnius String Quartet violinist, in May 2018, he burst out laughing at its reference to the Bolshevik Revolution.)[40]

The festival received no notice among regular concert listings in the daily press, and, indeed, its organization seems to have come together almost entirely through informal channels. The Estonian journalist Immo Mihkelson, who has done extensive research in the now-scattered archives of the Estonian SSR Philharmonic, confirms that Hortus Musicus traveled to Riga without filing any of the paperwork required for an official visit.[41] The musicologist Martin Boiko, brother of Lediņš's collaborator Juris Boiko, remembers that their family's Riga flat "suddenly became accommodations for two members of Hortus Musicus, because lodging hadn't been arranged."[42]

Still, the festival received one bit of advance press, penned by Lediņš himself, in the paper of the Latvian Komsomol, and it received brief mention in the weekly organ of the combined Latvian artists' unions. In the former, the DJ good-naturedly thumbed his nose at the Latvian SSR Philharmonic and other bureaucratic entities that had declined to support new music in recent years. Plugging the upcoming event, he wrote:

> Contemporary music, new music, modern music . . . What's the situation with such music in our republic? And throughout our country? You'll get answers to these and other questions about contemporary music if you come to the festival of Soviet music. Is it organized by the philharmonic? No, of course not! It's being organized by the Student Club of the Riga Polytechnic Institute.[43]

On the first day of the festival, an announcement in the paper of the Latvian artists' unions was full of errors: it claimed that both Schnittke and Gidon Kremer would attend, and also (remarkably) that the Composers' Union was among the sponsors. Nonetheless, its author's admiration for the work of Lediņš and his friends was clear. "The RPI Student Club deserves considerable praise," the author wrote. "The events it has organized—lectures, concerts, theatrical performances, meetings, discotheques—are of interest not only to youth at the institution but to society as a whole."[44]

Information about the festival programs is spotty, but an overview of at least some of the events is preserved among Lediņš's papers (fig. 4.5). On October 24, Lubimov, Pekarsky, and a saxophone quartet from Moscow gave a concert in the Anglican Church. An additional page provides the program: Edison Denisov's *Singing of the Birds* (*Penie ptits*, 1969), Sofia Gubaidulina's *Rumore e silenzio* (*Shum i tishina*, 1974) for harpsichord and percussion, an unidentified percussion piece by Martynov, and an unspecified selection of Russian classical and contemporary works performed by the saxophonists (Glazunov, Prokofiev, and Artemyev were among the composers represented).[45] The following day, at the Latvian Conservatory, a program of music by the Latvian composers Pēteris Vasks and Selga Mence. On October 26, the Vilnius String Quartet performed an unknown program, followed by a concert of unspecified works by Silvestrov, Martynov, Alexander Knaifel, and Viktor Suslin. At 3:30 in the afternoon of the twenty-eighth, Boomerang. At 10:30 that night, Hortus Musicus gave an all-Pärt concert. The next two days saw a pair of programs whose repertoire cannot be identified beyond the names of the composers represented: the Latvians Edvīns Zālītis, Imants Zemzaris, and Juris Ābols; the Estonians Mati Kuulberg and Raimo Kangro; and a Lithuanian, Osvaldas Balakauskas. A concert at the Latvian Conservatory featured a new choral work by Knaifel. Pärt was not the only composer to attend the festival in person. Silvestrov came from Kyiv, Knaifel came from Leningrad, and Suslin and Martynov traveled from Moscow. According to Avramecs, Tigran Mansuryan flew in from Yerevan, but I have not found any record or account of his music being performed.

At the time of the festival, Hortus Musicus, directed by Mustonen, was among the most famous early music ensembles in the USSR, second in renown only to Madrigal, the group from Moscow founded by Volkonsky and directed in 1977 by Davydova. The Estonians' performance of Pärt's music on the evening of October 28, recorded on reel-to-reel tape by Lediņš, showcased their early music sound as they delivered a program markedly more austere than the official premiere of Pärt's tintinnabuli-style works in Tallinn the year before.[46] Gone from the ensemble were the electric guitar and bass that played in *Calix* and *Modus*. Also missing from the Riga performance was the full, highly polished sound of the Tallinn Chamber Choir. In their place, the ensemble featured a handful of voices, crumhorns, recorders, a consort of viols, and brass. The first half of the evening's all-Pärt concert featured a new version of the *Tintinnabuli* suite, with four of its six constituent pieces receiving their first-ever public performances. The program began with the fanfare of *Arbos*, composed about a month before, with the familiar brass parts of its canonic 1987 recording played by reedy crumhorns.[47] *Arbos* was followed by a quick *Cantate Domino*, written in June, and then *Summa*, which Pärt had completed at the start of the year. Both of the latter were performed with their Latin texts clearly

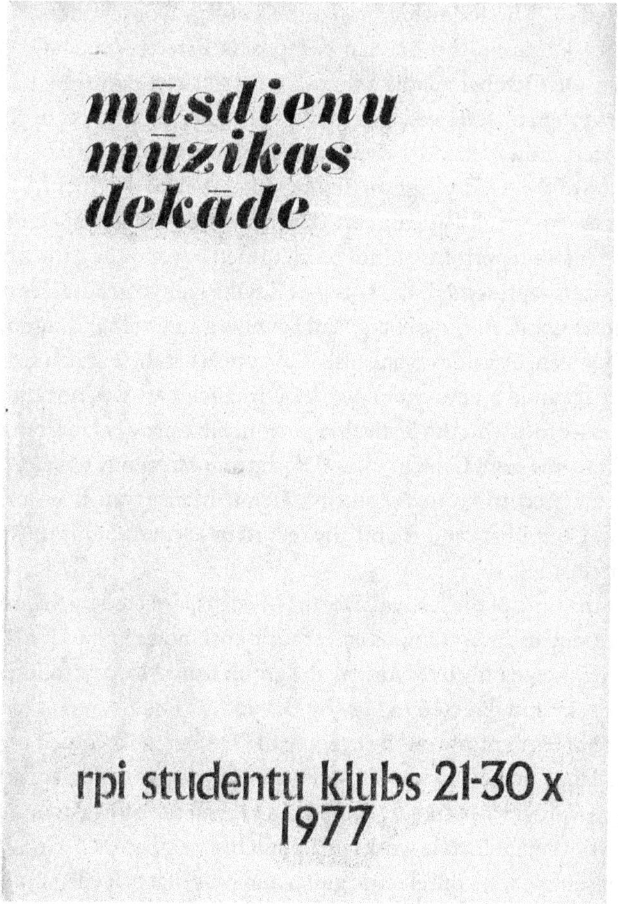

mūsdienu
mūzikas
dekāde

rpi studentu klubs 21-30 x
1977

FIGURE 4.5   Program for the Festival of Contemporary Music at the Riga Polytechnic Institute, October 1977. Collection of the Latvian Centre for Contemporary Art.

enunciated by the choir: Psalm 96 and the Nicene Creed, respectively. Then came *Fratres*, which Pärt had finished only three weeks before the festival, with each iteration of its generative algorithm performed by a different group of instruments: high recorders, then viols, then crumhorns, then low recorders, brass, and so on. The Riga version of the *Tintinnabuli* suite closed with two works from the previous year—*In spe*, performed by voices, and *Pari intervallo* on lute and viols.

```
24. oktobrī, pl. 18.00      RPI Studentu klubā

                            A.Ļubimovs, M.Pekarskis,
                            saksofonu kvartets (Maskava)

25. oktobrī, pl. 20.00      Konservatorijas zālē

                            N.Novika un R.Haradžanjans

            pl. 22.30       Jauno latviešu komponistu
                            skaņdarbu koncerts

26. oktobrī, pl. 20.00      RPI Studentu klubā

                            A.Knaifeļa, V.Martinova,
                            V.Silvestrova, V.Suslina
                            skaņdarbu koncerts

27. oktobrī, pl. 20.00      RPI Studentu klubā
26. OKTOBRĪ PL. 18.00       Viļņas stīgu kvartets

28. oktobrī, pl. 15.30      Dzelzceļnieku klubā, Suvorova
                            ielā 7

                            Maskavas elektroniskās mūzikas
                            studijas grupa "Bumerangs"

            pl. 22.30       RPI Studentu klubā

                            Ansamblis "Hortus musicus"
                            Programmā A.Pērta skaņdarbi

29. oktobrī, pl. 17.00      Straupes koncertzālē

                            Dekādes dalībnieku koncerts

30. oktobrī.                Dekādes noslēguma koncerts

                            (vietu un laiku paziņos
                            atsevišķi)

---------------------------------------------------

Abonementi un biļetes RPI Studentu klubā
Bibliotēkas ielā 2a no pl. 12.00
```

After the suite, something even more remarkable than the sacred vocal music just played: the *Missa syllabica*, performed in its entirety, which Pärt had written in the initial rush of discovering his syllabic method at the start of the year. It was the work's first-ever public performance. As we saw in chapter 3, on the cardboard box that houses the tape, Lediņš inscribed its title as "Mass (Test)," making clear his knowledge not only of the title that Pärt was sometimes using (*Test*), but also of the work's ritual function. In its rendering by Hortus Musicus that night, the vocalists were joined by instrumentalists, with Mustonen following the manuscript score precisely, a document that records Pärt's absolutely strict adherence to the generative algorithm.[48] The expressive lengthening of notes at the ends of phrases familiar from the score Pärt eventually published was nowhere heard in the premiere concert.[49] Word after word, line after line, for just over ten minutes in performance, the audience sat through the entire ordinary of the Latin Mass, from the *Kyrie* ("Lord, have mercy") to the *Credo* ("I believe in one God") to the concluding *Ite missa est* ("Go, it is concluded. Thanks be to God"). On October 28, at around eleven in evening, it was as if the building that housed the Student Club had become a church once again, the sacred rite resounding in its walls for the first time since the arrival of Soviet tanks some thirty-seven years before.

Pärt's was not the only sacred music to be performed at the festival. Martynov, too, had a premiere, his *Passionslieder* (1977) for soprano (Davydova) and a Baroque ensemble of strings and harpsichord. Comprising nine movements, each based on a single four-bar melody in G minor, Martynov's work is a highly repetitive, even hypnotic setting of a Lutheran chorale text written by the German theologian Johann Mentzer at the turn of the eighteenth century. *Der am Kreuz ist meine Liebe, meine Liebe ist Jesus Christ*: "He on the cross is the one whom I love, the one whom I love is Jesus Christ" (ex. 4.1).

This performance, too, was captured by Lediņš on reel-to-reel tape.[50] As Lediņš clarified in an interview of 2001, the *Passionslieder* and the all-Pärt concert were the only festival performances he recorded. When asked to explain, he replied simply: "Sacred music." Lediņš never professed or exhibited religious convictions himself. Rather, his selection of these two concerts for recording seems to attest to the sheer extraordinariness of such performances in the Soviet Union at that time.[51] As was the case with Pärt's sacred premieres, the identity of Martynov's *Passionslieder* was concealed on the xerographic schedule of festival events, which simply indicated the performance of "works" (*skaņdarbi*) by both composers (fig. 4.5). Still, the fact that these concerts, like the festival itself, were advertised to the general public makes one wonder how long they would have remained unnoticed by officials after the event, even if the festival organizers

1. Der am Kreuz ist meine Liebe! Meine Liebe ist Jesus Christ! Weg, ihr argen Seelendiebe

1. Satan, Welt und Fleischeslüst! Eure Lieb ist nicht von Gott Eure Liebe ist gar der Tod

EXAMPLE 4.1 Martynov, *Passionslieder* (1977), measures 17–28.

had not made the one terrible mistake they did. As Avramecs reports, one of them—not a core member of the group, he stresses—dropped typescript copies of Mentzer's text from the balcony of the Anglican Church, to land in the laps of concert attendees just as Martynov's piece was being played. The stunt, he notes, was observed by the KGB.[52] The rest, as they say, is history.

RESONANCE

I'll pause this story at a dramatic moment in hopes that you'll read something I think is important to this history, concerning Vladimir Martynov. Not widely known outside of Russia, Martynov is an unmissable presence in that country today, renowned as much as an author and public intellectual as he is as a composer. From this point forward, he will loom increasingly large in the story of the festival project that began at RPI, and of Pärt's own path as a composer of openly sacred music in the Soviet Union. What I wish to stress is that it is no surprise that the premiere of Pärt's *Missa syllabica* in Riga made such a deep impression on his Russian colleague. And in stressing that, I wish to point to some ways in which Pärt's music resonated so powerfully for many contemporary artists. Put simply, hearing the *Missa syllabica* just two days after the first performance of his own *Passionslieder* would surely have revealed to Martynov a uncanny intersection of both spiritual and aesthetic concerns—made all the more remarkable, perhaps, by the fact that neither the sound nor the nature of Pärt's tintinnabuli experiments were widely known in Moscow at the time. I noted earlier Martynov's aversion to the sounds and ambitions of the postwar Euro-American avant-garde and also his rhetorical investment in "discrediting the principle of self-expression" in art.[53] With the widely publicized premieres of Pärt's Third Symphony and *Song to the Beloved* in 1972–73, the Estonian composer had achieved a measure of renown for what seemed to be his own rejection of avant-garde modernism. But prior to the Riga festival of October 1977, Martynov would likely have heard little about Pärt's tintinnabuli project. And he could not have known that Pärt was striving, at that very moment in his own compositional practice, for Orthodox hesychasm: silencing the impulse to interpret the sacred texts he set, effecting—to paraphrase the painter Eduard Steinberg—his own renunciation of the creative ego.

Prior to his premieres at the RPI festival of 1977, Pärt's overtly religious tintinnabuli experiments were the silent provenance of his musical diaries. And it was only after settling in the West in 1980 that he began talking openly about the hesychastic nature of his work. "Tintinnabuli is like submission," Pärt wrote from Berlin. "Renunciation of one's own will." Or: "Become nothing (before all else)!"[54] As we have seen, Pärt's discovery of the syllabic method was a crucial step toward these goals, signaled by his composition of the *Missa syllabica* in February 1977. Martynov, in his own creative practice, took a different approach to similar ends, via means he would call "bricolage" and later "simulacra," involving an imaginary return to the musical materials and compositional methods of earlier ages. Specifically, Martynov sought to connect with musical practices characteristic of a time *before* the advent of thinking about the composer as a self-expressing artist. This meant, for him, the sixteenth century or earlier. Thus the deliberately archaic sounds of the *Passionslieder*.[55]

Whereas Pärt had arrived at his tintinnabuli style after years of musical and spiritual exploration, Martynov, in 1977, was still searching for his path. The son of a distinguished musicologist, he had taken his degree in composition from the Moscow Conservatory in 1971. After that, he headed east: to Soviet Tajikistan, where he spent his days working for a film studio and his nights with friends, listening to records by John McLaughlin and Shakti, Klaus Schulze, King Crimson, and Tangerine Dream. At a time when the sounds of Western progressive and experimental rock were attending and inspiring religious awakenings and visions of an "imaginary elsewhere" among young people throughout the USSR, Martynov was drawn in deeply.[56] In Dushanbe, he and his friends spent hours discussing what they heard on vinyl and the "Great Idea" (*Velikaia Ideia*) it seemed to reveal. And "by *Great Idea* we meant, of course, the *Great Religious Idea*," he later explained. Planted on the steppe of central Asia, their listening sessions and conversations carried them even further eastward. "We were united by a deep conviction that the West had long ago lost its Great Idea," he remembers. "At the same time, we were firmly convinced that the East had not only *not* lost its Great Idea, but that the Idea was revealed, in its full, luminous power, in the contemporary religious practices of India and Tibet."[57] In a move that seems unintuitive today but was widespread among Soviet youth of his generation, the principal vehicle for Martynov's imaginary travel was not Tibetan music but Western rock. As Lediņš recalled of these same years, "In truth, we could travel the world only through the means of literature—or we could do the same with music, which was easier for some."[58]

Within a year, Martynov was back in Moscow, where he tapped into what the anthropologist Terje Toomistu describes as "a subcultural network" of "alternative youth across the urban Soviet Union" of the 1970s, "a community of shared affect that was based on their engagements with the imaginary elsewhere and which drew them into mimetic communication with their imagined counterparts in the West as well as among themselves."[59] In the Russian capital, Martynov encountered Yevgeniya Zavadskaya just as her book *The East in the West* (1970) was circulating widely in creative circles. He studied with a yogi. And he took a job at the electronic music studio of the Skriabin Museum, at the moment when its equipment and staff were undergoing the generational shift he later described.[60] "By day," he recalls, "the studio operated like an ordinary Soviet institution," its staff conducting experiments with sound synthesis and creating scores for films. At night, however, it became a "laboratory of psychedelic art rock, in which the audio engineer Yurii Bogdanov transformed himself into a high priest administering the cult's sacred rites." The most hallowed of those rites were all-night listening sessions, accompanied by heated debates about religious questions and mystical themes.[61] Listening one night with his studio friends to King Crimson's 1974 album *Red*, Martynov had a vision: of music as a "sparkling stream embracing and penetrating everything," and of the task of the composer or musician as consisting, simply, in "lowering themselves into that stream." Up to that point, Martynov, always a writer, had been composing poetry alongside music. But with his studio epiphany, he gave up his literary ambitions. From that moment forward, he devoted himself fully to music.[62]

As he later recounted, Martynov's first inklings of the ideas that would lead to his thinking about simulacra and such works as the *Passionslieder* came when he read a pair of standard-issue music history texts, the polemical statements traded circa 1600 between the composer Giovanni Artusi and a brother of the composer Claudio Monteverdi. Technically, the Italians' debate focused on Claudio Monteverdi's then-radical treatment of musical dissonance, but it hit more broadly upon the role of any composer in relation to the texts they set. Artusi held that it was the composer's duty to subject himself (he thought only of men) to the norms and rules of inherited tradition. Monteverdi countered that the composer, as a freely interpreting intellect, was entitled to bend the rules however he saw fit to express his own interpretation of a poem. Martynov, who was just then starting to think about music as a "path toward religious understanding," sided with the conservative Artusi—and hard.[63] He discussed the centuries-old debate with friends whenever and wherever they were willing to listen, even adopting the sixteenth-century writers' terminology as his own, and he seriously pondered writing his own polemical treatise to set the record straight. Monteverdi's music, and most of the music composed after him, was, for Martynov, "artistic music," music created to give sounding expression to the mind or ideas of the artist. The music of earlier ages, in contrast, was "magical music," as he called it, music that resounds *through* the composer, music that sounds the voice of God. That was the kind of music Martynov wished to write.[64] In unknowing parallel to Pärt in Tallinn, Martynov immersed himself in study of early and pre-Baroque musics. And he began to seek, in his own compositions, ways of tapping into the sounds of earlier ages, creating musical structures with means that he would later call simulacra.

Although he had not yet committed fully to Orthodox Christianity, Martynov had arrived, by the time of the 1977 festival, at an understanding of his compositional project as a deeply spiritual act, with the sounds of his music important primarily for the metaphysical experience they might inspire or convey. Looking back, he writes of the "essence" or "destiny of music" (*prednaznachenie muzyki*) consisting "not in its sounds being heard by someone, but in the possibility of its sounds being heard as a certain 'support beam' of being." He speaks of the "unheard sounds of music," in which "there is realized a worldly order," an order that we allude to reflexively when we speak of "the singing of angels or the sounds of cosmic spheres." He continues: "Music is not what is heard and not what sounds, but that *through which* the sounds sound, and also that which sounds *within* the sound and provides, through its unheard sound, for the existence of forms of being."[65] Here too, his thinking intersects with Pärt's. "Gregorian chant," Pärt reflected in the 1980s, "has taught me what a cosmic secret is hidden in the art of combining two, three notes." It helped him to realize that "everything that is readable with the eyes is not everything. One never knows what music lies behind these notes."[66] Or, as Pärt confided to West German Radio shortly after his emigration, "It's actually this music of the angels, which is always there, that Mozart heard and wrote down, this music of the angels that the holy monks wrote down, which is sung today in the church. . . ." His interviewer interceded: "So you wouldn't say, 'I wrote this music, it is my music.' But rather, perhaps like Bach, 'I am the servant of a higher power'?" To which Pärt replied: "I'd imagine that every great composer would have said that."[67] The photo reproduced in figure 1.3, taken in Tallinn in 1978, appears in hindsight to capture something of the relationship between the two artists: conceptually profound even if never personally close. Amid the most intensive period of his own creative and spiritual searching, Martynov felt as if he saw in Pärt a vision of himself reflected in a musical mirror, as if he heard an echo of his own quest in the resonant harmony of Pärt's compositions. In Riga, as Martynov later recalled, he and Pärt presented a "united front."

AN ENDING

Shortly after the festival ended, this space for experiment and community-making, carved out from the gaps and holes in the system by Lediņš, Lubimov, and their friends, was flooded with unwelcome light, cast by authorities who charged them with engaging in "religious propaganda." To date, much of the material from Latvia's KGB archives remains inaccessible to researchers, and I have been unable to find any record of repercussions in the archives of the Komsomol, the Riga Polytechnic, or the Composers' Union, which is sometimes said to have tried to intervene in defense of the students and artists implicated.[68] Later, in the time of glasnost, Lediņš recalled the fallout he experienced. "After the repressions" in the wake of the festival, "I no longer involved myself with avant-garde music." Referring to the imaginary "travel" that such musical engagements had recently afforded him, he explained: "Because I was an architecture student, I was called in to see the rector, and that's why I ceased my travels around the world. I was given a choice: to continue with my studies, or to organize further festivals. . . ." Lediņš chose the former.[69]

For Lubimov, the repercussions were harsher. "After the festival in Riga," he recalls, "I was deprived of concert trips abroad for several years."[70] Avramecs recounts how Lubimov told him of what transpired when he was summoned for a conversation with the Latvian Minister of Culture: "He actually screamed, 'As long as I am Minister, do not put a foot inside Latvia!'"[71] Harsher still was the punishment given to the head of the Student Club, Aina Bērziņa, who, along with the club's student organizer of artistic activities, lost her job. The decisions behind these moves seem to have been made quietly, or in spaces still inaccessible to historians. When I spoke with Bērziņa's successor in the post, Asja Visocka, in summer 2018, I asked her directly about the circumstances surrounding the shakeup of late 1977. Visocka insisted that the event was a "completely normal festival," and she explained the cessation of Lediņš's organizational work simply: "There was no real desire to continue."[72] Martin Boiko recalls things differently. Although he did not attend the festival himself, he remembers arriving at the Student Club shortly after the scandal broke. "One day I stepped into the Anglican Church, and in the Student Club office at the entrance to the balcony, there sat one of the workers (the director or her deputy), a person who was usually gracious and smiling. Now, she was crying. Having seen me several times before, she asked, 'What do you think, is all of this unimportant, not needed?' She paid no heed to my reaction, as if she were talking into the void. And that was how it ended."[73]

At the start of November, the RPI rector published an essay in the student paper, thanking all of the students, professors, and others who had organized events in commemoration of the sixtieth anniversary of the October Revolution. He made no mention of Lediņš's discotheque festival or the Student Club's contributions to the institution's festivities.[74] Nevertheless, two weeks later, the music critic for the student paper published a brief overview of the festival events, highlighting performances by the Latvian Conservatory Chamber Choir and the Vilnius String Quartet. "The public was especially looking forward to A. Lubimov, who was appearing for the second time at our Student Club," she wrote. She made no mention of Pärt, Martynov, or the scandal unfolding in the wake of their premieres.[75] After that point, in official discourse, news of the festival simply disappeared.

Almost, that is—at least locally. For in one of the stranger twists in this story, the events of October 1977 were recounted in considerable detail in January of the following year, in a paper called *Voice of the Homeland* (*Dzimtenes Balss*), a weekly publication shipped overseas to Latvian émigrés in the West. It was a project of the same KGB-directed office that produced the émigré-targeted radio program for which Lediņš's mother reported, the Committee for Cultural Relations with Compatriots Abroad.[76] Much of the essay in *Voice of the Homeland* reprints or paraphrases the festival coverage published in the polytechnic's student paper. But it also broached something markedly different, treating the very premieres that led to upset at home as events to be trumpeted to Latvians abroad. "Alongside the distinctly contemporary works of V. Suslin and V. Silvestrov, one could hear V. Martynov's cantata, *Passionslieder*, in which the composer made use of texts by seventeenth- and eighteenth-century authors [*sic*]." To make things clear, the author emphasized: "*Passionslieder* was performed in German."[77]

In Riga, the performance of openly religious works spelled the end of the short-lived but vital tradition of the RPI festivals, at which Pärt and Martynov felt free enough to come out publicly as Christian composers of sacred music. A month after the close of the second festival, its traces had been all but scrubbed from public discourse in the Latvian SSR. But to audiences abroad, that very transgression was held up as an indicator of the ostensible openness of Soviet cultural life. On the pages of *Voice of the Homeland*, the Soviet Union was a place where a young composer could set music to a text whose sacred ori-

gins nearly every Western European reader would recognize immediately from the German title of the work. Shuttered at home, the
partly underground space of the polytechnic disco was celebrated to
audiences in the West, the creative freedoms it temporarily afforded
turned to a final, ironic end by the state. And yet, as with nearly every
story surrounding the RPI festivals, this one, too, is ambiguous, its
meanings probably multiple and in any case unclear. There is no way
to tell whether Hardijs's mother, Rute Lediņa, had a hand in planning
or shaping coverage of the festival on the pages of *Voice of the Homeland*. But given the small office in which she worked, in which that paper was produced, it does not seem out of the question. Maybe, just
maybe, she sought to support her son in this way as well. The events
that transpired had finally landed Hardijs in trouble, from which her
position could not shield him. But maybe she saw his festival project
as valuable nonetheless, its achievements worthy of memorializing
wherever and however might still be possible.

As the 1977–78 academic year drew to a close, changes were in the air.
Working diligently to complete his degree, Lediņš continued to organize discos, but he increasingly sought venues beyond the polytechnic's campus, with an ever-larger share of his programs devoted to rock
and new wave music, and with his own recording projects veering into
distinctly popular realms. Meanwhile, in Moscow, Lubimov and his
friends were busy making plans for a third festival of new music. The
events of October had compelled them to look outside the Latvian
SSR, and with Lediņš's departure from the scene they connected with
Andres Mustonen, director of Hortus Musicus, who leveraged his esteem with officials in Tallinn to open the doors of Estonia's musical es-
tablishment to a blowout event planned for November 1978. The tradition of the festivals in which Pärt's sacred tintinnabuli project took
root would continue after all, it seemed, but in a new locale—right in
Pärt's backyard.

Avramecs would not be involved in organizing the Tallinn festival of 1978.[78] For him, as for Martynov and Lubimov, the culminat-
ing moment for the scene he helped shape was and would remain the

RPI festival of 1977. Looking back nearly thirty years after the event, he described its significance largely in terms of its impact in the social realm, a realm at once aesthetic and spiritual—and also, perhaps, even slightly, vaguely political. Recalling the concert of October 26 at which Martynov's *Passionslieder* premiered, he wrote:

> The concert took place late in the evening, at the end of October. And that night, on the embankment beside the Anglican Church, there was a rehearsal for an army parade going on, because November 7 [the anniversary of the revolution] was approaching. You could hear the grumbling of truck drivers and commands shouted in Russian. But right next to all that, *it was a little oasis.*[79]

FIVE

TALLINN 1978

In a satirical essay published in the journal of the Latvian Komsomol in 1988, amid the flurry of biting social critique that attended glasnost and perestroika, Hardijs Lediņš, famous by then, was put on mock trial for a list of offenses supposedly committed against the mores of Soviet youth. These included, first and foremost, the role he played in sparking the disco craze still raging among Riga's students. But his ostensible crimes also included organizing the 1977 festival of new music at the RPI Student Club. "Is it not enough for you that the club's director and its head of artistic activities lost their jobs?" Lediņš pled to his fictitious prosecutor. "Ha ha!" The prosecutor answered. "The same thing will happen to anyone who organizes further festivals!" In the face of this threat, the accused was defiant. "But the following year," Lediņš retorted, "the very same festival was held in Tallinn, and it resounded around the world . . ."[1]

The festival to which Lediņš referred was and also was not the same as those he organized at the Riga Polytechnic Institute, where Pärt's *Sarah* premiered in 1976 and the *Missa syllabica* in 1977. The Tallinn event, officially billed as the Festival of Early and Contemporary Music, ran for six days in November 1978, and it indeed received coverage abroad—in the United Kingdom and West Germany, and also in the Estonian émigré press.[2] Arranged under the auspices of the Estonian SSR Philharmonic and drawing leading performers from throughout the Soviet Union, it was the culmination and also the endpoint of the organizational work of the community that coalesced in the cradle of Lediņš's discotheque. It marked the moment when official and unofficial cultures of music making merged and became one, with the unofficial largely absorbed into the official, and with the remaining handful of ideological offenses simply ignored by authorities. At the Tallinn festival, the Soviet underground emerged into the daylight, as it were, to be celebrated by one and all.

Pärt stood at the center of the festivities of November 1978. His recent music figured prominently on three of the festival's programs, with the premiere of his new *Italian Concerto* the grand finale of the week's events. And yet Pärt received the festival and surrounding celebration with ambivalence. At the moment that seemed outwardly to be his greatest professional triumph, he felt uncertain of his path forward as an artist and increasingly alone. Soon his life in the USSR would become increasingly difficult and eventually untenable. At the time of the festival, that outcome was still unimagined, unthinkable. For six days in November, it seemed that all of Tallinn was in thrall to whatever the next festival concert would bring, hoping against hope to secure a ticket to the evening's sold-out events.

FESTIVAL, FESTIVAL!

While the Riga festivals of 1976–77 received little attention in the press and official support only from student organizations (the Komsomol, the RPI Student Club), plans for Tallinn's Festival of Early and Contemporary Music were eagerly, even breathlessly covered in nearly all of the city's papers. It seems that no one in Tallinn knew of the scandal in Riga the prior autumn. As the Estonian journalist Immo Mihkelson notes, communications, even official ones, between the Baltic republics were generally poor, and an embarrassing lapse like the one that allowed the performance of sacred music at the Riga Polytechnic was unlikely to have been broadcast abroad by Latvian officials.[3] The Tallinn festival concerts were arranged through the Estonian SSR Philharmonic, which answered to the Central Committee of the Estonian SSR. On its programs were musical works composed by such consummate insiders as Boris Parsadanian, chair of the philharmonic, and Raimo Kangro, who had recently been appointed secretary of the

Estonian SSR Composers' Union.[4] As Inna Kivi, then a philharmonic official, recalls of preparations for the event, a degree of subterfuge was still required in order to accomplish all that its organizers envisioned. This time around, however, those engaged in the scheming were not just students and visitors from abroad but Parsadanian and other senior members of philharmonic leadership itself. Though Parsadanian would attend the festival and even had one of his compositions performed, he reportedly arranged to take a trip overseas with colleagues just as the festival program was taking shape. In doing so, he assured a lack of high-level official oversight—a lack of his *own* oversight—of key parts of the process. It was a situation reminiscent of the circumstance that enabled the premiere of Pärt's *Credo* almost exactly ten years earlier. This time, however, the absence of authority figures was planned by the authorities themselves. Only after the festival was over, it is widely claimed, did Parsadanian report to his supervisors in the Central Committee on what exactly had been performed.[5]

In the wake of the recent upset in Riga, Lediņš had retired from the festival-organizing business, and Lubimov was temporarily barred from visiting the Latvian SSR. Undiminished in his enthusiasm, Lubimov connected with Andres Mustonen, the conductor of Hortus Musicus, whose local esteem and philharmonic patronage went a long way toward opening doors in the Estonian capital.[6] On the one hand, the addition of early music to the program signaled a return to the artistic conception of Lubimov's short-lived concert series in Riga, "Works of the Past and the Present," the cancelation of which had inspired Lediņš's first festival foray in 1976. As Mustonen later recalled, however, the conductor's conversations with Pärt also played a key role in shaping the Tallinn events. The two first connected, Mustonen recalls, shortly after the *Credo* premiere, drawn together by their shared enthusiasm for early music. (Pärt's contacts in Moscow, Mustonen recounts, were invaluable sources of copied scores.) Mustonen remembers Pärt dropping in one day on a choral rehearsal he was conducting, possibly even before the founding of Hortus Musicus in 1972. In turn, Mustonen visited rehearsals for Pärt's Third Symphony and *Song to the Beloved*. A few years later, when Pärt's first experiments with his tintinnabuli style were coming together, the two saw each other almost daily, with Pärt bringing scores to Hortus Musicus rehearsals so that he could hear what he was working out.

Around mid-decade, Mustonen recalls, their conversations turned increasingly toward what Alexei Yurchak would call the "imaginary West": to sounds and lives in places like London and Vienna, cities they both had yet to visit. (Pärt's first trip to the West took place in June 1978, a state-sponsored group tour of Italy that inspired the title of the *Italian Concerto*.)[7] The imaginings of both musicians were distinctly outward-facing, Mustonen remembers, peering beyond the contemporary present into the historical past, and beyond the surrounding Soviet world to spaces beyond its borders. "Later," he recounted, "the 1978 Festival of Early and Contemporary Music came together as a reflection of our mindset. It was sort of the result."[8] In an interview with a Latvian reporter in 1979, Mustonen further linked the Tallinn project to his experience of the Riga festival of 1977. "I really liked the Riga public and the atmosphere at the RPI Student Club at the time of the music festival. We thought, why not continue the tradition and organize a similar event in Tallinn?"[9]

Official reportage of the events of November 1978 began a month before the festival's opening concert, in the form of an interview with Mustonen published in the weekly paper of the combined creative unions of the Estonian SSR. In a wide-ranging discussion of what he had lately accomplished and what projects he had in the works, Mustonen described an upcoming festival of new music by Schnittke, Denisov, Silvestrov, and Martynov, to be performed alongside works by contemporary composers from the West and the near abroad: Krzysztof Penderecki, Iannis Xenakis, Cage, Stockhausen, and Hans Werner Henze. He revealed that a new concerto by Pärt was planned for the festival's finale, and he highlighted the scheduled premiere of a new rock opera by Martynov, *Seraphic Visions of St. Francis of Assisi*, written specifically for the occasion.[10]

A week before the festival began, the same paper published a detailed preview of upcoming events, likewise highlighting Pärt's *Italian Concerto* and Martynov's *Seraphic Visions*, and including a spread of photographs of participants, among them the philharmonic director Parsadanian.[11] On November 4, five days before the opening, Tallinn's leading daily predicted "a memorable event for every musical enthusiast" in the city, and it too pointed to *Seraphic Visions* as one of the most eagerly awaited performances.[12] On the eve of the opening concert, in the journal of the Estonian Komsomol, the critic Ivalo

Randalu, an early advocate of Pärt's work, declared that the festival was sure to be "one of the most beautiful and exciting musical events in Estonia." He described Martynov's several upcoming performances in detail, clearly having heard the music in advance, or at least having spoken with the composer about it. Martynov's *Albumblatt* (*Listok iz al'boma*, 1976), Randalu reported, "is like an endless walking in circles, which enfolds into its circling a series of new musical sounds and colors." His *Seraphic Visions*, Randalu continued, "sets a text by a nineteenth-century English poet"—Robert Southey—"with a string quartet joined by amplified electric instruments and six brass players. Each section [of the eight that make up the work] expresses an unvarying, distinct, static condition."[13]

The festival events, which ran from the ninth to the fourteenth of November, were held in two of the capital's most prestigious venues, the Estonia Concert Hall and Tallinn's newly restored Town Hall (*Raekoda*). Its nine concerts featured some of the most widely feted classical performers in the Soviet Union. Grindenko and Kremer played on three different programs, as did Lubimov and the Lithuanian Chamber Orchestra conducted by Saulius Sondeckis. The cellist Ivan Monighetti made an appearance as did the Russian pianist Gleb Axelrod. The final concert featured the duo of Natalia Gutman on cello and Oleg Kagan on violin. And, of course, there was Hortus Musicus. Some of the programming was remarkably ambitious. The opening concert, performed by Lubimov's Moscow Contemporary Music Ensemble, was described in the press as a "marathon" event, lasting nearly four hours and ending just before midnight.[14] A Hortus Musicus concert two days later was nearly as long and divided into three parts. The first featured music from the twelfth and thirteenth centuries. The second, works by Penderecki, Cage, Denisov (*Singing of the Birds*), Martynov (*Asana* for contrabass, performed by Anatoly Grindenko), Silvestrov (*Kitsch-Music*, 1977), and Pärt: *In spe* and a new arrangement of *Fratres* for Kremer and the ensemble. (The score of the latter has been lost, but an archival recording of the festival concert reveals the ensemble part to have been identical to the version premiered in Riga the previous year, and the violin part to be the one Kremer played, in an arrangement for violin and piano, at the Salzburg Festival in 1980.)[15] The final third of the concert featured Venetian choral music by Giovanni Gabrieli and his contemporaries.

The following night, Kremer and Grindenko played *Tabula rasa* with the Lithuanian Chamber Orchestra, with whom they had returned in January from a blockbuster tour of West Germany and Austria.[16] On the same program, the duo played works by Henze and the Lithuanian composer Bronius Kutavičius as well as the premiere (according to the program) of Schnittke's *Moz-Art à la Haydn*.[17] The final concert of the festival featured music by Vivaldi and Bach, Parsadanian's concerto for violin and cello, and the premiere of Pärt's *Italian Concerto*, dedicated to Gutman and Kagan. In the midst of the festivities, Randalu registered his disappointment with *Seraphic Visions* (it "inclined toward the expected," he wrote), and also his excitement about the upcoming performance of the *Italian Concerto*: "A premiere. Arvo Pärt. Music about which we know nothing at all today, and about which we will still know nothing tomorrow."[18]

The closing concert was followed by an outpouring of critical assessments in the press. Several seconded Randalu's remarks about Martynov's opera. It "left a questionable impression," wrote a critic for the paper of the combined creative unions. Later, in the same journal, another writer asked, "Why dress up an unfamiliar [poetic] work in such an uninspired and tedious way?"[19] In the national daily, the critic Aurora Semper hit upon another widely articulated theme. "It's sad," she noted, "that only one of [the concerts] was dedicated to young Estonian composers"—Kangro, Lepo Sumera, and Alo Põldmäe, all of whom were ten to fifteen years younger than Pärt.[20] As another critic put it, "it appears from the concerts that performers in Estonia mostly perform music from other republics. . . . Where are our ensembles that advocate for contemporary music as consistently as the Moscow Ensemble of Soloists does?" That critic, who had reported to readers in Tallinn on the RPI festival the previous year, continued: "Presently, we don't dare stage a concert of works by young composers exclusively, of Kangro's and Põldmäe's generation. We need an interpreter who loves new music like Andres Mustonen and his ensemble love the old."[21]

And yet, in spite of complaints about individual concerts, the festival as a whole was celebrated as a brilliant success in seemingly every corner of the official commentariat, with many writers expressing eagerness for a follow-up festival they hoped to see in 1979. The November events, a weekly cultural journal reported, were sources of "rapture [or *inspiration*: in Estonian, *vaimustus*] on the part of the public."[22] The creative unions' weekly went so far as to observe that the festival had inspired a powerful sense of community and belonging among all who attended, a feeling not unlike the effect Avramecs ascribed to the 1977 festival in Riga. "What was the most enriching thing about listening through the lineup at the Festival of Early and Contemporary Music?" The author, Ines Rannap, asked. "It wasn't just the experience of all the beautiful concerts," she explained. Rather,

> there flowed through us a multifaceted feeling of solidarity, the threads of which bound thousands of listeners together with musicians coming from different places and the creative traditions of distant centuries. . . . Does this sound like an exaggeration? Figure for yourself: the Estonia [Concert Hall] filled four times, four times the *Raekoda*, with a seemingly infinite number of people who couldn't get a ticket![23]

Rannap concluded: "The festival has ended, but we will not soon forget the impressions . . . and we ask when the next one will be put on." The critic Semper concurred, already imagining "the next festival, for which we are all waiting."[24]

The festival audience consisted mostly of people residing in the Estonian capital. But as one musician visiting from Riga observed, "not only onstage but also among the listeners, one saw a good number of visitors from other Soviet cities."[25] Lediņš apparently attended the festival, as attested by programs, photos, and other materials preserved among his effects.[26] A handful of visitors came from outside the USSR as well. These included Alfred Schlee, head of the Vienna-based music publishing firm Universal Edition, which had already published Pärt's *Perpetuum mobile* and would soon help the Pärt family resettle in the West (fig. 5.1).

Another foreign visitor was the Helsinki-based music critic Seppo Heikinheimo, who published a detailed report on the festival in the *Allgemeine Zeitung* in Mainz. For the most part, Heikinheimo's impressions matched those of his Estonian colleagues. He was deeply impressed by the programming and the organization of the whole and by the level of the performances he attended. He too was disappointed by Martynov's opera (it seemed a good idea "in theory," he wrote, "but

FIGURE 5.1   Pärt and Alfred Schlee at the Festival of Early and Contemporary Music in Tallinn, November 1978. Photo by Nora Pärt. Estonian Theatre and Music Museum. Courtesy of the Arvo Pärt Centre and the Estonian Theatre and Music Museum.

it was less pleasant to listen to").[27] But Heikinheimo departed from Estonian commentary by describing a performance that took place outside of the official festival program, one that seems to have gone entirely unmentioned in the Soviet press. He revealed that Pärt's *Missa syllabica*, once again called *Test*, was also performed, apparently at the end of the Hortus Musicus concert of November 11.[28] "Whatever was tested," he wrote of *Test*, "it seemed successful indeed. And the work has already stood up to the test, since it is part of the repertoire of this fantastic ensemble—which will, we hope, soon have the chance to win over listeners in the West with its youthful *élan*."[29]

Of course, by the time of the Tallinn festival, the *Missa syllabica* was no longer new. As *Test*, it was premiered in Riga in 1977 and performed by Hortus Musicus in Tartu in May 1978. A few weeks after the Tallinn festivities, Mustonen's ensemble would bring *Test* to Leningrad for a performance at the House of Composers—a concert, the conductor later recalled, that was very well received.[30] The fact that the *Missa syllabica* was nowhere noted in official records or coverage of the Tallinn festival seems to make clear that the performance of Pärt's openly religious music was still deemed unacceptable in mainstream Soviet society, even within the relatively liberal environment that supported and celebrated other festival events. But this time around, in November 1978, one could hardly say that its performance took place underground. With so many famous artists taking part, and with several of Tallinn's most widely read and respected music critics attending the concert, it clearly did not go unnoticed by prominent representatives of Soviet officialdom. Rather, as if by tacit agreement, its performance was simply ignored.

Looking back, Mustonen described a key point of strategy employed when organizing the festival events. "I felt certain that it was very important [to assemble] a group of performers whose names were surrounded by a certain halo. With this group, we were able to do things that otherwise we could not."[31] In November 1978, the protective cover provided by an all-star cast indeed seemed to shield the festival organizers from anything like the troubles that followed the Riga events of the previous year. Pärt's own standing with Soviet officials had changed in the intervening months as well, for with the international success of *Tabula rasa* in the winter of 1977–78, he too had become a star. In hindsight, reading Mustonen's recollections, it can even seem that the religiously oriented contributions by Pärt and Martynov had, once again, made the most lasting impressions of all on festival participants. "The unobtrusive religiosity of early music and the covert religiosity of avant-garde music united [the] seemingly distant traditions" represented at the festival, Mustonen remarked. "Together, they sustained a spiritual resistance to the cultural politics of the totalitarian regime."[32]

Whatever the complexities of inspiration and reception might have been in 1978, the festival was widely recalled with nostalgia in later years. Reunited for an anniversary celebration some twenty years after the event, festival participants framed their impressions, one after another, in relation to all that had unfolded in the interim: foremost the unexpected, traumatic implosion of the Soviet world itself. For Martynov, reflecting in 1998, the Tallinn festival was emblematic of an age that saw the "last great compositional discoveries" in Western classical music, before deeply held social and artistic convictions had been emphatically displaced by market forces. "There is simply nothing like it happening today," he averred. For Mustonen, the festival marked the pinnacle achievement and also the end of what must be considered in hindsight as "a very good time for art."[33] Later still, an Estonian journalist relived highlights from the festival in conversation with the Hortus Musicus conductor. The festival as a whole, she remarked in summary, was "clearly the most legendary musical event in our music history."[34]

AUTUMN INTO WINTER

Outwardly, the events of November 1978 marked a major triumph for Pärt. As the critic Rannap reported afterward, "Pärt was on the program only . . . four times." (The dramatic ellipsis is hers.) "But recall the ovation for *Tabula rasa* and the *Italian Concerto*!" She admitted having trouble making sense of some of the music she heard over the course of the week, especially Martynov's. But she experienced Pärt's in much the same way as she had experienced the premiere of *Tabula rasa* the previous year. "This too is new music," she wrote of the *Italian Concerto*. "But its simplicity, harmonic purity, and extraordinary static tension are unlike almost anything else we've heard."[35] For Rannap's colleague Aurora Semper, Pärt's new concerto was "lively, one could even say joyful," its closing moments imbued with what she described as "peaceful tension."[36] Among critics, the only remarks not wholeheartedly enthusiastic about Pärt's contributions were registered by Heikinheimo, the visitor from Helsinki. "Of all the composers performed in Tallinn, it was an Estonian composer, Arvo Part [*sic*], who attracted most attention." But of the *Italian Concerto*, Heikinheimo continued: "In it, Part uses the same compositional techniques as in *Tabula rasa* but does not quite attain the same level of inspiration."[37]

A photo taken at the close of the festival shows Pärt celebrating with friends: Grindenko and Kremer on the left and Pärt on the far right. Mustonen holds Lubimov in the air, the pianist's right fist raised above him in a sign of victory (fig. 5.2). But two weeks after the festivities ended, on the twenty-eighth of November, Pärt gave a wideranging interview to Randalu, and his mood was decidedly dark. Their conversation would not be published in its entirety until 1988. Filmed by the director Andres Sööt, excerpts from their talk were spliced

FIGURE 5.2 Celebrating at the Festival of Early and Contemporary Music, Tallinn, November 1978 (*left to right*): Tatiana Grindenko, Gidon Kremer, Alexei Lubimov held by Andres Mustonen, Arvo Pärt. Photographer unknown. Estonian Theatre and Music Museum.

together with scenes from festival rehearsals and concerts, yielding a documentary motion picture entitled *Arvo Pärt in November 1978*. That document, too, would not be seen by the public until the time of perestroika.[38]

Early in their conversation, Randalu asked Pärt about the *Italian Concerto*, and the composer demurred. "A first performance is like sketching," Pärt reflected. "Only afterward does the real work begin, breathing life into this lump of clay. You have to make a lot of improvements."[39] At that point, Nora Pärt chimed in, reminding her husband that the situation had been much the same with *Cantus* and *Calix*, after which their conversation drifted off to other topics. But soon, Randalu returned to the matter of the *Italian Concerto*, asking Pärt whether he was as happy with it as he had been with early performances of his *Tintinnabuli* suite. "I am quite unhappy on account of the *Italian Concerto* at the moment," Pärt replied, "because I don't feel that it succeeded." Nora Pärt interjected: "But nothing succeeds immediately." To which the composer responded: "Well, yes. But it was served up so pretentiously, with venerable soloists and orchestra, and at the festival . . ."[40]

In November 1978, Pärt was at the pinnacle of his career in the USSR. Following the sensational premiere of *Tabula rasa* in September 1977, Kremer and Grindenko took that work on a two-month tour of Western Europe, and they had recently performed it at the prestigious Warsaw Autumn Festival.[41] Pärt's *Cantus in Memory of Benjamin Britten* had also been a hit. Premiered in Tallinn in April 1977, it had already been performed twice more in that city as well as in Leningrad, Riga, and Tbilisi. The celebrated Estonian conductor Neeme Järvi had just taken it on tour in Finland.[42] In May 1978, Pärt received the Annual Award in music (*Aastapreemia*) from the Ministry of Culture for his achievements.[43] That same month, a retrospective concert of his music took place in the Georgian capital, spanning his career from *Perpetuum mobile* (1963) through the Third Symphony and his early tintinnabuli-style compositions. The Tbilisi concert even included *Credo*, performed under the title *Fantasy in C Major*—an event documented in another film by Sööt, which likewise remained unseen for a decade.[44]

Against the backdrop of these successes and the adulation he received even for the *Italian Concerto*, it is not clear what exactly depressed the composer about the festival experience. In hindsight, Mustonen recalled the concerto troubling his friend for months, during which he revised it repeatedly before setting it aside for good. (The compositional diaries bear this out; Pärt eventually withdrew the work from his catalog, it remains unpublished, and it has never been commercially recorded.)[45] In Mustonen's view, the unqualified success of *Tabula rasa*—Pärt's first concerto in the tintinnabuli style—might have overshadowed its successor in a fateful way, setting the bar so high for a second work in the genre that disappointment was all but inevitable.[46] To be sure, the *Italian Concerto* was not as novel as its predecessor had been. Its slow movement made use of material that audiences had heard before—namely, the passage from *Modus* reworking music from the soundtrack to the film *Colorful Dreams*. And its finale was dreamy rather than haunting, as the ending of *Tabula rasa* had been. But Pärt's postfestival interview with Randalu revealed his unease with more than just this single work. When asked about the Tbilisi concert at which *Credo* had been revived, Pärt responded: "It was a horrible experience. . . . It's a shame that I took so much time from people." And then: "I don't have any relationship with my own works at all, especially those written so long ago. I don't have any contact with them. I've lost closeness with them, the bodily warmth."[47]

At the end of November 1978, Pärt found himself at a creative crossroads. He had accomplished so much, so quickly and unexpectedly. Yet he felt that he could not rest where he was, and he definitely felt he could not move forward by revisiting musical spaces he'd inhabited before. Still, he seemed to have no firm idea about where he should go next. His discovery of the syllabic method in early 1977 had been such a tremendous breakthrough. In the months that followed, new ideas came to him daily, and he had composed with such certainty, such conviction. The entire *Missa syllabica* had come together in under a week, and *Cantate Domino* had taken him a day. But something seems to have shifted for him after the Riga festival in October of that year. Between December 1977 and the beginning of August 1978, he largely traded his syllabic work for an almost single-minded focus on the *Italian Concerto*.[48] The only significant breaks came on March 15, when he composed the entirety of *Spiegel im Spiegel*, and in mid-April, when he paused to work on the soundtrack for a documentary film, *Footsteps in the Snow* (*Jäljed lumel*).[49] Between August and October he shifted his attention to the movie *The Test of Pilot Pirx*. From late October to the start of December, he seems to have composed nothing at all.[50]

The months surrounding the Tallinn festival were those of Pärt's greatest professional triumphs. He was lionized by critics and performed by famous musicians, while still remaining an idol for the community of younger, alternative artists that coalesced in Lediņš's discotheque. Inwardly, however, he felt himself lost and increasingly alone. For the first time since the underground premiere of *Sarah* in April 1976, he seems to have felt uncertain about the direction his music and career should take. If the Tallinn festival seems in hindsight to have marked the end of one particular line of work within the Soviet alternative music scene, it also seems to have marked, in some vaguely palpable way, the ending of a chapter of Pärt's life. Or at least the beginning of an ending.

A photograph survives of Pärt receiving his award from the Estonian SSR Ministry of Culture on May 16, 1978. Labeled on its back

FIGURE 5.3 Pärt receiving his Award of the Year from the Ministry of Culture of the Estonian SSR, May 1978. Photographer unknown. Estonian Theatre and Music Museum.

"A. Pärt in the Presidium of the Supreme Soviet," it shows him flanked by other award winners, looking distinctly out of place.[51] His body language is stiff and awkward, his expression betraying boredom or discomfort. To dress for the formal presentation, he wore a baggy, woolen sweater, in sharp contrast to other recipients, and also to the suit he favored for performances of his music (fig. 5.3; compare with figs. 5.1 and 5.2 above). Earlier in his life, in the 1960s, Pärt presented well among Soviet officials. With works like *Perpetuum mobile* and *Pro et contra* (1966), he managed to push the boundaries of what had been officially permissible while also remaining in the good graces of the bureaucracy.[52] But after the *Credo* scandal of 1968, he seems to have begun regarding himself as an outsider, an artist likely irredeemable within the bounds of mainstream Soviet society. He resigned himself to earning a living by composing soundtracks for films (work he came to despise), while spending his free time on the radically impractical task of searching for a musical language to embody his vision of the divine. When opportunities for concert engagements arose, he took them, especially in collaboration with Hortus Musicus. But for the public unveiling of the music that was most meaningful to him, his sacred compositions in the tintinnabuli style, he looked to venues underground, his ideal audience consisting of underground figures more or less like himself.

Then, at the end of 1977 and the start of 1978, his life took a series of unexpected turns. He had written *Tabula rasa* and *Cantus*, and suddenly there he was: an underground figure, committed to a distinctly alternative vision of Soviet art, with a pair of major successes under his belt, receiving one of the highest honors his republic bestowed upon its artists. The photograph of the award ceremony provides a glimpse of just how disorienting recent months had been. As we will see, however, Pärt was not the only member of his circle who felt himself unmoored at this time. In late 1978, Martynov, probably unbeknownst to Pärt, was on the cusp of forsaking music altogether and embarking on a wholly different life. And Lediņš, compelled to move his disco out of the RPI Student Club, was charting new creative directions as he sought—following what he may have taken to be Pärt's lead—his own, distinctive voice as a composer. Still in Tallinn, Pärt was wrestling with an array of unfamiliar insecurities, not least the pressure exerted by Soviet political culture upon its artists who achieved fame in the West. Though he did not yet know it, 1979 would be Pärt's last year in the USSR. The sense of an ending, vaguely haunting at the time of his interview with Randalu, would soon be inescapable.

SIX

AFTERSOUNDS

———

Bolderāja, Sergiyev Posad, and a Train to Brest-Litovsk

After Tallinn, the community of musicians that had formed in Lediņš's disco fell apart. There was no scandal, there were no disagreements. Its underground festival-organizing activity, inaugurated in Riga in 1976, had emerged into the daylight less than three years after its start, to be embraced by Soviet officialdom and celebrated by audiences far and wide. In light of this, its crowning achievement, the group's work seemed simply to be done. And yet, viewed from another angle, the dissolution of the collective can seem like a natural result of the very same experimentalist mindset that had animated its activities all along. Since its beginnings, what had brought its central figures together was something they shared with experimentalist collectivities throughout the world: a "restless desire to be elsewhere," to quote again from Benjamin Piekut, a "searching for an otherwise."[1] That searching inspired the launch of Lediņš's discotheque at RPI, and it led to the formation of the communal, experimental space of the Riga festivals of new music. It underlay his friends' explorations of new sounds, new forms of performance, new conceptions of the artwork, new religious engagements. And it had a great deal to do with their embrace of Pärt's openly devotional works of music.

This final chapter considers how three members of the group—Pärt, Lediņš, and Vladimir Martynov—never ceased exploring. But it also documents how their restless searching for an "elsewhere" ultimately took them into deeply personal spaces, beyond the concerns or the capacity of the group to realize. Between late 1978 and the turn of the decade, each of these artists constructed or found an alternative space of his own: beyond new music as they conceived of it together, or beyond the production of music itself. In Pärt's case, it was literally beyond the geographical and political confines of the Soviet world. With these turns, the "elsewheres" they sought became, for each of them, concrete geographies, their future work an aftersound of the underground scene that each had helped to shape.

SILENCE

The Orthodox practice of hesychasm, of prayer in inner silence, was not something Pärt would discuss openly until after his emigration to the West.[2] But the trope of silence (in Estonian, *vaikus*) nonetheless figured broadly in conversations about Pärt's life and work in what would be his last years in the Soviet Union. First, there was the acoustic silence into which the concluding movement of *Tabula rasa*—itself entitled *Silentium*—dissolves. Struggling to describe the effect of the ending after attending the premiere of the work in September 1977, the Estonian critic Ines Rannap fell into a silence of her own, leaving a blank space on the page to convey what her words could not:

Pärt's *Tabula rasa* is . . .

. . .

For those who heard it, no verbal description is needed, and it would be pretty much useless anyway. And to those who did not hear it, it's impossible to convey a sense of the unearthly atmosphere that surrounded the performance.[3]

In conversation shortly after the premiere with another Estonian critic, Nora Pärt described how silence had literally been composed into the score of the work, which had, at the time, only been seen by those who had performed it. "With increasing calm," she related of the ending of *Tabula rasa*, "the conductor conducts the silence"— four bars of rests notated at the end—"like a continuation of the music, which is resolved only a dozen seconds later, with the start of the applause."[4]

Then, there was a different variety of silence broached in Pärt's searching conversation with Ivalo Randalu shortly after the November 1978 festival. "Does concert activity help you?" Randalu asked the composer. Pärt replied: "It only disturbs me. Silence is much more helpful."[5] A gifted interviewer, Randalu let the issue drop, but he returned to it later, indirectly. "Have you ever thought about what Mozart would have composed had he lived into old age?" Randalu wondered. "Or would he not have written anything anymore, like Sibelius or Pushkin, who exhausted themselves as far as writing goes?" "I don't know," Pärt reflected. "Maybe those people didn't exhaust themselves at all." And then:

PÄRT: Maybe they just went silent [*vaikisid*], lived another life. We just don't know. Their silence didn't mean they weren't evolving any longer. They simply expressed themselves in a new way.
RANDALU: Do you want to go silent? . . .
PÄRT: And not write music anymore? I don't know.[6]

Pärt, of course, never took that step. He remained prolific, his work unabated. But the silence for which he sometimes longed—into which he sometimes might have wished to flee—was embraced more fully by an acquaintance whose presence was unmissable at all three festivals considered in this book. Little more than a month after the close of the festival events in Tallinn in November 1978, Martynov, whose *Seraphic Visions* had been among the festival's most eagerly anticipated performances, joined a monastery, the Trinity Lavra of St. Sergius in the Russian town of Sergiyev Posad. With that move, he fell silent to the world outside, not composing any longer, expressing himself in a new way.

When Martynov had returned to Moscow from Tajikistan around 1972, he was convinced that the paragons of progressive rock and the spiritual leaders of India and Tibet were together onto something important. As he later recounted this period of his life, they all seemed to sense a "new Renaissance" (*novyi Renessans*) dawning upon the world. That movement, as he saw it, was a global one, arising spontaneously in far-flung locales, and it was "diametrically opposed to the goals and aspirations of the earlier Renaissance of Europe." While the latter had arisen in the fourteenth and fifteenth centuries from the desire of artists and intellectuals to "overcome the dictates of religion, to strive for the ideal of emancipating humanistic culture," the "new Renaissance" of the 1970s saw diverse individuals working in the opposite direction, seeking alternatives to scientific secularism and to revivify the life of the spirit.[7] As a young man, Martynov dove headlong into that project, reading the Upanishads and studying with a yogi. At the electronic music studio of the Skriabin Museum, he found a community of fellow travelers who encouraged him to refashion his musical practice in line with his emerging spiritual convictions.[8] It was around that time, in 1973, that he composed *Asana* for the contrabassist Anatoly Grindenko, one of his several works performed at the Tallinn festival of 1978. Each of its sections, Martynov explained, reflected on one of the eight components of yogic practice outlined by the Hindu sage Pantajali: *yama* (abstinence), *niyama* (observance), *asana* (posture), and so on. As he later recalled of *Asana* and this period in his life more generally, "music became for me a path toward religious experience [or cognition, or understanding: *poznanie*]. And in that moment, on that path, I believed I had found my calling."[9]

Soon, however, the locus of Martynov's spiritual explorations began to shift, as he befriended a pair of individuals who directed his attention away from South Asian metaphysics and toward Orthodox Christianity. First, there was the archpriest Vladimir Rozhkov, an eccentric figure known for advising Soviet filmmakers on their depictions of Christian ritual in their work, and no less for the lavish meals he hosted for members of Moscow's bohemian circles, Martynov included. Rozhkov owned an extensive library of books on Orthodox spirituality, and Martynov borrowed extensively. Then there was the art historian Valery Baidin, professor at the Moscow State University and a devout yet mostly private Orthodox practitioner, who further helped Martynov ground his spiritual explorations philosophically. "In time," Martynov recalled, "all of this reading and more reading in books, all these endless conversations and meditations on religious questions began to feel rather insufficient and incomplete. I sensed that it was necessary to somehow put all of this into practice internally.

But just how to do so, I did not know."[10] As a composer, he ceased his yoga-inspired experiments and devoted himself to work on compositions like the *Passionslieder* (1977), setting Christian texts in a deliberately historicizing manner and using materials he would later call *simulacra* to circumvent his subjective will to express himself in the music he wrote. Beyond those artistic moves, however, he was deeply uncertain of his path forward and increasingly anxious about what his future as both artist and believer might bring.

At this point, we should recall Alexei Yurchak's words about just how nonnormal it was to engage in overt religious practice in the Soviet public sphere. While "tolerated by the state," organized religion was "disconnected" from every aspect of officially sanctioned daily life: "education, media, industry, public associations, army, bureaucracy, etc." To come out publicly as a practicing Christian was to court "suspicion and hostility." To take the step Martynov was already pondering—devoting his life to his faith entirely—was worse.[11] Indeed, Martynov describes his spiritual journey as a kind of "emigration," through which he transplanted himself "from [the realm of] culture into the Church," and he has compared that move to the literal emigration of so many of his friends and idols in the later 1970s: the composers Alexandre Rabinovitch and Andrei Volkonsky, both of whom had already left, and Pärt himself, who would soon make a new home in West Berlin.[12] Martynov's analogy captures something of the peril he believed himself to be facing, for when a person left the USSR for the West, the costs were high and the attendant transition often traumatic. To take such a step was to become a nonperson in the only home one had ever known.

As Martynov wrestled with the decision before him, he confided his fears to Baidin, who urged him to embark on a three-day fast in a monastery beyond the city. Joined by a friend from the rock band Outpost in March 1978, Martynov did as Baidin prescribed, and he emerged feeling certain of his calling. "After that, I understood that it was time for me to accept my decision, because the decision had already been made for me. All that remained was for me to dedicate my life to carrying out that decision."[13] Back in Moscow, things moved quickly. With Baidin's help, he became a novice in the Orthodox Church. He traveled by car to several area monasteries but found himself drawn back to St. Sergius. The only problem that remained, it seemed, was that he still had to compose.

For the Tallinn festival, he had promised a rock opera, and he delivered *Seraphic Visions*. But the work disappointed; even Tatiana Grindenko, whom Martynov would later marry, would later admit that, "honestly speaking, I don't really remember what the music was like."[14] It was not just *Seraphic Visions* that gave him trouble. "All of my attempts at composition," he recalls, "started seeming dull and unexciting to me. My professional work and responsibilities began to feel like a burden." He remembered an Outpost performance of 1978 that felt like a "tiresome obligation." He had a commission from his friends Alexei Lubimov and Mark Pekarsky for a new work slated for premiere in Leningrad. The resulting composition, which Martynov described as "very unsuccessful," would turn out to be his last for over half a decade. "I quite simply did not want to write anything anymore, as my interests had shifted entirely to things concerning the Church."[15] Ever since returning to Moscow, he'd had ample work composing for television and film, but "emigrating from the sphere of culture meant that I had to renounce all of those commissions."[16] At the end of the year, he took the final step, retreating into the silence of St. Sergius. With that move, he was left unemployed. But much as Pärt had mused about Sibelius and possibly himself during that same autumn of 1978, Martynov's renunciation of his music did not mean that he had ceased to evolve. Going forward, in Sergiyev Posad, Martynov expressed himself in new ways. There, for a while, he felt free.[17]

"HIS OWN MANNER OF COMPOSITION"

Hardijs Lediņš did not go silent in 1978. When he lost access to the RPI Student Club as a venue for his discotheque after the scandal of the previous year, he responded by moving his operation to a cultural center in the suburbs, and he laid plans for the future. In an interview of 1980, noting an explosion of interest in discos in the city (he estimated that as many as fifty had opened in Riga by that point), he lamented that the kind of institutional instability he'd recently experienced had limited the artistic quality of discotheques and hindered the professionalization of DJs. And, he added, "one of the most difficult problems facing discos is that we still don't have any [appropriate musical] repertoire produced locally."[18] That year, he took an important step toward resolving at least some of those problems. With the help of friends, he secured a permanent home for his disco in the heart of central Riga. For the foreseeable future, his new disco, which he christened Cosmos (*Kosmoss*), would host weekly multimedia events in a cultural center called October, each presenting a new musical program as well as artworks by a painter friend, along with a constantly evolving light show and other special effects.[19]

Lediņš continued composing as well—and prolifically. A list he compiled of music he recorded or produced through early 1978 includes twenty-one reels of tape ("albums" or "records," he called them: *skaņuplates*), some with illustrations on their cardboard covers, many in collaboration with Juris Boiko, and all in what the pair were calling their "Seque Records Avant-Garde Series" of recordings (*seque* being a nonsensical but distinctly foreign-looking word).[20] Seventeen reels appear to have been devoted to music composed by Lediņš and his friends, with the rest featuring performances by others recorded at the Student Club. (Several reels have been lost or are unplayable; those that survive include his recordings of Pärt's *Missa syllabica* and Martynov's *Passionslieder* from the 1977 festival.) The earliest albums of his own music, from 1976, consist of free improvisations, inspired in part by his experience of seeing Lubimov and Grindenko play Stockhausen and Cage at the start of that year. On one of those reels, entitled *Best of Seque 76*, the track "On the Right Way" features Lediņš plucking the strings of a piano while Boiko improvised a percussion part with empty bottles. Another track, "Pool in Clouds," features a prepared piano accompanied by further improvised percussion, bubbles blown in a cup of water, and someone playing on what sounds like a toy or wooden flute, possibly a Latvian *stabule*. Other works are more technologically adventurous. "Composition for Dog & Piano—Electronic Version" is an experiment with magnetic tape, featuring a pentatonic piano improvisation with a dog barking loudly in the background, recorded and then played backward in order to yield the finished product.[21]

In what is likely his first recording made after hearing Pärt's tintinnabuli-style music at the Riga festival of 1977, Lediņš broached something new. In his *Kuncendorf's China Notes*, recorded in February 1978 as part of the Seque series, the instrumentation is sparse (Lediņš sits alone at the piano), the melodic structures are unambiguously

EXAMPLE 6.1 Lediņš, *Kuncendorf's China Notes* (1978), opening measures of track 2, "Abschied." Transcribed by the author from a tape recording (www.pietura.lv).

modal, triadic, and repetitive, and the atmosphere is distinctly medi-tative.[22] The album's second track, "Abschied" ("farewell" in German), the opening of which is transcribed in example 6.1, typifies the sound of the whole. His left hand cycling as if endlessly through a simple ar-peggiation of an E-minor triad, he seems freely and slowly to impro-vise up and down the E-minor scale with his right.

We do not know whether Lediņš's work on *Kuncendorf's China Notes* was inspired by listening to Pärt. But among the items preserved in his estate are programs for two concerts featuring Pärt's music at the Tallinn festival of 1978. On one of those documents, Lediņš charted his reading of Nora Pärt's program notes by underlining in pencil what he seems to have considered its most important passages. Among those underlined passages, in notes for the performance of *Tabula rasa* on November 12, was this: "The work of the past two years clearly indi-cates that Arvo Pärt has found his own manner of composition."[23] For Lediņš, it seems, it was still unclear what *his* own manner of composi-tion might be. But it seems in hindsight that he was clearly searching for *something* in the months surrounding the festival. After Tallinn, his production of experimental recordings in the Seque series dropped off significantly. Increasingly, he turned his attention to a project that ap-peared on the surface not to be musical at all.

At three in the morning on the last day of November 1980, Lediņš,

Boiko, and an architect friend departed Lediņš's Riga home and followed ten kilometers of railroad tracks to the forsaken coastal suburb of Bolderāja. They walked into the sunrise. Along the way, they drank tea, took photographs, and paused frequently to take in what they encountered. When they arrived, they bought bus tickets back home. The following June, Lediņš and Boiko repeated the journey (fig. 6.1).

FIGURE 6.1 Lediņš walking to Bolderāja, June 14, 1981. Photo by Juris Boiko. Collection of the Latvian Centre for Contemporary Art. Courtesy of Martin Boiko.

In January 1982, they took the journey again. Their treks evolving into an annual pilgrimage, they took on ritual trappings. The walkers ate hardboiled eggs at pretimed intervals. They left mementos for themselves along the tracks.[24] Reflecting later about what they were after, Lediņš described their walks as exercises in spiritual renewal, as a kind of "new religion." Bolderāja, he explained, was in fact a "terrible place," the train tracks littered with industrial detritus, passing by metallurgy shops, skirting a shipyard where workers broke down old warships. But in its very awfulness, he reflected, it was "like the Christian catacombs, which inspire a new kind of sensitivity to life."[25] Boiko, in turn, described the Bolderāja walks as an extension of their contemporary interest in experimental music. "Stockhausen's ideas, Cage's ideas, we grasped those ideas viscerally. . . . We were simply seeking substantiation of those ideas in the surrounding reality." He continued: "The walks to Bolderāja can be compared to Cage's silent piece, 4'33", [Martynov's] *Albumblatt* or [Stockhausen's] *Aus den sieben Tagen*."[26]

Other comparisons are revealing as well, perhaps none more so than those Journeys beyond the City organized by Andrei Monastyrsky and the Collective Actions group in Moscow starting in 1976. It is unclear whether Lediņš and Boiko knew of Monastyrsky's project at the time, but the latter's journeys were likewise highly ritualized affairs, and they were similarly described by their initiator as a form of "spiritual practice" aimed at effecting a change in perception and self-reflection on the part of participant-observers.[27] Like the members of Monastyrsky's circle, who memorialized their journeys in photos and written recollections, Boiko and Lediņš documented their walks in a variety of ways. They took photographs, often framed or modified artistically (fig. 6.2). Once, they brought along a boom box, not to accompany their walking with music but to record the ambient soundscapes through which they traveled (fig. 6.3).[28]

During their journeys, they also wrote poetry.[29] One of their poems, entitled "A House in Bolderāja," pictures an impossible home in an imaginary locale, without doors or walls, from which they would sell passersby bus tickets to "another Bolderāja." Another, called "The Ballad of Deep Bolderāja," implores anyone and everyone—an imagined minicommunity of misfits—to take the journey with them:

FIGURE 6.2 Juris Boiko and Hardijs Lediņš, *Empty/Alone* (walking to Bolderāja, June 14, 1981). Collection of the Latvian Centre for Contemporary Art. Courtesy of Martin Boiko and Pēteris Lediņš.

If you have galoshes on your feet
but someone else has wooden legs,
no matter, take them with you
to far-off Bolderāja.

If someone's deaf and cannot hear
those wooden legs clacking along,
then let them walk without hearing,
to soundless Bolderāja.

FIGURE 6.3 Juris Boiko walking to Bolderāja, January 16, 1982. Photo by Hardijs Lediņš. Collection of the Latvian Centre for Contemporary Art. Courtesy of Pēteris Lediņš.

. . . .

> And if someone cannot walk
> because they don't have legs,
> then put them on a stretcher
> and head to Bolderāja.

As it happened, and however improbably, it was through his experience of the Bolderāja walks that Lediņš ultimately succeeded in finding what would turn out to be his own distinctive manner of composing. In doing that, he helped to solve yet another of the key problems facing Soviet disco culture that he had recently diagnosed.

Immediately after returning from the first of their walks in November 1980, Lediņš, Boiko, and a handful of friends recorded a magnitizdat album unlike any they had produced before. Completed over
the course of thirteen months, *Bolderāja Style* (*Bolderājas Stils*, 1980–
82) featured fourteen tracks, few of which bore much resemblance to
their earlier, experimental work. Notably, all the tracks on *Bolderāja
Style* are *songs*, performed in simple pop-like arrangements, many setting the poetry composed along their journeys, and all reflecting upon
what they had seen and experienced over the course of their treks.[30]
The first "side" of *Bolderāja Style* opens with "A House in Bolderāja,"
setting the poem described above where they imagined selling bus
tickets in a house without walls or windows. It closes with the ballad
"Deep Bolderāja," setting the poem where they invited a ragtag group
of the deaf and the legless to join them on their trip. Other tracks on
Bolderāja Style recall sights seen on their walks: trains, buses, snow on
cars. Still others meditate on the experience of walking itself:

> It's still not light,
> it's not dark anymore,
> I walked to Bolderāja.
>
> I walked to who knows where,
> probably nowhere.
> So one goes to Bolderāja.[31]

Significantly, the very years in which Lediņš and Boiko began setting their Bolderāja poetry to song saw the first attempts at creating
new wave music in the USSR, barely trailing the coalescence of a new
wave aesthetic in the West.[32] Local acts drew sonic vocabularies from
Western bands like Ultravox, the Eurythmics, and Soft Cell, whose
music first circulated, via pirated tapes and smuggled LPs, in marginal
venues like Lediņš's Cosmos discotheque. In Riga, one of the first
new wave bands to hit the scene was the Yellow Postmen (*Dzeltenie
Pastnieki*), whose leader, Ingus Baušķenieks, attended the Riga Polytechnic alongside Lediņš and was captivated by *Bolderāja Style* from
the moment he heard its first-recorded tracks. On their own debut album, the Yellow Postmen covered four of Lediņš and Boiko's Bolderāja

songs in their polished, reggae-inflected style evocative of the British band The Police. They acknowledged their debt to the pair of walkers by titling their album *Bolderāja Railway* (1981).[33] Returning the tribute, Lediņš and Boiko enlisted Baušķenieks to produce their second album of songs set to Bolderāja poetry, with the resulting recording, *There's No One in My Forest* (1982), moving clearly in the direction of the pulsing rhythms and synthesizer-driven arrangements for which the Yellow Postmen were already becoming famous.[34] Later that year, Boiko and Lediņš consolidated their production efforts by forming a band of their own, NSRD, a Latvian acronym for Workshop for the Restoration of Unfelt Feelings, whose distinctly danceable, synth-centered tracks would play on Riga's disco scene until the end of the Soviet Union itself.[35] With his new work fronting NSRD as principal songwriter and sometime singer, Lediņš addressed directly the principal problem of which he had recently complained: a lack of high-quality, disco-appropriate music made in the USSR. But his band accomplished something else as well. With its roots in the Bolderāja walks, it extended a distinctly Soviet strain of experimentalist performance art—one that regarded the ritualized journey beyond the city as a means of experiencing social and expressive freedom—into the socially cohering, broadly accessible realm of the disco hall. In doing these things, Lediņš found his own, distinctive path as a composer.[36]

ON THE BORDER

The sense of being adrift, of being caught between an irrecoverable past and an indiscernible future apparent in Pärt's interview with Randalu of November 1978, would soon envelop the whole of the Estonian composer's professional life. After Grindenko and Kremer returned from their tour of Western Europe at the end of 1977, making waves with *Tabula rasa* everywhere they played, Pärt began receiving invitations to attend performances of his music abroad. On December 6, 1978, the British Broadcasting Corporation planned a performance of *Cantus* in London, with Pärt scheduled to appear. Two days before the concert, however, the vaunted Russian conductor Kirill Kondrashin defected while touring the Netherlands, and officials abruptly canceled Pärt's exit visa, wary of him following Kondrashin's lead. In summer 1979, Pärt's request to attend a performance of *Tabula rasa* in Kuhmo, Finland, was similarly denied.[37] Other invitations and denials followed. To an extent, Pärt's experience was shared by many Soviet artists who achieved fame abroad, whom the Ministry of Culture considered to be flight risks and who were consequently barred from foreign travel. But Pärt's experience also reflected personal circumstances. "I had married a young woman whose parents lived in Israel," he told a French journalist in 1987, referring to Nora Pärt's family and the government's policy of allowing Soviet Jews to move to Israel in the 1970s. "Since Jews were permitted to leave the USSR, it seemed that I had publicly declared my intention to emigrate. For ten years, I hung on. But I began to be known abroad. When I was invited to Finland or Canada, a visa was systematically refused to me."[38]

It was not only the denial of travel that led to Pärt's crisis of relations with officials. As the off-schedule performance of his *Missa syllabica* at the Tallinn festival made clear, his sacred music, the composition of which had motivated and animated nearly the whole of his tintinnabuli project, was and seemed destined always to remain officially unacceptable: unplayable in aboveground spaces, unmentionable in public discourse, unpublished and unacknowledged by the state. Demand for Pärt's film scores remained strong, so he would always have creative work to do. But that work had never been more than a means to an end, and he found the experience of scoring *The Test of Pilot Pirx* to be deeply disheartening.[39] He tried to sink himself into work on more practical creative projects—revising the *Italian Concerto*, working on something for Kremer, composing a Schnittke-like cadenza for Haydn's C-major cello concerto—but none of them proved to be sustaining, and he returned repeatedly in his compositional diaries to his radically impractical *Passio*.[40] In winter 1979, he staged a protest at a meeting of the Estonian SSR Composers' Union, wearing a wig he borrowed from a film studio and sarcastically declaring himself a dissident.[41] Over the course of that year, as Nora Pärt put it to me in late November 2019, Pärt's relations with the Composers' Union and other branches of Soviet officialdom seemed simply to evaporate. "He had no use for them, and they had no use for him."[42]

When recalling his decision to enter the monastery in Sergiyev Posad, Martynov described the move as his emigration. But the trauma of literally emigrating from the USSR is hard to overstate and nearly impossible to imagine for anyone who did not live it. Writing of Pärt's experience in 1980, the musicologist Christopher J. May has tried. The moment when a person crossed the border with a one-way exit visa, May writes, in a powerful essay whose title inspired that of the present chapter, was "that moment where everything changes forever," when "old friendships [were] bent and broken," when "'home' was no longer itself."[43] Communications and physical contact were lost with no prospect (it then seemed) of ever being restored. When he took that step, Pärt's music instantly became unplayable in his former home. Studies of his compositions were pulled from the presses. His history was erased, his continued life unacknowledged, his future work to be unheard.[44] And in his new place of residence, initially Vienna, Pärt lived at first as a complete unknown. As a Viennese journalist described his meeting with the composer during that first, unfathomable year in the West, "he regrets that a number of musicians who lobbied for him earlier don't even know that he's here. And many of his compatriots who are still 'over there' can no longer perform his work."[45] With emigration, Pärt's career itself became a tabula rasa, a blank slate upon which he had no choice but to fashion himself anew.

In January 1980, accompanied by the musicologist Toomas Siitan, a filmmaker friend, and Nora Pärt's aunt, the composer and his family boarded a train to the border station of Brest-Litovsk in Soviet Belarus.[46] There, the family alone entered the railway hall and proceeded onward to customs. Nora Pärt recalls the scene that unfolded in that place:

A remarkable event occurred at the border station of Brest-Litovsk at customs control. When we arrived with our two children and our small amount of luggage, the customs officer asked, "Where is your luggage? Is that all?" Other people waiting at the station were heavily laden with baggage of all kinds. They even had furniture, and someone even had a piano. We only had a few suitcases, and even those were half empty! But we still had to open them, and so they noticed the cassettes with the recordings of Arvo's first works. One of the customs officers said, "Oh, you're musicians! I too played music in Estonia." Immediately, they wanted to check the cassettes with our tape recorder. And so, we heard the *Missa syllabica*, then *Arbos*, and after that *Cantus*. The station was a gigantic building with a domed roof as high as a church, and we were inside this huge place alone with the border police. There I could really feel the effect that this music had on people: suddenly everything was so normal, so relaxed, so beautiful. Our Michael lay in his cradle. A friend had knitted him a new coat, and all the female border police tried to copy the pattern. A policewoman led us into a room where they undressed Michael to check if we had perhaps hidden something in the clothing he was wrapped in. From all the icons we had at home, we had taken just one with us, one so small that we could hide it in one of Michael's pockets. They didn't find it. Michael started crying and the police let us bring him some cookies. It was an unforgettable scene, not least because everything was accompanied by Arvo's music. Everything turned out all right, and after a short time we boarded the train to Vienna. We knew that emigrants were to be brought together in a camp there, where they would await travel onward to Israel.[47]

It is impossible now to know exactly which recordings accompanied the family's hours at the border. But one of their cassettes from that time survives. Labeled in the composer's unmistakable hand, in both Roman and Cyrillic script, it includes live recordings of a number of Pärt's earliest tintinnabuli-style works (fig. 6.4).[48] Side 1 opens with *Tabula rasa*. Then, *Arbos*, *Cantate Domino*, and *Summa*. Side 2 begins with *Fratres*, followed by *In spe*, *If Bach Had Kept Bees*, another performance of *In spe*, and *Calix*, closing with the opening part of *Trivium*. (Despite the labeling on the cassette, *Pari intervallo* is not on it.) The date, the locale, and even the performers on *Tabula rasa* are not known. But *Arbos*, *Cantate Domino*, *Summa*, and *Fratres*, along with the cassette's first rendering of *In spe*, were clearly recordings of the same performances captured by Lediņš on reel-to-reel tape on October 28, 1977. That is, the cassette's recordings were made at the second Riga Polytechnic festival, when all of those works, and the *Missa syllabica* as well, had their underground premieres.[49]

We do not know whether this cassette was among those played at Brest-Litovsk. But the possibility is real and poignant. When Pärt and

FIGURE 6.4 Cassette preserved in the Pärt estate. Photos by Doug Maskew. Courtesy of the Arvo Pärt Centre and the Arvo Pärt Recorded Archive/Doug Maskew.

his family stepped across the border, they left behind a Soviet world they would never see again and that would never be the same. For Mustonen, the year 1980 was a "year of mourning" (*leina-aasta*) following Pärt's departure.[50] That the final sounding of Pärt's music in the territory of the USSR, performed by Mustonen's Hortus Musicus and played from cassette on a portable deck, might well have echoed a pinnacle achievement of the underground scene in which Pärt's tintinnabuli project took root seems both unfathomable and wholly natural. An aftersound of that scene itself, it marked an ending, and a beginning.

———————

A catalog of Pärt's music published in Austria by Universal Edition, prepared in July 1980, a half-year after the family settled in Vienna, includes the *Missa syllabica*, no longer called *Test*. It includes *Credo* from 1968 and *Cantate Domino* and *Summa* of 1977, none of which were published or publishable in the USSR. It also includes the *Passio*, to which Pärt had returned in his new home, which had yet to receive the performance by the Hilliard Ensemble through which it would later become famous. The Universal catalog also features *Calix*, inspired by Schnittke in another age. No longer referred to by the neutral Latin title under which it had been premiered ("Chalice"), it was now listed under the devotional incipit that animated its composition in the first place: *Dies irae*, from the requiem mass.[51]

Also at the front of Pärt's mind during that first, disorienting year in the West was the *Italian Concerto*, a work he would eventually disown, the memory of which remains painful today. Even after the Tallinn festival and his tortured interview with Randalu from autumn 1978, Pärt continued to work on the piece, and it was among those performed during his first season living abroad. Programmed as part of the Wiener Festwochen in June 1981, it was played by Gidon Kremer, the Russian cellist Karine Georgian, and the Polish Chamber Orchestra under the direction of Jerzy Maksymiuk. Before his emigration, the concerto had seemed Pärt's best shot at a large-scale, officially acceptable composition in 1978–79. A work without text, it was plausibly separable from the devotional project that had animated his tintinnabuli project to date, and its title recalled impressions of his state-sponsored trip to Italy. Premiered by Natalia Gutman, Oleg Kagan, and the Lithuanian Chamber Orchestra, it had crowned Tallinn's Festival of Early and Contemporary Music to considerable acclaim. Yet now, in the Wiener Festwoche program, the concerto and its history were reframed. Its pensive first movement, recasting material debuted in *Sarah Was Ninety Years Old*, was "conceived as a passageway to attentiveness and full concentration." The quick second movement, the program continued, "radiates spiritual activity." And the third—the elegiac, incontrovertible beauty of which was surely part of what drove Pärt to continue working on the piece for so long—resounded with the "joy of the promised land." Notes for the Festwoche performance continued with a quote from the composer: "My initial impulse, in working on the concerto, was the impression made by hearing Psalm 102, 'Hear my prayer, Lord,' in an Orthodox cloister in Estonia."[52]

It is not clear where Pärt might have heard Psalm 102 sung in the Estonian SSR. But his musical diaries indicate that it was a psalm for which he had sketched a setting all the way back in October 1977.[53] In fact, that sketch was the very last compositional project—unrealized at the time—that he undertook before heading to Riga to attend the festival premieres of the first openly religious compositions he had braved since the *Credo* scandal. Now, in Vienna, he revealed that even the *Italian Concerto*, his last work completed in the Soviet Union, had likewise originated, however distantly, in the devotional project from which his tintinnabuli style itself had emerged, and in the very season of his most intensive period of collaboration with Mustonen, Lubimov, Lediņš, and others who made the performances of his officially unacceptable music possible. Today, more than forty years after he took his fateful step across the border, Pärt's music is ubiquitous on the soundscape of the global West, attesting to the persistence of his faith and the clarity of his vision as it coalesced so long ago. And still, in its present sounding, in numberless guises, in place after place and year after year, the sound of his work can conjure traces of something else as well: a vanished world of strictures, repressions, and breathtaking possibilities, the world of the 1970s Soviet underground.

ACKNOWLEDGMENTS

First and foremost, I wish to thank Arvo and Nora Pärt for entrusting me not only with a story about this period in the composer's life but with the still unbelievable, life-changing experience of being granted unlimited access to Pärt's musical diaries. The archive housing the diaries and related materials, the Arvo Pärt Centre (Arvo Pärdi Keskus) in Laulasmaa, is a dream space for a scholar to work in: quiet, beautiful, friendly, and deeply caring, staffed by a community of individuals dedicated to cultivating knowledge and learning about Pärt's music and its histories. Among them I wish to thank especially Kristina Kõrver, Anneli Kivisiv, Anu Kivilo, and Ardo Västrik.

My other archive home for this project is just as amazing in different ways: the Latvian Centre for Contemporary Art (Latvijas Laikmetīgas mākslas centrs) in Riga. Beginning with a gift of documents and photographs from the Lediņš family following the death of Hardijs Lediņš in 2004, the center has become the principal repository of materials related to Lediņš's life and work for many who knew and made art with him. There too a stunningly knowledgeable and helpful staff—especially Māra Žeikare—provided me with unlimited access over many visits. Māra in particular was and remains an expert guide through the archive, and through the not-always-transparently linear course of Lediņš's life and creative engagements.

When it comes to acknowledging all the many individuals who helped me with this project, I'll start with Martin Boiko, who read drafts of chapters, answered many questions, shared recollections, and went out of his way on numerous occasions to help establish connections and advance my project in Riga and beyond. Christopher J. May, whose inspiring work blazed a trail for us all in the realm of archival work on Pärt, was a key interlocutor at several points in the early stages of my research. Andrea Bohlman read an early version of the manuscript from start to end, and her insightful comments and suggestions have shaped every chapter in this final version. Kristina Kõrver's reading of a later version helped tremendously on many points. Boriss Avramecs met with me several times to share his recollections as co-organizer of the Riga festivals, without which much of chapter 4 could not have been written. Lauris Vorslavs, curator of the online archive Pietura nebijušām sajūtām, shared with me some crucial archival materials at just the right moments, as did Doug Maskew, curator of the Arvo Pärt Recorded Archive in Tallinn.

There are many others without whose help I could not have written this book, at least not in the way that I did. Donatus Katkus, Urve Lippus, Alexei Lubimov, Immo Mihkelson, Georgs Pelēcis, Toomas Siitan, Kirils Šmeļkovs, Rūta Stanevičiūtė, and Asja Visocka shared recollections of events, projects, and the conditions under which they took shape. Anda Beitāne, Peter Bouteneff, Laura Emmery, Jeffers Engelhardt, Daniel Grimley, Peter Höyng, Lisa Jakelski, John Lysaker, Meredith Schweig, and Richard Taruskin shared thoughts or suggestions about my research or writing, sometimes after a talk or during a visit, sometimes over months or years. Pēteris Lediņš, Kirils Šmeļkovs, and Ilya and Emilia Kabakov shared materials from their personal archives or pointed me in some valuable directions. Jeffers Engelhardt and Ilze Karnes helped decipher some tricky passages of Estonian and Latvian, respectively. Marta Tonegutti and Dylan Montanari at the University of Chicago Press were helpful and encouraging partners throughout. Chris Fenger did a nice job with the musical examples. Over the course of this project, Peter Schmelz shared materials, helped track things down, entertained questions, traded ideas, and generally helped in many ways.

Among the institutions on which my research has relied, I wish to thank the staff of the Estonian Theatre and Music Museum (Eesti teatri- ja muusikamuuseum), the National Archive of Latvia (Latvijas Valsts arhīvs; especially Anita Krastiņa), the National Library of Estonia (Eesti Rahvusraamatukogu; especially Helen Põldmäe), the National Library of Latvia (Latvijas Nacionālā bibliotēka), Estonian Public Broadcasting (Eesti Rahvusringhääling; especially Immo Mihkelson and Ilona Hausmann), and Riga Technical University (Rīgas Tehniskās universitāte; especially Alīda Zigmunde and Asja Visocka). Financial support for the extensive travel this project has entailed was provided by the College of Arts and Sciences of Emory University. Emory College also provided a subsidy to make this book as affordable as possible. Thank you.

Some material in chapter 4 appeared in an earlier guise as Kevin C. Karnes, "Arvo Pärt, Hardijs Lediņš and the Ritual Moment in Riga, October 1977," *Res Musica* 11 (2019): 115–27. A revised version of that article was reprinted under the title "Arvo Pärt's Tintinnabuli and the 1970s Soviet Underground," in *Arvo Pärt: Sounding the Sacred*, ed. Peter C. Bouteneff, Jeffers Engelhardt, and Robert Saler (New York: Fordham University Press, 2021), 68–85.

APPENDIX

Key Premieres and Early Performances of Pärt's
Tintinnabuli-Style Works, 1976–78

MARCH 23, 1976   First public performance of *Aliinale* [*Für Alina*], played as a recital encore by the pianist Rein Rannap in Tallinn's Estonia Concert Hall.[1]

APRIL 27, 1976   First public performance of *Saara* [*Sarah Was Ninety Years Old*] at the Student Club (formerly Anglican Church) of the Riga Polytechnic Institute, as part of the club's first festival of avant-garde music organized by Hardijs Lediņš under the auspices of his discotheque. Performers uncertain.[2]

OCTOBER 25, 1976   First public performance of the *Tintinnabuli* suite, given by Hortus Musicus under the direction of Andres Mustonen in an Estonian SSR Philharmonic concert at Tartu University. The suite consisted of *Modus* [*Sarah*], *Für Alina*, *If Bach Had Kept Bees*, *Pari intervallo*, and *In spe*.[3]

OCTOBER 27, 1976   Tallinn premiere of the *Tintinnabuli* suite in an Estonian SSR Philharmonic concert in the Estonia Concert Hall, performed by Hortus Musicus under the direction of Andres Mustonen, with Rolf Uusväli (organ), the Tallinn Chamber Choir, and others. The suite consisted of the same works performed in Tartu on October 25, plus *Calix* and *Trivium*.[4]

APRIL 7, 1977   Premiere of *Cantus in Memory of Benjamin Britten* by the Estonian SSR Philharmonic Orchestra, conducted by Eri Klas in Tallinn's Estonia Concert Hall.[5]

SEPTEMBER 30, 1977   Premiere of *Tabula rasa* at the Tallinn Polytechnic Institute, performed by Tatiana Grindenko, Gidon Kremer, and the RAT (national opera) "Estonia" Chamber Orchestra conducted by Eri Klas (Alfred Schnittke playing prepared piano). The concert was repeated in Leningrad on October 27—the first known performance of Pärt's tintinnabuli music beyond the Baltic republics. In November and December, Grindenko, Kremer, and Schnittke performed the work on tour in Austria and West Germany, with the Lithuanian Chamber Orchestra conducted by Saulius Sondeckis.[6]

OCTOBER 28, 1977   First public performance of the *Missa syllabica* (as *Test*) and a new version of the *Tintinnabuli* suite at the Student Club of the Riga Polytechnic Institute, as part of the club's Festival of Contemporary Music Dedicated to the Sixtieth Anniversary of the Great October Socialist Revolution. Performed by Hortus Musicus under the direction of Andres Mustonen, the suite consisted of *Arbos, Cantate Domino, Summa, Fratres, In spe,* and *Pari intervallo.*[7]

MAY 15, 1978   Premiere of a new version of the *Tintinnabuli* suite, given by Hortus Musicus under the direction of Andres Mustonen in an Estonian SSR Philharmonic concert at Tartu University. The suite consisted of *Arbos, Cantate Domino, Summa, Test* [*Missa syllabica*], and *Fratres.*[8]

NOVEMBER 14, 1978   Premiere of the *Italian Concerto* at the Festival of Early and Contemporary Music in Tallinn, performed by Natalia Gutman, Oleg Kagan, and the Lithuanian Chamber Orchestra conducted by Saulius Sondeckis.[9]

DECEMBER 19, 1978   Performance of a new version of the *Tintinnabuli* suite, given by Hortus Musicus under the direction of Andres Mustonen at the Leningrad House of Composers. The suite consisted of *Arbos, Cantate Domino, Für Alina, Spiegel im Spiegel, Variationen zur Gesundung von Arinuschka, In spe, Test* [*Missa syllabica*], *Pari intervallo, Summa,* and *Fratres.*[10]

NOTES

CHAPTER ONE

1. Lubimov is quoted in Avramecs, "Neoficiālie laikmetīgās mūzikas festivāli," 20; Silvestrov is quoted in Liubimov (Lubimov), "Vremia radostnykh otkrytii," 152.

2. Iankilevskii (Yankilevsky), "Iz 1960-x v 1970-e," 356 (emphasis added).

3. Liubimov, "Vremia radostnykh otkrytii," 151.

4. The first-ever public performance of Pärt's tintinnabuli-style music, the composition *Aliinale* (later published and recorded as *Für Alina*) was given a month before, on March 23, as an encore closing a recital by the Estonian pianist Rein Rannap in Tallinn. The only record of the performance is passing mention in a single review: Mets, "Rein Rannapi klaveriõhtult," 10. On tropes of reception surrounding Pärt and his tintinnabuli-style music since that year, see Karnes, *Arvo Pärt's Tabula Rasa.*

5. The recording of the concert was made by Hardijs Lediņš, who cataloged it as 1016 in his "Seque Records Avant-Garde Series" of tapes. It is preserved in the private collection of the Lediņš family/Lauris Vorslavs in Riga. For more on the concert and the Seque series, see chaps. 4 and 6. A different recording of portions of the same concert, possibly made by Arvo or Nora Pärt, is preserved on a cassette tape at APK, 5–2.499 (cassette 156 in the Arvo Pärt Recorded Archive, maintained by Doug Maskew). I am grateful to Lauris and Doug for providing me with digital copies of the tapes.

6. For instance, Dohoney, *Saving Abstraction*; Iverson, *Electronic Inspirations*; Piekut, *Experimentalism Otherwise*; and Bernstein, ed., *The San Francisco Tape Music Center.*

7. On Pärt's work and its reception prior to 1976, see May, "System, Gesture, Rhetoric," 96–170; and Karnes, *Arvo Pärt's Tabula Rasa*, 17–36.

8. Kabakov, *60e-70e*, 51–52 (at 51). Published only later, Kabakov composed these memoirs in 1982–84; see Kabakov, *On Art*, 68.

9. I follow Alexei Yurchak and Victor Tupitsyn in describing the artistic scenes

on which I focus as "alternative," reserving the term "unofficial" for those contexts in which I intend to emphasize the not-officially-sanctioned (or not-*explicitly*-officially-sanctioned) nature of an event. Never stable, the lines between official and unofficial art in the Soviet Union are widely considered to have become so fluid and confused after 1974 that the applicability of the terms is vigorously debated with respect to that period. For a sampling of views on the issue, see the position papers published in Thiemann, ed., *(Non)conform: Russian and Soviet Art, 1958–1995,* 136–67. On unofficial music scenes in the 1950s and 1960s, see Schmelz, *Such Freedom.* On the looser notion of "alternative" scenes in the 1970s and 1980s, see Yurchak, "Necro-Utopia"; and V. Tupitsyn, *Museological Unconscious,* 35. Yurchak has recently shown a preference for describing these scenes as "informal"; see Kurg, "Interview with Alexei Yurchak." In seeking to move beyond the official/unofficial binary, I also follow Astahovska's foreword (*priekšvārds*) to Astahovska, ed. *Atsedzot neredzamo pagātni/Recuperating the Invisible Past,* 12–13.

10. Yurchak, *Everything Was Forever,* 7; and Iurchak (Yurchak), *Eto bylo navsegda,* 43. Aygi's statements are quoted from Schmelz, *Such Freedom,* 322; the whole section of Schmelz's book in which Aygi's words appear ("The End of the Soviet Sixties," 322–24) is helpful for understanding them.

11. Lubimov's recollections, quoted above, are published in a volume of reminiscences by several Soviet artists active in the decade: Kizeval'ter, ed., *Eti strannye semidesiatye.* Also important are the recollections of Kabakov (*60e-70e*), partly translated in Kabakov, *On Art,* 68–138. A massive store of documents produced in Soviet alternative art circles of the 1970s is available online in Russian and English at *Moskovskii kontseptualizm,* http://conceptualism.letov.ru. Among contributions by historians and others, see Bryzgel, *Performance Art in Eastern Europe*; Crowley and Muzyczuk, eds., *Notatki z podziemia/Notes from the Underground*; Eşanu, *Transition in Post-Soviet Art*; and Seiffarth, Stabenow, and Föllmer, eds., *Sound Exchange.*

12. Liubimov, "Vremia radostnykh otkrytii," 151; Martynov is quoted in Katunian, "Unikal'nyi eksperiment so vremenem," 4. For Lediņš's statement, see the documentary film *Manā mežā nav neviens* at 0:10:01. A similar retrospective assessment of the decade is offered by the Russian critic Artemy Troitsky: "in a time of enormous shortages, the population spent their time slogging around the shops looking for food and other vital products. But young people were buzzing with excitement." See Troitsky, *Subkultura,* 132.

13. Yurchak elaborates: "the performative reproduction of the form of rituals and speech acts [expected by Soviet officialdom] actually *enabled* the emergence of diverse, multiple, and unpredictable meanings in everyday life, including those that did not correspond to the constative meanings of authoritative discourse." Yurchak, *Everything Was Forever,* 25 (emphasis in original); Iurchak, *Eto bylo navsegda,* 74.

14. Piotrowski, "No komunisma uz postkomunisma situāciju/From Communist to Post-Communist Condition," 18–19. See also Piotrowski, *In the Shadow of Yalta*; and IRWIN [collective], ed., *East Art Map.*

15. Piekut, "Pigeons," 118.

16. Jackson, *Experimental Group*, 2 (emphasis added).

17. A copy of the program is preserved in ETMM, M238:1/4.

18. Mustonen is quoted in Kautny, *Arvo Pärt zwischen Ost und West*, 118. On the official premiere of Pärt's tintinnabuli music in Tallinn, see Mihkelson, "The Cradle of Tintinnabuli."

19. I trace this history in Karnes, *Arvo Pärt's Tabula Rasa*, 92–99.

20. The program for the Tartu concert of October 25, 1976 is preserved in ETMM, MO20. The title and date of the Riga premiere (April 27, 1976) are recorded in Pärt's "musical diaries" (*muusikapäevikud*) preserved at APK, 2–1.10. On the diaries, see chap. 3. A manuscript score of *Modus* with the heading "Tintinnabulum 1" is preserved in ETMM, M238:2/13.

21. Liubimov, "Vremia radostnykh otkrytii," 151; Kizeval'ter (Kiesewalter), introduction to Kizeval'ter, ed., *Eti strannye semidesiatye*, 16. See also Solomon, *Irony Tower*, 46.

22. Quoted in Katunian, "Unikal'nyi eksperiment so vremenem," 3.

23. Martynov, *Zona opus posth*, 132–33. Lubimov recalls his own impressions similarly; see his "Vremia radostnykh otrkytii," 157. On the widely available recording by Sergey Yakovenko and Ilya Scheps on the ECM label (ECM New Series 1898/99), the title of the collection is given as *Silent Songs*.

24. Martynov, "Povorot 1974–1975 godov," 169–70; and Martynov, *Avtoarkheologiia (1978–1998)*, 18–21. On the Skriabin Studio from Murzin's time through the beginnings of the shift Martynov describes, see Schmelz, "From Skriabin to Pink Floyd," 254–77. On the studio as experienced by Artemyev, see Egorova, *Vselennaia Eduarda Artem'eva*, 41–44, 65–67. The generational and technological transitions were subjects of an hour-long Estonian radio broadcast from 1978, which includes substantial excerpts of music composed at the studio by Schnittke, Artemyev, and Martynov. It is archived at https://arhiiv.err.ee/vaata/moskva-rock-ja-tehismuusika-stuudios. Artemyev's soundtrack for the 1972 film *Solaris* (*Soliaris*), dir. Andrei Tarkovsky, excerpts of which are widely available online, provides an indication of the new sound worlds opened by the Synthi-100.

25. Martynov, "Povorot 1974–1975 godov," 172–77.

26. Martynov, *Zona opus posth*, 115–37 (quoted at 118, 124). Martynov first broached this thesis at the turn of the millennium under the rubric "the end of the age of composers," when he credited Cage's work, Stockhausen's "intuitive music," Happenings, and other developments of the 1960s and early 1970s with having contributed to the "destruction [or erosion: *razrushenie*] of the idea of the text, the idea of the work, the idea of the author." See Martynov, *Konets vremeni kompozitorov*, 220. Martynov's thesis remains influential in Russian music historiography, undergirding at least one attempt to write an expansive history of music in late twentieth-century Russia; see Cherednichenko, *Muzykal'nyi zapas*.

27. Martynov, *Zona opus posth*, 136.

28. Jackson makes a similar point with respect to the relation between the

young painters, poets, and sculptors clustered around Kabakov and some of their older colleagues, noting "the growing distance between Kabakov's circle and those who, like [the painter Ülo] Sooster, had experienced Stalin's camps firsthand." Jackson, *Experimental Group*, 107.

29. Piekut, *Experimentalism Otherwise*, 19; Gottschalk, *Experimental Music since 1970*, 2. Recent projects have cast considerable light on experimental music scenes beyond the US and UK, yet those in the Soviet Union remain largely unexamined in Anglo-American musicology. See, e.g., Piekut, ed., *Tomorrow Is the Question*; and Alonso-Minutti, Herrera, and Madrid, eds., *Experimentalisms in Practice*.

30. Unless otherwise noted, my account in this paragraph and the one that follows is taken from Jackson, *Experimental Group*, 52–55, 136–40; V. Tupitsyn, *Museological Unconscious*, 43–44, 74–81; Solomon, *Irony Tower*, 69–77, 89–90; and Scammel, "Art as Politics and Politics as Art," 52–56.

31. Kizeval'ter, introduction to Kizeval'ter, ed., *Eti strannye semidesiatye*, 19.

32. Kabakov, *60e-70e*, 62–63; his discussion of the event is translated in Kabakov, *On Art*, 114–15.

33. The graph was published in Kabakov, *60e-70e*, 63. On these changes, see also Iankilevskii, "Iz 1960-x v 1970-e," 357–58.

34. Eşanu, *Transition in Post-Soviet Art*, 68–69. See also Degot', *Russkoe iskusstvo XX veka*, 154–55.

35. M. Tupitsyn, "On Some Sources of Soviet Conceptualism," 303–4 (at 304). For other thoughts on Conceptualism, see Degot', *Russkoe iskusstvo XX veka*, 165–84; V. Tupitsyn, *Museological Unconscious*, 101–21; and V. Tupitsyn, "Immaculate Conceptualism," *Parkett* 83 (2008): 206–9. Kabakov's relationship with the group is the subject of Jackson, *Experimental Group*.

36. In a classic and influential treatment of *Opasno*, Margarita Tupitsyn reads the painting as exemplary of "sots art," a late-Soviet take on Anglo-American pop art; see M. Tupitsyn, *Margins of Soviet Art*, 61–97. Jackson disagrees in a helpful discussion, where he also connects the graphic impression of the painting's textual layout to the "inflected diagonals of the German military medal, the Iron Cross," awarded to Nazi soldiers in World War II. See Jackson, *Experimental Group*, 115–20 (at 117).

37. Martynov, *Zona opus posth*, 137–38.

38. M. Tupitsyn, "On Some Sources of Soviet Conceptualism," 304.

39. Schmelz, *Such Freedom*, 11–12 (at 12). Schmelz also treats polystylism in *Such Freedom*, 303–11, and in greater detail in Schmelz, *Alfred Schnittke's Concerto Grosso No. 1* and Schmelz, *Sonic Overload*. Although polystylism is widely associated with Schnittke's work, Schnittke credited Pärt's inspiration in such works as the latter's *Collage über B-A-C-H* (1964). See Karnes, *Arvo Pärt's Tabula Rasa*, 28–29.

40. Monastyrskii (Monastyrsky) et al., *Poezdki za gorod. Kollektivnye deistviia*, 25, 36 (description and documentation of *Appearance*), 123–24, 131–32 (the same for *Ten Appearances*). For accounts of these and other early actions, see Eşanu, *Transition in Post-Soviet Art*, 92–122. For helpful introductions to Collective Actions'

work more broadly, see Jackson, *Experimental Group*, 184–91; and Bishop, "Zones of Indistinguishability."

41. Monastyrskii, "Predislovie," 24.

42. Quoted in M. Tupitsyn, "Some Russian Performances," 11. M. Tupitsyn and Jackson report that Monastyrsky briefly corresponded with Cage, but I have been unable to verify this. In any case, the debt is openly acknowledged. In an interview of February 2011 published on the website of the Moscow Museum of Modern Art, Monastyrsky is asked the question, "Who do you consider your teachers?" His reply: "Cage and Kabakov." See http://www.contemporaries.mmoma.ru/en/personality.php?id=31. See also Jackson, *Experimental Group*, 290n55 (reporting the author's interview with Monastyrsky); and M. Tupitsyn, *Margins of Soviet Art*, 53.

43. Eşanu, *Transition in Post-Soviet Art*, 102, 106. See also Monastyrskii, "Predislovie," 19–24.

44. Kabakov, *60e-70e*, 53. For the actions Kabakov attended, see Monastyrskii et al., *Poezdki za gorod*, 781.

45. B. G. (Boris Groys [Grois]), "Moskovskii romanticheskii kontseptualizm," 50–65. Groys's essay was revised and published alongside an English translation, titled "Moscow Romantic Conceptualism," in the Parisian Russian émigré journal *A-Ya*. That translation, further revised, was later republished in Groys, *History Becomes Form*, 35–55. Since the *A-Ya* version was most widely circulated and cited in the period, my quotations are based on that translation, which I have adjusted in relation to the Russian and English versions published in *Tridtsat' sem'* and *History Becomes Form*.

46. Groys, "Moscow Romantic Conceptualism," 11 (*Tridtsat' sem'*, 64; *History Becomes Form*, 51, 54).

47. Groys, "Moscow Romantic Conceptualism," 11 (*Tridtsat' sem'*, 64–65; *History Becomes Form*, 54–55).

48. Liubimov, "Vremia radostnykh otrkytii," 157.

49. Quoted in Brotbeck and Wächter, "Lernen, die Stille zu hören," 15.

50. On yoga, the Hare Krishna movement, and other facets of the phenomenon in the late Soviet bloc, see Fürst and McLellan, eds., *Dropping Out of Socialism*. On the Orientalist fetishizing of Russia by early writers from Western Europe, see Karnes, "Inventing Eastern Europe," 75–108.

51. Liubimov, "Vremia radostnykh otkrytii," 159.

52. Astahovska and Žeikare, eds., *Nebijušu sajūtu restaurēšanas darbnīca/Workshop for the Restoration of Unfelt Feelings*, 54. On *Kuncendorf's China Notes*, see chap. 6.

53. Astahovska and Žeikare, eds., *Nebijušu sajūtu restaurēšanas darbnīca/Workshop for the Restoration of Unfelt Feelings*, 28.

54. Liubimov, "Keidzh (Cage) Dzhon," 2:768–69 (at 768); Quillen, "After the End: New Music in Russia," 9. Quillen treats Lubimov's role in promoting Cage's work on 9–29; he translates much of Lubimov's encyclopedia article on 10–11. Cage's appearance with Merce Cunningham at the Warsaw Autumn Festival in

1964 marked a significant opening of minds and ears in the Soviet bloc to his music and ideas; see Jakelski, *Making New Music in Cold War Poland*, 115–20.

55. Zavadskaia (Zavadskaya), *Vostok na zapade*; Stanevičiūtė, interview with the author (in English), Vilnius, May 31, 2018; Solomon, *Irony Tower*, 85–86 (at 85). On the impact of Zavadskaya's work on the Moscow Conceptualists and the Collective Actions group, see also Eşanu, *Transition in Post-Soviet Art*, 80–83.

56. Cage, "East in the West," 15–18; Zavadskaia, *Vostok na zapade*, 90; Zavadskaia, *Kul'tura vostoka v sovremennom zapadnom mire*, 148–51.

57. Zavadskaia, *Kul'tura vostoka*, 149.

58. Yurchak, "Necro-Utopia," 200; see also Yurchak, "Suspending the Political," 713–33.

59. Iankilevskii, "Iz 1960-x v 1970-e," 362.

60. See Restagno, ed., *Arvo Pärt im Gespräch*, 32–34 (quoted at 33); an alternate translation is given in Restagno, ed., *Arvo Pärt in Conversation*, 25–27 (at 26). On the premiere and initial reception of *Credo*, see Kautny, *Arvo Pärt zwischen Ost und West*, 83–91.

61. Siitan, "Arvo Piart—pesni izgnannika," 185.

62. Savenko, "Vozvyshennoe i smirennoe," 18.

63. Pärt's discovery of Orthodoxy is recounted in Bouteneff, *Arvo Pärt: Out of Silence*.

64. On Pärt's music for Soviet films, see May, "System, Gesture, Rhetoric," 86–91; and May, "Colorful Dreams."

65. See Fairclough, "'Don't Sing It on a Feast Day.'"

66. Documents related to the founding and early activities of Hortus Musicus are preserved in ETMM, MO20. On the early years of Madrigal, see Schmelz, *Such Freedom*, 208–13.

67. Siitan, interview with the author (in English), Tallinn, October 31, 2017; Avramecs and Traumane, "Mūzikas avangards 70. gadu Rīgā," 312.

68. Boris Berman, who conducted Madrigal between 1970 and 1973, recalls that performances of Russian church music were "often banned"; see Schmelz, *Such Freedom*, 210–11 (at 211).

69. Yurchak, *Everything Was Forever*, 112; Iurchak, *Eto bylo navsegda*, 230. Yurchak discusses the techniques and social importance of performing "normalcy" (*normal'nost'*) in *Everything Was Forever*, 102–22, and in *Eto bylo navsegda*, 212–41.

70. In Dvoskina, "Tat'iana Grindenko," 51.

71. Kabakov, *60e-70e*, 51–52.

72. See Schmelz, *Such Freedom*, 246–47 (quoted at 246); and Ivashkin, *Alfred Schnittke*, 160.

73. See Ivashkin, ed., *Besedy s Al'fredom Shnitke*, 266–67, 298. A photograph of Schnittke and Kaljuste together in Tallinn is reproduced on p. 106.

74. Avramecs, interview with the author (in Latvian), Riga, November 2, 2017; Avramecs and Gailītis, "Between Communist Party Bosses and Individual Courage." The circumstances surrounding Schnittke's reported visit to Riga are un-

clear. It is not documented in the archives of the Latvian SSR Composers' Union (Latvijas PSR Komponistu savienība), but neither is any comparable activity during the period. A note in the union's fond at LVA, added in 1982 by its chairman Ģederts Ramans, indicates that of the 253 files that had recently documented the group's activities between 1973 and 1979, "148, which have lost their historical or practical significance, were removed and destroyed" (LVA, fonds 423, historical note [vēsturiska izziņa] appended to the fond description). Still, an overview of the union's plans for the 1975–76 season indicates that organizing "visits to the Composers' Union by [composers] from brotherly republics" was a priority, and another planning document from the time indicates that Schnittke in particular should be invited "to lead a seminar for members of the C[omposers'] U[union] about various issues in Soviet music." See LVA, fonds 423, apraksts 6, lieta 29 (Oļģerts Grāvītis, untitled list of plans for 1976, dated December 8, 1975); and fonds 423, apraksts 6, lieta 43 (Pauls Dambis, undated document headed "LPSR Komponistu savienības darba plāns republikas darbaļaužu internacionālajā audzināšanā 1976.–1980.").

75. Pärt, "Greatly Sensitive: Alfred Schnittke in Tallinn," 198.

76. Sketches for Calix indicating its setting of the Dies irae text are preserved in ETMM, M238:2/61; a partial transcription and description of the work are given in chap. 3. Calix was performed in Tallinn on October 27, 1976; in Leningrad on January 27, 1977; and once again in Tallinn on March 18, 1977 (programs preserved in ETMM, M238:1/4). A recording of the concert of October 27, 1976, is preserved at ERR, ÜPST-2734/KCDR-1020. A recording of the performance of either January 27 or March 18, 1977, is preserved on a cassette tape at APK, 5–2.499 (cassette 156 in the Arvo Pärt Recorded Archive). Pärt would later incorporate revised portions of Calix into his Miserere (1989), recorded by the Hilliard Ensemble on ECM Records in 1991 (ECM New Series 1430).

77. See Restagno, ed., Arvo Pärt im Gespräch, 33; Restagno, ed., Arvo Pärt in Conversation, 26; and Kautny, Arvo Pärt zwischen Ost und West, 86.

78. Kaktus, interview with the author (in English), Vilnius, May 31, 2018; Schmelz, Such Freedom, 207–8.

79. Avramecs, interview with the author (in Latvian), Riga, November 2, 2017; Avramecs, "Neoficiālie laikmetīgās mūzikas festivāli," 26. These administrative structures are described in Samsons, ed., Latvijas PSR Mazā enciklopēdija, 1:513–14, 3:115, 3:339–40.

80. For example, Troitsky: "my first visit to Estonia, at the end of 1975, was a real shock. . . . It was all unbelievably impressive and unexpected—like Tallinn's Latin script and gothic architecture. The dazed Russians in attendance [at the rock festival he recounts] walked around thoughtfully whispering to themselves about 'the West.'" Troitsky, Back in the USSR, 44–45.

81. Toomistu, "Imaginary Elsewhere," 41–62. On the Riga black market, see Yurchak, Everything Was Forever, 187–88; Iurchak, Eto bylo navsegda, 366; and Rudaks, Rokupācija, 47–49.

82. On the vitality and outsized influence of early Baltic rock scenes, see Ryback, *Rock around the Bloc*, 111–14. On Baltic origins of the disco movement, see Zhuk, *Rock and Roll*, 215–38.

83. In Dvoskina, "Tat'iana Grindenko," 54.

84. See Yurchak, *Everything Was Forever*, 80–108 (quoted at 85, 87–88); Yurchak, *Eto bylo navsegda*, 170–212. One of Zhuk's interviewees paints a vivid picture of Komsomol authorities in the Ukrainian city of Dniepropetrovsk: "All these Komsomol activists drank too much. They were openly dating each other." See Zhuk, *Rock and Roll*, 260.

85. See Iakovlev, "Diskoteki: vchera, segodnia, zavtra."

86. See Reed, *Laurie Anderson's Big Science* and Piekut, *Henry Cow*.

87. The recording is preserved ERR, ÜPST-2734/KCDR-1020, where the climactic point in *Modus* occurs between 15:50 and 16:32 (the performance is recounted in chap. 3).

88. Avramecs and Traumane, "Mūzikas avangards 70. gadu Rīgā," 312.

89. Martynov, "Povorot 1974–1975 godov," 170. See also Dvoskina, "Tat'iana Grindenko," 54–55. Fripp was famous for such statements. For instance: "I've gotten to the point now where I see music as being something other than what most people see. I would say that the crux of my life is the creation of harmony, and music you take to be one of the components of that harmony"; quoted in Rosen, "King Crimson's Robert Fripp." On the centrality and significance of improvisation across musical genres in alternative East European scenes, see Crowley, "Sceny improwizowane/Scenes of Improvisation," 74–115.

90. Pelēcis, interview with the author (in Latvian), Riga, November 3, 2017.

91. A musical counterpart to samizdat, "magnitizdat" refers to the practice of making and distributing tape-recorded copies of music informally, beyond the control of Soviet institutions that limited access to official music production and distribution networks. Lediņš's engagement with the practice is considered in chap. 6.

92. Lediņš, "Centra mūzikas dzīve dienu ritumā," undated, unpaginated essay in an untitled and undated red manuscript notebook, preserved at LLMC in a box labeled "Klades." For more on Lediņš's recordings, see chap. 6.

93. Chuikov, "Navernoe, my byli i dissidentami," 309–10.

94. Yurchak, "Suspending the Political," 715.

95. Avramecs, "Neoficiālie laikmetīgās mūzikas festivāli," 31.

96. V. Tupitsyn, *Museological Unconscious*, 19–23 (at 20).

97. V. Tupitsyn, *Museological Unconscious*, 42–47 (at 43 and 47; emphasis added).

98. Yurchak, *Everything Was Forever*, 8. In the revised Russian edition of his book, Yurchak continues: "The positive, creative, ethical side of life was just as organic a part of socialist reality as feelings of alienation and meaninglessness"; see Iurchak, *Eto bylo navsegda*, 45. As Piotrowski notes in a discussion of East Germany in the 1970s, such artistic commitments to socialist ideology—as distinct

from commitments to political structures—were not confined to the USSR; see Piotrowski, *In the Shadow of Yalta*, 263.

99. In Kurg, "Interview with Alexei Yurchak" (emphasis in original).

100. In Gillen, "Ungefähre Kunst in Riga," 47.

101. For a thoughtful consideration of nostalgia in firsthand accounts of the Soviet 1960s, see Schmelz, *Such Freedom*, 328–36. For a consideration of Kabakov's wrestling with ideas of utopia in the wake of the collapse of the USSR, see Boym, *The Future of Nostalgia*, 309–26. Martynov reflects on his own feelings of nostalgia for the 1970s in Ulanova, "Vladimir Martynov."

102. Solomon, *Irony Tower*, xix.

103. Boiko, "NSR Darbnīca," 253.

104. In Gillen, "Ungefähre Kunst in Riga," 33.

CHAPTER TWO

1. Lediņš, "Disko. Disko? Disko!"

2. See Zhuk, *Rock and Roll*, 215–38; and Kveberg, "Shostakovich versus Boney M.," 211–27.

3. Zhuk, *Rock and Roll*, 219.

4. Lediņš is quoted in Prape, "Diskotēka: Agrāk—Tagad," 8. For Troitsky's claim, see his *Back in the USSR*, 32–33. My sense of "listening discos" in Tallinn and Tartu owes to interviews with Toomas Siitan (in English), Tallinn, October 30, 2017, and Immo Mihkelson (in English), Tallinn, November 26, 2019.

5. Cushman, *Notes from Underground*, 20.

6. Handwritten protocols from the disciplinary hearing are preserved at LLMC in a box labeled "Lediņa arhīva papildinājums." They are transcribed and published in the exhibition catalog *Lediņš. Starp to un kaut ko citu*, ed. Lindenbauma (no pagination given in the catalog). The single issue of *Zirkahbols* known to have survived, in private collection, is available at http://www.pietura.lv/seque/txt/samizdats/1972_zirkahbols_Nm_11.pdf. On *Zirkahbols* and its successor, *WCZLS*, see Astahovska and Žeikare, eds., *Nebijušu sajūtu restaurēšanas darbnīca/Workshop for the Restoration of Unfelt Feelings*, 22–23.

7. Some of their correspondence from this period is preserved at LLMC, in a box labeled "Lediņa arhīva papildinājums."

8. *WCZLS* 3, copy in private collection, available at http://www.pietura.lv/seque/txt/samizdats/1973_74_wczls_03.pdf.

9. *WCZLS* 5, copy in private collection, available at http://www.pietura.lv/seque/txt/samizdats/1973_74_wczls_05.pdf.

10. *The Riesling Brothers on Tour in Latgalia!*, copy in private collection, available at http://www.pietura.lv/seque/txt/samizdats/1974_ontourinlatgalia.pdf.

11. Ījabs, "Lediņš savos Rietumos."

12. Red and green notebook labeled "Melody Maker from 1970," preserved at LLMC in a box labeled "Klades." Lediņš's account of visiting these library col-

lections is given in Līdums, "Velvēs skan disko." On *Roksi*, see Kushnir, *Zolotoe podpol'e*, 55–61; and McMichael, "'After All, You're a Rock and Roll Star,'" 664–84.

13. Interview with the author (in Latvian and English), Riga, November 29, 2019.

14. See Yurchak, *Everything Was Forever*, 187–88; Iurchak, *Eto bylo navsegda*, 366; and Rudaks, *Rokupācija*, 47–49.

15. Zake, "Soviet Campaigns," 91–114 (at 100). Further information referenced in this paragraph is drawn from interviews with Boriss Avramecs (in Latvian), Riga, November 2, 2017; Māra Žeikare (in English), Riga, June 1, 2018; and most importantly Martin Boiko (in Latvian and English), Riga, November 29, 2019; as well as from Žeikare and Popova, "Hardija Lediņa diskotēkas."

16. Boriss Avramecs, a frequent collaborator with Lediņš in these years, has recently suggested this explicitly with respect to the disco-sponsored festivals of 1976–77 at which Pärt's sacred tintinnabuli works were premiered. We'll consider this possibility in chap. 4. See Avramecs and Gailītis, "Between Communist Party Bosses and Individual Courage."

17. Unlabeled blue school notebook, preserved at LLMC in a box labeled "Klades."

18. Piekut, *Henry Cow*, 387.

19. Zhuk, *Rock and Roll*, 178–79.

20. Bērziņa, "Jaunie studenti!"

21. Liepiņš, "Skanējumu sāk diskotēkas"; Oliņa, "Kāda celtne Vecrīgas panorāmā"; Asja Visocka, interview with the author (in Latvian), Riga, September 5, 2018.

22. Preserved at LLMC in a binder labeled "Rokraksti."

23. Preserved at LLMC in a binder labeled "Manuskripti."

24. Sketches for these lectures are preserved at LLMC in a binder labeled "Rokraksti."

25. The Wyatt and Gentle Giant lectures are preserved at LLMC in a binder labeled "Rokraksti." The Davis lecture is found in a separate notebook at LLMC labeled "M. Davis."

26. Preserved at LLMC in a binder labeled "Rokraksti."

27. Yurchak, *Everything Was Forever*, 236–37 (at 236); Iurchak, *Eto bylo navsegda*, 458–59.

28. Avramecs and Traumane, "Mūzikas avangards 70. gadu Rīgā," 312 (an alternative translation is given on 318).

29. Siitan, interview with the author (in English), Tallinn, October 30, 2017.

30. Šauriņš, "Šoruden—pirmā diskotēka."

31. Šauriņš, "Šoruden—pirmā diskotēka."

32. Martin Boiko stresses this point: as the son of an elite family in Soviet Latvian society, Lediņš understood intuitively how to communicate and operate within elite, official circles (interview, in Latvian and English, Riga, November 29, 2019).

33. Visocka, interview with the author (in Latvian), Riga, September 5, 2018.

34. On the renovation of the church as home for the Student Club, see Briedis, ed., *Augstākās tehniskās izglītības vēsture Latvijā*, vol. 3, *Rīgas Politehniskais institūts 1958–1990*, 190; and Oliņa, "Kāda celtne Vecrīgas panorāmā."

35. Visocka, interview with the author (in Latvian), September 5, 2018.

36. An organizational chart of the RPI Komsomol's structure in 1974 is preserved at LVA, fonds PA-4263, apraksts 8, lieta 2.

37. Visocka, interview with the author (in Latvian), September 5, 2018; *Jaunais Inženieris*, May 13, 1976, February 24, 1977, and April 28, 1977.

38. RPI Komsomol protocols of December 16, 1974, preserved in LVA, fonds PA-4263, apraksts 8, lieta 2.

39. These documents from the archives of the Latvian SSR Composers' Union (Latvijas PSR Komponistu savienība) are preserved at LVA, fonds 423, apraksts 6, lieta 29 (Oļģerts Grāvītis, untitled list of plans for 1976, dated December 8, 1975); fonds 423, apraksts 6, lieta 29 (Pauls Dambis, undated document headed "LPSR Komponistu savienības darba plāns republikas darbaļaužu internacionālajā audzināšanā 1976.–1980. gadam"); and fonds 423, apraksts 6, lieta 43 (Dambis, "Spravka," December 1976).

40. Liepiņš, "Skanējumu sāk diskotēka." See also Oliņa, "Kāda celtne Vecrīgas panorāmā."

41. Šauriņš, "Šoruden—pirmā diskotēka."

42. Komsomol protocols of January 26, 1976, and September 20, 1976, preserved in LVA, fonds PA-4263, apraksts 10, lietas 1 and 2.

43. Zhuk, *Rock and Roll*, 215, 223–25.

44. Šauriņš, "Šoruden—pirmā diskotēka." Protocols and other materials documenting the activities of the Composers' Union in this period are preserved in LVA, fonds 423, apraksts 6, lietas 25 and 29.

45. Kadile, "Tikāmies ar vārda un mūzikas daili." My account in this paragraph and all quotations are based on and taken from this source.

CHAPTER THREE

1. On Pärt's presentation to the Composers' Union of the Estonian SSR (Eesti NSV Heliloojate Liit), see Kautny, *Arvo Pärt zwischen Ost und West*, 114–15. The canonic recording, by Sergej Bezrodny, was released on Pärt's 1995 ECM album *Alina* (ECM New Series 1591).

2. This nomenclature, along with the reduction of understandings of the style to this contrapuntal structure, derives from Hillier, *Arvo Pärt*, 86–97. The complete score to *Aliinale/Für Alina* in its first published form for piano (Universal Edition, 1980; now Universal Edition UE 19823 [1990]) is given on pages 88–89 in Hillier's book. On the use of the work in film, see Maimets-Volt, *Mediating the "Idea of One."* Recently, our conception of tintinnabuli structures have been enriched by the work of Leopold Brauneiss especially; see his *Arvo Pärdi tintinnabuli-stiil*.

Several of Brauneiss's essays are available in English, including "Tintinnabuli: An Introduction," 107–62, and "Musical Archetypes: The Basic Elements of the Tintinnabuli Style," 49–72.

3. Kareda, "'Dem Urknall entgegen,'" 59n3. The sketch is found in APK, 2–1.7. Arvo and Nora Pärt locate and discuss the sketch in the documentary film *Arvo Pärt: 24 Preludes for a Fugue*, at 0:55:30.

4. For consideration and critique of this mythology, see Karnes, *Arvo Pärt's Tabula Rasa*, 3–15.

5. April 27, 1976; APK, 2–1.10. On the concert and the premiere, see chap. 4.

6. *Värvilised unenäod*, at 0:27:30. A copy is preserved in the film collection of the National Archive (Rahvusarhiiv) in Tallinn, filmi nr. 5173; the manuscript is preserved in ETMM, M238:2/38.

7. The manuscript score (fig. 3.1) is preserved in ETMM, M238:2/13; the sketch (fig. 3.2) in ETMM, M238:2/61.

8. Robinson, "Analyzing Pärt," 96–97; the now-canonical version of *Sarah* is published as Universal Edition UE 30300. Notably, Robinson theorized Pärt's compositional procedure by analyzing the published score of *Sarah* alone, without (it seems) knowledge of the manuscript sources or the music Pärt wrote for *Colorful Dreams*—in other words, without knowing that his hypothesis seems to comport exactly with what Pärt actually did.

9. The rule in *Modus* being something like this: *let the final pitch of iteration x be the first pitch of iteration x+1.*

10. Soomere, "Simfonizm Arvo Piarta," 212. For Soomere's remarks to the Composers' Union on October 5, 1976, see Kautny, *Arvo Pärt zwischen Ost und West*, 116.

11. Vaitmaa, "Hortus Musicus—muusika aed," 10. With "intonation" (*intonatsioon*), Vaitmaa referred to the theoretical notion of musically referencing sounds or ideas from the natural or social worlds.

12. Vaitmaa, "*Tintinnabuli*—eluhoiak, stiil ja tehnika," 37.

13. The score of *Laul Armastatule*, which Pärt would soon withdraw from his catalog, is preserved in ETMM, M238:2/10. Archival recordings from performances of 1973 and 1974 are preserved at APK, cataloged as APRA 0010282 and APRA 0010506 in the Arvo Pärt Recorded Archive, maintained by Doug Maskew in Tallinn. I am grateful to Doug for providing me with digital copies of the recordings.

14. My description of the work and its performance is based on the manuscript fair copy of the full score, preserved in ETMM, M238:2/13; manuscript drafts, preserved in ETMM, M238:2/61; and a recording of the concert preserved at ERR, ÜPST-2734/KCDR-1020. No recordings of *Calix* are known to exist in broad circulation, but much of its material was later revised as part of Pärt's *Miserere* (1989). Recorded by the Hilliard Ensemble on ECM Records in 1991 (ECM New Series 1430), material from the opening section of *Calix* can be heard at 05:47, and from its closing section at 32:09.

15. This was first noted in Vaitmaa, "Arvo Pärdi vokaallooming," 22.

16. Preserved in ETMM, M238:2/13.

17. The rock musicians who participated in the performance were not named in the program. On the archival recording (ERR, ÜPST-2734/KCDR-1020), this climactic point occurs at 15:50. In the canonical 1990 version of *Sarah*, recorded by the Hilliard Ensemble on their *Miserere* album of 1991 (ECM New Series 1430), the moment once seized by electric guitar and bass is handled instead by the organ (at 21:45).

18. Lippus, interview with the author (in English), Tallinn, February 7, 2015. Mustonen similarly recalled the "absolute simplicity" of *Modus* causing "complete puzzlement" (*täielik hämming*) among members of the premiere audience; see Randalu, "Muutumised," 34.

19. Vaitmaa, "*Tintinnabuli*—eluhoiak, stiil ja tehnika," 43.

20. A copy of the program is preserved in ETMM, M238/1:4. All quotations from Arvo and Nora Pärt in this paragraph are from this source.

21. Also from the program preserved in ETMM, M238/1:4.

22. Karnes, *Arvo Pärt's Tabula Rasa*, 50–52; Taruskin, *Oxford History of Western Music*, 5:43–44.

23. Program preserved in ETMM, M238:1/4.

24. Martynov, *Zona opus posth*, 118, 282.

25. Liubimov, "Vremia radostnykh otkrytii," 156. In that source, Lubimov recalls the event taking place in 1971, and the organizer simply as the "head of a club" (*rukovoditel' kluba*). He recounted the story somewhat differently in an interview with Peter Schmelz, identifying the organizer as Mark Mil'man and the club as being structured around the performance of chamber music at Moscow's House of Composers. Schmelz identifies the event as having taken place in 1969. See Schmelz, *Such Freedom*, 205.

26. A copy of the program note for the Leningrad concert of January 27, 1977, is preserved in ETMM, M238:1/4. It is reprinted with an English translation as Arvo and Nora Pärt, "Arvo Pärt—*Tintinnabuli* (1976)," trans. Shushan Avagyan, *Music & Literature* 1 (Fall 2012), 20–21.

27. Program preserved in LLMC in a box labeled "Rokraksti." All quotations in this paragraph are from this source.

28. Also from the program preserved in LLMC in a box labeled "Rokraksti."

29. Unless otherwise indicated, this and subsequent references to Pärt's sketches and compositional process are to the composer's unpublished "musical diaries" (*muusikapäevikud*) preserved at APK; his work on *Bees* and the vocabulary list just described is in APK, 2–1.18. In the 1970s, Pärt's diaries typically consisted of oblong notebooks of manuscript paper, which he would fill from beginning to end, dating his work as he went. When one or two shelf-inches of notebooks were filled—usually around eight of them—he would have them bound together, labeling the cover of the first with the range of dates they collectively span (i.e., "3 IX—27 XI 76" for September 3 through November 27, 1976; that particular composite

volume is cataloged as APK, 2–1.18). For a look at the diaries, see *Arvo Pärt: 24 Preludes for a Fugue*, at 0:38:11, and the documentary film *Arvo Pärt: Even if I Lose Everything*, which is broadly structured around Pärt's reading through his diaries and other manuscript materials.

30. APK, 2–1.18.

31. APK, 2–1.18.

32. Yurchak, *Everything Was Forever*, 102–22; Iurchak, *Eto bylo navsegda*, 212–41. On the performance of normalcy in relation to religious practice, see chap. 1.

33. APK, 2–1.18.

34. Kristina Kõrver, interview with the author (in English), Laulasmaa, January 21, 2019. On the algorithm, see Brauneiss, *Arvo Pärdi tintinnabuli-stiil*, 88–90; and Motte-Haber, "Struktur als Programm," 1:14–25.

35. APK, 2–1.18.

36. APK, 2–1.19.

37. APK, 2–1.21.

38. For detailed treatments of the method, see Brauneiss, "Tintinnabuli: An Introduction," 122–25; and Hillier, *Arvo Pärt*, 106–14.

39. APK, 2–1.21.

40. APK, 2–1.21.

41. Pärt's work on the *Passio* described here spans two composite volumes of musical diaries: APK, 2–1.20 (March 1–5, 1977), and APK, 2–1.21 (February 24–March 14, 1977). Pärt considered both *De Profundis* and *Passio* incomplete at the time of his emigration. The former was completed in 1980 and premiered in Kassel the following year; the latter he finished in 1982, shortly before its first performance in Munich.

42. Siitan, introduction to *In Principio*, 11.

43. Engelhardt, *Singing the Right Way*, 44, 36. See also Bouteneff, *Arvo Pärt: Out of Silence*, 119–22.

44. Engelhardt, "Perspectives on Arvo Pärt after 1980," 42.

45. Martynov, *Zona opus posth*, 118.

46. APK, 2–1.22.

47. Program preserved in ETMM, M238:1/2.

48. APK, 2–1.22. On the commission and preparations for the premiere, see Karnes, *Arvo Pärt's Tabula Rasa*, 61–65.

49. APK, 2–1.23, 2–1.24, 2–1.25.

50. APK, 2–1.26.

51. APK, 2–1.26.

52. A manuscript copy of the soloists' parts to *Ludus*, the first movement of *Tabula rasa*, dated July 1977, is preserved in ETMM, M238:2/58. Pärt continued working on the violin figuration of *Ludus* until July 23, and he was still working out the movement's cadenza on September 18–20, a little over a week before the work's premiere (APK, 2–1.26 and 2–1.27).

53. APK, 2–1.27.

54. APK, 2–1.27.

55. APK, 2–1.27 (Pärt's emphasis).

56. The first entry in the notebook whose cover bears this inscription is dated October 30, 1977. Theophan's letter, penned in August 1888, and the collection in which it originally appears, *Letters on Spiritual Life* (*Pis'ma o dukhovnoi zhizni*), has been widely reprinted and circulated since his death in 1894. The letter is available online at https://rutlib5.com/book/26876/p/147.

57. Hillier, *Arvo Pärt*, 6–10.

58. Bouteneff, *Arvo Pärt: Out of Silence*, 121n101.

59. Bouteneff, *Arvo Pärt: Out of Silence*, 111, 120.

60. Engelhardt, *Singing the Right Way*, 106, 43–44.

61. Siitan, introduction to *In Principio*, 11.

62. Unless otherwise noted, information provided in this paragraph is taken from Manewitsch, "Eduard Steinberg. Eine biographische Skizze," 17–36; Riese, *Eduard Steinberg*, 10–36; and Riese, "Wahrnehmung des Seins/The Perception of Existence," 42–71.

63. See, e.g., Steinberg's *Composition* (1969), reproduced in Riese, *Eduard Steinberg*, 23; in Brossard, *Eduard Steinberg*, 49; and in Thiemann, ed., *(Non)conform: Russian and Soviet Art, 1958–1995*, 410 (plate 560).

64. The letter is published in its entirety in Brossard, *Eduard Steinberg*, 67–68, and reprinted from there in Riese, *Eduard Steinberg*, 40–41.

65. In Brossard, *Eduard Steinberg*, 67–68; Riese, *Eduard Steinberg*, 41.

66. See Jackson, *Experimental Group*, 101–5 (at 102).

67. Kabakov, *60e-70e*, 56.

68. Steinberg, "Notizen zu einer Ausstellung," in Brossard, *Eduard Steinberg*, 76.

69. Degot', *Russkoe iskusstvo XX veka*, 185.

70. Schmelz, *Such Freedom*, 12.

71. Savenko, "Strogii stil' Arvo Piarta," 19. Vaitmaa makes a similar point in "Hortus Musicus—muusika aed," 10.

72. The tape, cataloged as 1016 in Lediņš's Seque Records Avant-Garde Series of recordings, is preserved in the private archive of the Lediņš family/Lauris Vorslavs in Riga. I am grateful to Lauris and to the staff of LLMC for providing me with a copy of the tape and photographs of its container.

73. Programs preserved in ETMM, M238:1/4.

74. The list, dated February 15, 1978, is preserved at the Estonian Composers' Union (Eesti Heliloojate Liit) in Tallinn (EHL, Pärt 1956–1978).

75. See May, "Colorful Dreams," 56; and May, "System, Gesture, Rhetoric," 88–89. This event was first described by Oliver Kautny, though he records some of its details incorrectly; see his *Arvo Pärt zwischen Ost und West*, 125–26.

76. These materials are preserved in ETMM, M238:2/48, M238:2/49, M238:2/50, M238:2/62, and M238:2/TA.

77. The music derived from *If Bach Had Kept Bees* can be heard in the opening scene of *Test Pilota Pirxa/Navigaator Pirx*.

78. *Test Pilota Pirxa/Navigaator Pirx*, at 1:00:00.

79. May, "Colorful Dreams," 57–58 (at 58).

80. The musicologist Monika Topmann and the journalist Avo Hirvesoo, respectively, quoted in Kautny, *Arvo Pärt zwischen Ost und West*, 126.

81. Jackson's words about Kabakov's reluctance to display his ideologically questionable works in the late 1960s could apply just as well to the situation Pärt faced after the *Credo* scandal: "To show his big, ragged paintings once could be chalked up to a lapse in judgment, but to show them twice might have suggested anti-Soviet provocation." Jackson, *Experimental Group*, 105.

CHAPTER FOUR

1. Lediņš, "Mūzikas dekāde."

2. Programs preserved in ETMM, M238:1/3 (*Tabula Rasa* in Leningrad on October 28, 1977, and in Moscow on January 7, 1979), M238:1/4 (*Tabula Rasa* in Tallinn on September 30, 1977; the *Tintinnabuli* suite in Tallinn on October 27, 1976, and in Leningrad on January 27, 1977), and MO20 (the *Tintinnabuli* suite in Tartu on October 25, 1976). On the premiere of *Tabula rasa*, see Karnes, *Arvo Pärt's Tabula Rasa*, 92–94.

3. The date of the premiere, April 27, 1976, is recorded in Pärt's musical diaries: APK, 2–1.10.

4. Katkus, interview with the author (in English), Vilnius, May 31, 2018.

5. Lediņš, "Vai esmu iegājis vēsturē kā mūziķis . . ." (ellipsis in original).

6. Vīlipa, "A. Lubimova koncertā."

7. Advertisement in *Rīgas Balss*, December 3, 1975.

8. Kārkliņa, "Decembris mūzikā."

9. Lediņš, "Vai esmu iegājis vēsturē kā mūziķis . . ." (ellipsis in original).

10. Lediņš's notebooks and early discotheque programs are discussed in chap. 2. A selection of his early tape compositions is available online: http://www.pietura.lv/seque/. For more on Lediņš's music and the Seque series, see chap. 6.

11. Avramecs, "Neoficiālie laikmetīgās mūzikas festivāli, 24–25 (at 24). Avramecs has recounted these events more recently in Avramecs and Gailītis, "Between Communist Party Bosses and Individual Courage." On *Drama* as cause of the upset, see Zelmane, "Vai 'under' nozīmē 'zem'?" In a letter to Silvestrov of February 16, 1976, Lubimov confirmed that he would be performing *Drama* on February 28, the date of the second installment of his Riga concert series; the letter is preserved at the Paul Sacher Stiftung, Basel. His second concert of the series was included, without any special advertising, in a daily listing of upcoming events published in *Rīgas Balss*, February 27, 1976.

12. Avramecs, interview with the author (in Latvian), Riga, November 2, 2017.

13. Information in this paragraph is relayed from Avramecs, interview with the author (in Latvian), Riga, November 2, 2017.

14. Muzyczuk, "Odcienie niezależności/Hues of Independence," 72.

15. Avramecs, "Neoficiālie laikmetīgās mūzikas festivāli," 26. Protocols and other materials recording discussions within the Komsomol during this period

are preserved at LVA, fonds PA-4263, apraksti 8–10. On Komsomol support for Lediņš's disco, see chap. 2.

16. The concert was advertised in *Rīgas Balss*, April 28, 1976.

17. APK, 2–1.10.

18. Avramecs, interview with the author (in Latvian), Riga, November 2, 2017; Avramecs and Gailītis, "Between Communist Party Bosses and Individual Courage."

19. Lubimov, letter to Silvestrov of July 12, 1977, preserved in the Paul Sacher Stiftung, Basel.

20. Lubimov, conversation with Peter Schmelz, Seattle, January 2017; conveyed in an email from Schmelz to the author, January 20, 2017. I'm grateful to Peter for this information.

21. Avramecs, interview with the author (in Latvian), Riga, November 2, 2017. Pärt disclosed this detail to Christopher J. May in 2015; see May, "System, Gesture, Rhetoric," 227n143.

22. Arvo and Nora Pärt, interview with the author (in German), Laulasmaa, November 28, 2019.

23. Avramecs, interview with the author (in Latvian), Riga, November 2, 2017; Arvo and Nora Pärt, interview with the author (in German), Laulasmaa, November 28, 2019; Kristina Kõrver, interview with the author (in English), Laulasmaa, November 1, 2017.

24. The photograph is preserved at LLMC. Šmeļkovs shared his recollections with me in an email of November 6, 2020. Pärt's response was related to me by Kõrver, interview with the author (in English), Laulasmaa, January 21, 2019.

25. All photographs are preserved at LLMC.

26. Avramecs, "Neoficiālie laikmetīgās mūzikas festivāli," 27; Avramecs and Gailītis, "Between Communist Party Bosses and Individual Courage"; Avramecs and Traumane, "Mūzikas avangards 70. gadu Rīgā," 311–13. See also Rovner, "Riga—moe muzykal'noe prizvanie," 62–63.

27. Cherednichenko, *Muzykal'nyi zapas*, 475–76 (at 475) and 545; on Pärt's participation in Happenings in Tallinn in the late 1960s, see Vaitmaa, "Eesti muusika muutumises," 154, with photos of Pärt performing on 155–74.

28. Akvo, "Avangarda mūzika."

29. Zelmane, "Vai 'under' nozīmē 'zem'?"

30. Liubimov, "Vremia radostnykh otkrytii," 159; Martynov, "Povorot 1974–1975 godov," 174–75. See also Ulanova, "Vladimir Martynov."

31. Avramecs's recollections are related in Rovner, "Riga—moe muzykal'noe prizvanie," 63. See also Avramecs and Gailītis, "Between Communist Party Bosses and Individual Courage."

32. Voss, "Par republikas partijas organizācijas uzdevumiem," 2–4.

33. Composers' Union protocols of June 14, 1977, preserved in LVA, fonds 423, apraksts 6, lieta 52; Albina, "Filharmonija oktobra jubilejai," 5; Viba, "Otkryt put' v tvorchestvo."

34. Avramecs, interview with the author (in Latvian), Riga, November 2, 2017.

35. LVA, fonds 423, apraksts 6, lieta 38 (protocols of November 23, 1976; the quotation is from this source); and fonds 423, apraksts 6, lieta 43 (undated document signed by Pauls Dambis, headed "LPSR Komponistu savienības darba plans republikas darbaļaužu internacionālajā audzināšanā 1976.–1980. gadam"). The organizers' musicologist helpers were Ingrīda Zemzare and Guntars Pupa.

36. Avramecs, "Neoficiālie laikmetīgās mūzikas festivāli," 28–29. The reference to "brotherly republics" and the official billing of the festival as a *dekāde* (after the Russian *dekada*, or ten-day festival; see fig. 1.1) plays upon the tradition of Soviet *dekady* inaugurated in 1936, which "aimed to bring the individual cultures of non-Russian Soviet nations to the attention of the broader, multiethnic audiences of the USSR," as the historian Isabelle R. Kaplan writes. On the Stalinist roots of the *dekada* as a vehicle for Soviet nationalities policy, see Kaplan, "Comrades in Arts," 78–94 (at 80). On Soviet nationalities policy as it inflected music-related conversations in the Baltic republics, see Karnes, "Soviet Musicology."

37. LVA, fonds PA-4263, apraksts 8, lieta 14 (document headed "Plan provedeniia meropriiatii po dostoinoi vstreche 60-letiia Velikogo Oktiabria v studencheskikh otriadakh RPI v III trudovom semester 1977 g.").

38. Lubimov, letter to Silvestrov of July 12, 1977, preserved in the Paul Sacher Stiftung, Basel.

39. Avramecs, "Neoficiālie laikmetīgās mūzikas festivāli," 29. No record of discussion of the festival plans is preserved in the archives of the Latvian SSR Composers' Union; see LVA, fonds 423, apraksts 6, lietas 25, 43, 52, and 54. However, it is possible that material related to the event was purged from the files of the Latvian Composers' Union during a housecleaning operation of 1982; on this, see chap. 1, n. 74.

40. Katkus, interview with the author (in English), Vilnius, May 31, 2018. A copy of the flyer is preserved at LLMC.

41. Mihkelson, interview with the author (in English), Tallinn, November 26, 2019; Mihkelson, emails to the author, November 29 and 30, 2019.

42. Martin Boiko, email to the author (in Latvian), January 30, 2020.

43. Lediņš, "Mūzikas dekāde" (ellipsis in original).

44. Pupa, "Studenti oktobra 60. gadadienai," 14.

45. The festival overview and program for the concert of October 24 are preserved at LLMC in a binder labeled "Pirmās diskotēkas Anglikāņos (RPI)." Programs for the other festival concerts are not known to survive, if they were ever printed at all. My recounting of information about further concerts in this paragraph is derived from reading and cross-referencing these surviving documents with published reviews and accounts of festival events: Rais, "Nüüdismuusikafestival Riias," 11; Petrova, "Aizvadīta modernās mūzikas dekāde"; and Avramecs's recollections given in Rovner, "Riga—moe muzykal'noe prizvanie," 63–64. I am grateful to Peter Schmelz for identifying the Gubaidulina work, given on the program with the Latvian title "Troksnis un klusums" (*Noise and silence*).

46. The tape of the Riga festival concert, cataloged as 1016 in Lediņš's Seque Records Avant-Garde Series of recordings, is preserved in the private archive of the Lediņš family/Lauris Vorslavs in Riga. I am grateful to Lauris and to the staff of LLMC for providing me with a digital copy of the tape and photographs of its container. A recording of the Tallinn concert of October 27, 1976, is preserved at ERR, ÜPST-2734/KCDR-1020. Events and sounds of the latter concert are described in chap. 3.

47. The canonical recording is found on Pärt's *Arbos* disc on ECM (1987), performed by the Brass Ensemble Staatsorchester Stuttgart conducted by Dennis Russell Davies (ECM New Series 1325).

48. A fair copy of the score of the Mass, prepared for the Riga performance and labeled *Test*, is preserved at APK, 2–2.1.131.

49. Universal Edition, UE 30431 (1996).

50. Cataloged as 1015 in Lediņš's Seque Records Avant-Garde Series, the recording is preserved in the private archive of the Lediņš family/Lauris Vorslavs in Riga. The authoritative recording, featuring Tatiana Grindenko and the ensemble Opus Posth led by Grindenko and Martynov, is widely available on a Long Arms Records release of 2004, *Vladimir Martynov: Passionslieder* (CDLA 04022).

51. The interview, previously unreleased, was broadcast on the Radio NABA program *Absolūtais Minors* on June 2, 2010; archived at http://sturm.lv/absolutais -minors/9/Absolutais_Minors_-_2010.06.02_-_Hardijs_Ledins_1955–2004 .mp3 (quoted at 0:19:41).

52. Avramecs, interview with the author (in Latvian), Riga, November 2, 2017; Avramecs, "Neoficiālie laikmetīgās mūzikas festivāli," 30; Avramecs and Gailītis, "Between Communist Party Bosses and Individual Courage." Martin Boiko, brother of Juris Boiko, also recalls that the individual who distributed copies of Mentzer's text was not one of the festival's principal organizers; rather, he observes, "things got too big, and they [Lediņš and other key figures] lost control" (Martin Boiko, interview with the author, in English and Latvian, Riga, November 29, 2019).

53. Martynov, *Zona opus posth*, 124.

54. Pärt, "Tintinnabuli—Flucht in die freiwillige Armut," 269.

55. Martynov introduces the notion of *simulacra* in *Zona opus posth*, 17–18. On his earlier, kindred notion of *bricolage* (the "reproduction [or regeneration: *vosproizvedenie*] of archetypal models"), see his *Konets vremeni kompozitorov*, 53–54 (at 54).

56. See Toomistu, "Imaginary Elsewhere," 41–62; and Zhuk, *Rock and Roll*, 200–11. Avramecs suggests (or recalls?) that Martynov's father, Ivan Ivanovich, supplied his son with Western LPs acquired during his professional trips abroad, much as Lediņš's mother is supposed to have done for her son; see Avramecs and Gailītis, "Between Communist Party Bosses and Individual Courage." Cherednichenko notes the general support Martynov received from his father during his early period of explorations in her *Muzykal'nyi zapas*, 557–58.

57. Martynov, *Avtoarkheologiia (1978–1998)*, 14–15 (at 15; italics added).

58. Quoted from the documentary film *Manā mežā nav neviens*, at 0:07:03. In a similar vein, Zhuk documents a connection attested by some Soviet listeners between their fascination with the Beatles and their own emerging attraction to the Hare Krishna movement in the early 1970s. See Zhuk, *Rock and Roll*, 201.

59. Toomistu, "Imaginary Elsewhere," 42–43.

60. Martynov, *Avtoarkheologiia (1978–1998)*, 16, 18–19. On Zavadskaya and the Skriabin Museum studio, see chap. 1.

61. Martynov, *Avtoarkheologiia (1978–1998)*, 21. As the historian Juliane Fürst documents, such "emotionally charged rituals and practices" surrounding the collective listening to rock recordings were fairly widespread among Soviet youth in the period, especially in Moscow and in the larger cities of the Baltic Republics. See Fürst, "Love, Peace and Rock 'n' Roll," 565–87 (at 573).

62. Martynov, *Avtoarkheologiia (1978–1998)*, 22 and 27. A selection of Martynov's poetry from the early 1970s is published in Martynov, *Avtoarkheologiia (1952–1972)*, 214–36.

63. Martynov, *Avtoarkheologiia (1978–1998)*, 23.

64. Martynov, *Avtoarkheologiia (1978–1998)*, 31–33.

65. Martynov, *Zona opus posth*, 81–82 (emphasis added).

66. Elste, "Interview with Arvo Pärt," 340 (interview of 1987); Jamie McCarthy, "An Interview with Arvo Pärt," 133 (interview of 1986).

67. Brotbeck and Wächter, "Lernen, die Stille zu hören," 16.

68. Avramecs, interview with the author (in Latvian), Riga, November 2, 2017; Rovner, "Riga—moe muzykal'noe prizvanie," 64. It is possible that material related to the event was purged from the files of the Latvian Composers' Union during a housecleaning operation of 1982; on this, see chap. 1, n. 74.

69. Quoted in Vasiļjevs, "Tiesa," 14. See also Lediņš, "Vai esmu iegājis vēsturē kā mūziķis. . . ." (ellipsis in original). Lediņš's "travels" were entirely metaphorical at this time, as referenced above; his first opportunity to literally voyage abroad came in summer 1988, when he traveled to West Berlin to work on installation of the exhibition *Riga: Lettische Avantgarde*. See Astahovska and Žeikare, eds., *Nebijušu sajūtu restaurēšanas darbnīca/Workshop for the Restoration of Unfelt Feelings*, 83–85, and Neue Gesellschaft für bildende Kunst, ed., *Riga: Lettische Avantgarde/ Latviešu Avangards*.

70. Liubimov, "Vremia radostnykh otrkytii," 156.

71. Avramecs and Gailītis, "Between Communist Party Bosses and Individual Courage."

72. Visocka, interview with the author (in Latvian), Riga, September 5, 2018. Bērziņa's firing is recounted by Lediņš in Vasiļjevs, "Tiesa," 14; and by Avramecs in "Neoficiālie laikmetīgās mūzikas festivāli," 30.

73. Martin Boiko, email to the author (in Latvian), January 30, 2020.

74. Veiss, "Paldies par labu un aktīvu darbu."

75. Petrova, "Aizvadīta modernās mūzikas dekāde."

76. See Zake, "Soviet Campaigns," 98.

77. Indra, "Septiņi priekšnojautas vakari."
78. Avramecs, interview with the author (in Latvian), Riga, May 7, 2019.
79. Avramecs, "Neoficiālie laikmetīgās mūzikas festivāli," 30 (emphasis added). The Bolshevik Revolution is generally considered to have started on October 25 in the Julian (Old Style) calendar, November 7 today.

CHAPTER FIVE

1. Vasiļjevs, "Tiesa," 14 (ellipsis in original).
2. In its official bilingual billing, *Varajase ja nüüdisaja muusika festival/Festival' starinnoi i sovremennoi muzyki.* For international coverage, see Heikinheimo, "As Kondrashin Defects," 10; Heikinheimo, "Russische Musik-Avantgarde"; and "Soome muusika-arvustaja muljeid Tallinnast," 3.
3. Mihkelson, interview with the author (in English), Tallinn, November 26, 2019. As late as 1992, a noted Estonian art critic observed: "Despite the common political background," the Baltic states of Estonia, Latvia, and Lithuania "still belong to different cultural areas." Juske, "Times of Transition," seventh unnumbered page.
4. On Raimo's work and station during this time, see "Khudozhestvennyi mir Raimo Kangro," anonymous typescript preserved in ETMM, M422 (p. 37).
5. Kivi discusses her involvement in these machinations in an interview broadcast on Estonian Public Radio on January 28, 2016, archived at http://arhiiv.err.ee/guid/104794 (at 0:03:01). For other recollections of planning for the festival both within and outside of the philharmonic, see Katunian, "Unikal'nyi eksperiment so vremenem," 1; and Garšnek, "Uus ja vana," 41.
6. Unless otherwise indicated, information in this paragraph and the one that follows is based on Mustonen's recollections, recorded in an interview with the Estonian journalist Ivalo Randalu: Randalu, "Muutumised," 33–37.
7. Yurchak, *Everything Was Forever,* 158–206; Iurchak, *Eto bylo navsegda,* 311–403. The itinerary of Pärt's trip to Italy, June 15–29, 1978, is recorded in his musical diaries: APK, 2–1.35 and 2–1.40.
8. In Randalu, "Muutumised," 37.
9. "Hortus Musicus," *Liesma,* June 1, 1979.
10. "Mis on valmis, teoksil, kavas?" 10.
11. "Varajase ja nüüdisaegse muusika festival," 10.
12. Torn, "Varajase ja nüüdisaja muusika festival," 3.
13. Randalu, "Kontserdiafišš" (November 8), 4.
14. Rannap, "Kontserdi päevik," 5. Programs for the festival concerts are preserved in ETMM, M238:1/4; and at LLMC, in a binder labeled "Rokraksti."
15. A recording of the festival performance is preserved at ERR, ÜPST-3094.4. Information on the possible whereabouts of the score (perhaps with Kremer) was relayed to me in an interview with Nora Pärt (in German), Laulasmaa, November 28, 2019. The Salzburg version of *Fratres,* for violin and piano, was recorded by Kremer and Keith Jarrett for Pärt's *Tabula rasa* album of 1984 (ECM New Series 1275).

16. On the tour, see Karnes, *Arvo Pärt's Tabula Rasa*, 95–100.

17. The identity of the work by Schnittke performed on the concert is not entirely clear. The title given in the program is unambiguous (*Moz-art a'la* [*sic*] *Haydn*), as is the fact that it was a premiere performance (*pervoe ispolnenie; esiettekanne*). According to Schnittke's biographer Alexander Ivashkin, *Moz-Art à la Haydn*, for two violins and chamber orchestra, was composed in 1977 but not premiered until 1983 in Tbilisi. An earlier work simply called *Moz-art*, for two violins alone, was dedicated to Kremer and Grindenko and premiered in Vienna in 1976. See Ivashkin, ed., *Besedy s Al'fredom Shnitke*, 283.

18. Randalu, "Kontserdiafišš" (November 12), 3.

19. Rais, "Festival, festival," 11; Rannap, "Festival on lõppenud," 10.

20. Semper, "Varajase ja nüüdisaja muusika festival Tallinnas," 3.

21. Rais, "Festival, festival," 11.

22. Rannap, "Kontserdi päevik," 5.

23. Rannap, "Festival on lõppenud," 10 (ellipsis in original).

24. Semper, "Varajase ja nüüdisaja muusika festival Tallinnas," 3; Rannap, "Festival on lõppenud," 10.

25. Klotiņš, "Mūzikas festivāls Tallinā," 3.

26. Among them, the photo of Pärt and Martynov reproduced in fig. 1.3; annotated festival programs that will be discussed in chap. 6; and a photo of Lediņš in Tallinn, taken by Imants Žodžiks circa 1978, published in Astahovska and Žeikare, eds., *Nebijušu sajūtu restaurēšanas darbnīca/Workshop for the Restoration of Unfelt Feelings*, 31.

27. Heikinheimo, "Russische Musik-Avantgarde" (unpaginated clipping preserved in ETMM, M238:1/14).

28. The printed program, which does not include *Test*, is preserved in ETMM, M238:1/4. *Test* is also not included in the archival recording of the concert made by Estonian Radio: ERR, ÜPST-3094. However, the radio journalist Immo Mihkelson explains that, at that time, concert encores were typically not recorded for archival purposes; Mihkelson, interview with the author (in English), Tallinn, November 26, 2019.

29. Heikinheimo, "Russische Musik-Avantgarde." Heikinheimo's words make clear that the title of the work—*Test*—was shared with the audience, or at least with him: "Was damit getestet wird, ist einleuchtend, und bisher hat das Werk auch den Test bestanden, denn es gehört zum ständigen Repertoire dieses großartigen Ensembles, das hoffentlich bald die Gelegenheit bekommt, auch im westlichen Ausland die Hörer mit seinem jugendlichen Elan zu erobern."

30. Randalu, "Muutumised," 34; the program of December 19, 1978, is preserved in ETMM, M238:1/4.

31. Quoted in Katunian, "Unikal'nyi eksperiment so vremenem," 1.

32. Quoted in Garšnek, "Uus ja vana," 41.

33. Both quoted in Katunian, "Unikal'nyi eksperiment so vremenem," 3 (Martynov) and 2 (Mustonen). Consider also the discussion with Mustonen, Grindenko, Kagan, and other reunion participants recorded by Estonian Public Radio

on December 2, 1998: "Muusika kurbusevärvi maalt," archived at http://arhiiv.err.ee/guid/31773.

34. Remme, "Ristirüütlid Brežnevi ajast."

35. Rannap, "Festival on lõppenud," 10. For her review of the premiere of *Tabula rasa*, see Rannap, "Muusikasündmus TPI aulas," 10; for discussion, see Karnes, *Arvo Pärt's Tabula Rasa*, 91–94.

36. Semper, "Varajase ja nüüdisaja muusika festival Tallinnas," 3.

37. Heikinheimo, "As Kondrashin Defects," 10.

38. The interview was published as "Arvo Pärt novembris 1978," *Teater. Muusika. Kino* 1988, no. 7, 48–55; the genesis of the film and its fate is described on p. 48. The film—*Arvo Pärt novembris 1978*, dir. Andres Sööt (Eesti telefilm, 1978)—is available online at http://www.efis.ee/et/filmiliigid/film/id/1874/err-video.

39. "Arvo Pärt novembris 1978," 49.

40. "Arvo Pärt novembris 1978," 50–51 (ellipsis in original).

41. On the tour and Warsaw Autumn Festival performance, see Karnes, *Arvo Pärt's Tabula Rasa*, 95–101. A copy of the program for Warsaw Autumn is preserved in ETMM, M238:1/5.

42. Programs for these concerts are preserved in ETMM, M238:1/2, M238:1/4, and M238:1/5.

43. The award is preserved in ETMM, 238:1/7.

44. Program preserved in ETMM, M238:1/4. The film is *Fantaasia C-dur*, dir. Andres Sööt (Eesti telefilm, 1979); available online at http://www.efis.ee/et/filmiliigid/film/id/2435/err-video. The fact that the film had not yet been aired by mid-1988 is attested in "Arvo Pärt novembris 1978," 48.

45. APK, 2–1.37, 2–1.38, and 2.1–39. An archival recording of its premiere performance at the 1978 festival is preserved at ERR, KCDR-1019.3–5. The manuscript conductor's score is preserved in ETMM, M238:2/54.

46. In Randalu, "Muutumised," 34–35.

47. "Arvo Pärt novembris 1978," 48.

48. APK, 2–1.27, 2–1.28, 2–1.29, 2–1.31, 2–1.32, 2–1.36.

49. APK, 2–1.32 (*Spiegel im Spiegel*); 2.1–33 and 2.1.34 (*Footsteps in the Snow*). On *Footsteps*, some of the music for which might have been further developed into *Annum per annum* (1980), see Christopher J. May, "Colorful Dreams," 58–62.

50. APK, 2–1.37.

51. ETMM, M238:1/11.

52. See, e.g., the photograph of Pärt with Boris Kõrver, chair of the Estonian Composers Union, taken around 1966, in Normet and Vahter, *Soviet Estonian Music*, 8; reprinted in Karnes, *Arvo Pärt's Tabula Rasa*, 30.

CHAPTER SIX

1. Piekut, *Experimentalism Otherwise*, 19.

2. For early statements registered in West Germany, see Pärt, "Aufzeichnungen," 7–8; and Pärt, "Tintinnabuli—Flucht in die freiwillige Armut," 269–70. On

notions of Orthodox hesychasm as they figure in conversations about Pärt and his music, see chap. 3.

3. Rannap, "Muusikasündmus TPI aulas," 10 (the ellipses and line spacing are reproduced as in the original).

4. In Kudu, "Collage teemal P–Ä–R–T," 3.

5. "Arvo Pärt novembris 1978," 49.

6. "Arvo Pärt novembris 1978," 53.

7. Martynov, *Avtoarkheologiia (1978–1998)*, 17.

8. Martynov, *Avtoarkheologiia (1978–1998)*, 17–19.

9. Martynov, *Avtoarkheologiia (1978–1998)*, 23. The program for the festival concert featuring *Asana* is preserved in ETMM, M238:1/4. The work was never published, but an archival recording of the festival performance is preserved at ERR, ÜPST-3094.6.

10. Martynov, *Avtoarkheologiia (1978–1998)*, 39–41 (at 41).

11. Yurchak, *Everything Was Forever*, 112; Iurchak, *Eto bylo navsegda*, 230.

12. Martynov, *Avtoarkheologiia (1978–1998)*, 5–6 (at 5).

13. Martynov, *Avtoarkheologiia (1978–1998)*, 43.

14. Quoted in Elena Dvoskina, "Tat'iana Grindenko," 54.

15. Martynov, *Avtoarkheologiia (1978–1998)*, 55.

16. Martynov, *Avtoarkheologiia (1978–1998)*, 59.

17. A few years later, Martynov did in fact return to the public sphere as a composer, and ultimately a prolific one. It began in 1984, with the premiere of his *Opus posthumum* (or *Opus posth*) for piano, which he described as "music for worship—a reconstruction of famous and old works." Composed with intensive reliance on *simulacra*, described in chap. 4, the piece is an epic minimalist meditation in a minor mode, framed by passages gesturing toward nineteenth-century common-practice tonality. For Tat'iana Cherednichenko, the work, composed between 1980 and 1983, is a signal testament to Martynov's sense, shaped by his Orthodox faith, that the source of true creativity resides in a metaphysical realm somewhere *beyond* the authorial subject, with the creative act consisting in subjecting oneself to the prototypical gestures (*simulacra*) dictated by and within that realm. See Cherednichenko, *Muzykal'nyi zapas*, 540–44 (Martynov is quoted on p. 540). Martynov's *Opus posthumum* was recorded by Alexei Lubimov on Long Arms Records in 2018 (CDLA 18100).

18. Lediņš, "Vai sasniegts viss?"

19. On Lediņš's discotheques of the 1980s, see Žekare and Popova, "Hardija Lediņa diskotēkas"; and Karnes, "Disko kultūra." His artist friend was Leonards Laganovskis.

20. The handwritten list is preserved at LLMC in a binder labeled "Dziesmu teksti." In conceiving and packaging their work in this way, Boiko and Lediņš were early contributors to a "magnetic-tape album culture" in the 1980s USSR. On that, see Kushnir, "Vkus magnitnogo khleba," 8–55 (at 8); and McMichael, "'After All, You're a Rock and Roll Star,'" 665–69.

21. Lediņš cataloged *Best of Seque 76* as number 1008 in the Seque Records

Avant-Garde Series. The tape is preserved in the private archive of the Lediņš family/Lauris Vorslavs in Riga and can be heard at http://www.pietura.lv/seque/?grupa=seque&disk=best_seque.

22. The recording date is given on a manuscript track-listing for the album; it is preserved at LLMC in a binder labeled "Dziesmu teksti." The album itself, cataloged as 1021 in the Seque Records Avant-Garde Series, is preserved in the private archive of the Lediņš family/Lauris Vorslavs in Riga; selections can be heard at http://www.pietura.lv/seque/?grupa=seque&disk=china_notes. Lediņš's copy of the tape gives the title of the album in English and Russian: *Kuncendorf's China Notes/Kitaiskie zametki Kuntsendorfa*.

23. Preserved at LLMC in a binder labeled "Rokraksti."

24. Lediņš and Lācis, "*HL*: NL," 50–55. Photographs, documents, and descriptions of the walks are provided in Astahovska and Žeikare, eds., *Nebijušu sajūtu restaurēšanas darbnīca/Workshop for the Restoration of Unfelt Feelings*, 153–60. For discussion, see also Žeikare, "Bolderājas stils mākslā." The architect friend who accompanied them on their first Bolderāja walk was Imants Žodžiks.

25. Undated interview broadcast on the Radio NABA program *Absolūtais Minors* on June 18, 2014; archived at http://sturm.lv/absolutais-minors/103/Absolutais_Minors_-_2014.06.18_-_NSRD_izlase.mp3 (at 0:10:45).

26. Quoted in Traumane, "NSRD pieturas punkti/NSRD: Points of Reference," 296 (an alternate translation is given on p. 305).

27. Monastyrsky, as quoted in M. Tupitsyn, "Some Russian Performances," 11.

28. These photographs are preserved at LLMC in a binder labeled "Bolderājas gājieni" and in a file box labeled "Bolderājas gājieni NSRD."

29. Drafts of these texts are preserved at LLMC in a binder labeled "Dziesmu teksti," with additional related material in a binder labeled "Dzeja ārpus albumiem."

30. Preserved in the private archive of the Lediņš family/Lauris Vorslavs in Riga, and available at http://www.pietura.lv/seque/?grupa=seque&disk=bolderajas_stils.

31. "It's Still Not Light" (*Gaismas vēl nav*), the final track on *Bolderājas Stils*; available at http://www.pietura.lv/seque/?grupa=seque&disk=bolderajas_stils.

32. The Soviet phenomenon remains largely unstudied, beyond Artemy Troitsky's recollections (see his *Back in the USSR*, 48–67). But radio shows and internet archives such as Radio NABA's *Absolūtais Minors* are invaluable sources of information and materials; see http://sturm.lv/absolutais-minors/. On origins in Western spaces, see Cateforis, *Are We Not New Wave?* and Reynolds, *Rip It Up and Start Again*.

33. A magnitizdat production, *Bolderājas Dzelzceļš* (later spelled *Bolderājas Dzelzsceļš*) was rereleased in 2003 by Baušķenieks on vinyl and cassette on his independent label, Ingus Baušķenieka Ieraksti. Biographical information on Baušķenieks is available on the website of Radio NABA's *Absolūtais Minors*, https://naba.lsm.lv/lv/raksts/absoluts-minors/ingus-bauskenieka-retrospekcija-19861993.a53920/.

34. The album, *Manā Mežā Nav Neviens*, is preserved in the private archive of

the Lediņš family/Lauris Vorslavs in Riga, and available at http://www.pietura .lv/seque/?grupa=seque&disk=mana_meza. Listen especially to the fourth track, "Alone in the Woods" (*Viens pats meža*).

35. See Astahovska and Žeikare, eds., *Nebijušu sajūtu restaurēšanas darbnīca/ Workshop for the Restoration of Unfelt Feelings*, 42; and Žekare and Popova, "Hardija Lediņa diskotēkas." A number of NSRD's albums are available at http://www .pietura.lv/nsrd/; the album *Medicīna un Māksla* (*Medicine and Art*, 1985; recorded 1982–84) is exemplary of the work they created for the Riga disco scene.

36. Lediņš and Boiko expanded NSRD in the later 1980s into a prolific multiarts collective, with works ranging widely between music, performance art, and video art. Although they lacked the means to distribute their music legally prior to perestroika, audio tapes produced by the outfit were widely copied and shared; Martin Boiko, brother of Juris Boiko, recalls that Lediņš possessed two reel-to-reel decks and was constantly copying and distributing tapes by NSRD and others (Martin Boiko, interview with the author in English and Latvian, Riga, November 29, 2019). The collective's work became, in turn, a crucial source of ideas, sounds, and materials for a "second wave" of Latvian new wave bands in the 1980s. The musician Lauris Vorslavs, member of the Riga-based second-wave band T.U.M.S.A., later recalled that NSRD "had connections with everyone" in that decade (*Absolūtais Minors*, Radio NABA, June 8, 2011, at 21:06). The final recording to feature music by Lediņš, who died in 2004, was released on the Idea Media Baltija label (06–06/1522-IMB-001): *NSRD Hardijs Lediņš + draugi: Dziesmas neuzrakstītai lugai* (*NSRD Hardijs Lediņš + friends: Songs for an Unwritten Play*).

37. See Heikinheimo, "As Kondrashin Defects"; and Heikinheimo, "Matkustuskiellon syyt epäselvät."

38. In Rey, "Arvo Pärt, le saint excentrique," 11.

39. APK, 2–1.36, 2–1.37.

40. APK, 2–1.37, 2–1.39. He returned to the *Passio* at least twice, in March and May 1978 (APK, 2.1–32 and 2–1.34).

41. Pärt gives his fullest account of this episode in his 1987 conversation with the French journalist Anne Rey; see Rey, "Arvo Pärt," 11; translated in Karnes, *Arvo Pärt's Tabula Rasa*, 103–4. Photographs of the protest are preserved in ETMM, M238:1/58. Also useful are Andres Mustonen's reflections on the event, in Randalu, "Muutumised," 36.

42. Nora Pärt, interview with the author (in German), Laulasmaa, November 28, 2019.

43. May, "Train to Brest," 130–31.

44. For example: an analytical essay on Pärt's *Perpetuum mobile*, slated for publication in *Sovetskaia muzyka* in 1980, was pulled from production, not to appear in print until 1991. See Liubov' Berger, "Arvo Piart, 'Perpetuum mobile,'" 59–63. For a contemporaneous account of the "return" of Pärt's music to Soviet concert life in the time of perestroika, see Savenko, "Maksimalizm Arvo Piarta," 11.

45. Gürtelschmied, "Viele wissen noch nicht, daß ich hier bin," 12.

46. The journey is described in May, "Train to Brest," 129–30.

47. Quoted in Restagno, ed., *Arvo Pärt im Gespräch*, 54–55; with an alternate translation in Restagno, ed., *Arvo Pärt in Conversation*, 47.

48. The cassette is preserved at APK, 5–2.499 (cassette 156 in the Arvo Pärt Recorded Archive, maintained by Doug Maskew). I am grateful to Doug for providing me with a digital copy and photos of the cassette.

49. The tape from the Riga festival concert, cataloged as 1016 in Lediņš's Seque Records Avant-Garde Series, is preserved in the private archive of the Lediņš family/Lauris Vorslavs in Riga. I am grateful to Lauris and to the staff of LLMC for providing me with a digital copy. The identity of some of the performances on the Pärts' cassette has been established by Doug Maskew of the Arvo Pärt Recorded Archive. In particular, Doug has determined that the cassette preserves recordings of the same performances recorded by Lediņš at the Riga festival, but that the recordings themselves were made independently of each other—i.e., that neither is a copy of the other (email to the author, December 31, 2017).

50. Quoted in Randalu, "Muutumised," 37.

51. The Universal Edition catalog is preserved in ETMM, M238:1/48. The pathbreaking, canonical recording of *Passio* by the Hilliard Ensemble was released on ECM Records in 1988 (ECM New Series 1370).

52. The program is preserved in ETMM, M238:1/48.

53. APK, 2–1.27 (October 20, 1977).

APPENDIX

1. Mets, "Rein Rannapi klaveriõhtult," 10.

2. The performance date and location are given in APK, 2–1.10. For additional information, see chap. 4.

3. Program preserved in ETMM, MO20.

4. Program preserved in ETMM, M238:1/4.

5. Program preserved in ETMM, M238:1/2.

6. Program for the premiere performance preserved in ETMM, M238:1/4; further programs in ETMM, M238:1/3, M238:1/5, and M238:1/6.

7. Tape recording by Hardijs Lediņš (Seque Records Avant-Garde Series, 1016), preserved in the private archive of the Lediņš family/Lauris Vorslavs in Riga. For additional information, see chaps. 3 and 4.

8. Program preserved in ETMM, M238:1/4.

9. Program preserved in LLMC in a binder labeled "Rokraksti."

10. Program preserved in ETMM, M238:1/4.

SOURCES

PHYSICAL ARCHIVES

Arvo Pärdi Keskus (Arvo Pärt Centre), Laulasmaa (cited as APK).

Arvo Pärt Recorded Archive, maintained by Doug Maskew, Tallinn.

Eesti Heliloojate Liit (Estonian Composers' Union), Tallinn.

Eesti Rahvusringhääling (Estonian Public Broadcasting), Tallinn (cited as ERR).

Eesti Teatri- ja Muusikamuuseum (Estonian Theatre and Music Museum), Tallinn (cited as ETMM).

Latvijas Laikmetīgas mākslas centrs (Latvian Centre for Contemporary Art), Riga (cited as LLMC).

Latvijas Valsts arhīvs (National Archive of Latvia), Riga (cited as LVA).

Lediņš family/private archive of Lauris Vorslavs, Riga.

Paul Sacher Stiftung, Basel.

Rahvusarhiiv (National Archive), Tallinn.

ONLINE ARCHIVES

Absolūtais Minors, Radio NABA: http://sturm.lv/absolutais-minors/.

Eesti filmi andmebaas: http://www.efis.ee/.

ERR Arhiiv: http://arhiiv.err.ee/.

Moskovskii Kontseptualizm: http://conceptualism.letov.ru/.

Pietura nebijušām sajūtām: http://www.pietura.lv/.

Project for the Study of Dissidence and Samizdat, University of Toronto Libraries: https://samizdatcollections.library.utoronto.ca/.

PUBLISHED PRINT MATERIALS

Akvo, A. "Avangarda mūzika." *Jaunais Inženieris*, May 6, 1976.

Albina, Diāna. "Filharmonija oktobra jubilejai." *Literatūra un Māksla*, October 21, 1977, 5.

Alonso-Minutti, Ana R., Eduardo Herrera, and Alejandro L. Madrid, eds. *Experimentalisms in Practice: Music Perspectives from Latin America*. Oxford: Oxford University Press, 2018.

"Arvo Pärt novembris 1978." *Teater. Muusika. Kino* 1988, no. 7: 48–55.

Astahovska, Ieva, ed. *Atsedzot neredzamo pagātni/Recuperating the Invisible Past*. Riga: Latvijas Laikmetīgas mākslas centrs, 2012.

Astahovska, Ieva, and Māra Žeikare, eds. *Nebijušu sajūtu restaurēšanas darbnīca/ Workshop for the Restoration of Unfelt Feelings*. Riga: Latvijas Laikmetīgas mākslas centrs, 2016.

Avramecs, Boriss. "Neoficiālie laikmetīgās mūzikas festivāli 1976. un 1977. gados Rīgā." In *Robežu pārkāpšana. Mākslu sintēze un paralēles. 80 gadi*, ed. Ieva Astahovska, 20–31. Riga: Laikmetīgas mākslas centrs, 2006.

Avramecs, Boriss, and Viestarts Gailītis. "Between Communist Party Bosses and Individual Courage." *Unearthing the Music: Sound and Creative Experimentation in Non-democratic Europe*, July 15, 2020; http://database.unearthingthemusic.eu/Between_Communist_Party_Bosses_and_Individual_Courage.

Avramecs, Boriss, and Māra Traumane. "Mūzikas avangards 70. gadu Rīgā/The Musical Avant-garde in 1970s Riga." In *Nebijušu sajūtu restaurēšanas darbnīca/ Workshop for the Restoration of Unfelt Feelings*, ed. Ieva Astahovska and Māra Žeikare, 310–22. Riga: Latvijas Laikmetīgas mākslas centrs, 2016.

Berger, Liubov'. "Arvo Piart, 'Perpetuum mobile' ('Interferentsiia'): khudozhestvennyi obraz i kompozitsionnaia ideia" [1980]. *Sovetskaia muzyka* 1991, no. 2: 59–63.

Bernstein, David W., ed. *The San Francisco Tape Music Center: 1960s Counterculture and the Avant-Garde*. Berkeley: University of California Press, 2008.

Bērziņa, Aina. "Jaunie studenti!" *Jaunais Inženieris*, October 17, 1974.

Bishop, Claire. "Zones of Indistinguishability: Collective Actions Group and Participatory Art," *E-flux* 29 (November 2011); https://www.e-flux.com/journal/29/68116/zones-of-indistinguishability-collective-actions-group-and-participatory-art/.

Boiko, Juris. "NSR Darbnīca." *Avots* 1988, no. 4: 22–23. Reprinted with an English translation in *Nebijušu sajūtu restaurēšanas darbnīca/Workshop for the Restoration of Unfelt Feelings*, ed. Ieva Astahovska and Māra Žeikare, 253–54. Riga: Latvijas Laikmetīgas mākslas centrs, 2016.

Bouteneff, Peter C. *Arvo Pärt: Out of Silence*. Yonkers, NY: St. Vladimir's Seminary Press, 2015.

Bouteneff, Peter C., Jeffers Engelhardt, and Robert Saler, eds. *Arvo Pärt: Sounding the Sacred*. New York: Fordham University Press, 2021.

Boym, Svetlana. *The Future of Nostalgia*. New York: Basic Books, 2001.

Brauneiss, Leopold. *Arvo Pärdi tintinnabuli-stiil: arhetüübid ja geomeetria*. Ed. and trans. Saale Kareda. Laulasmaa: Arvo Pärdi Keskus, 2017.

———. "Musical Archetypes: The Basic Elements of the Tintinnabuli Style." Trans. Martin Wittenberg. In *The Cambridge Companion to Arvo Pärt*, ed. Andrew Shenton, 49–72. Cambridge: Cambridge University Press, 2012.

————. "Tintinnabuli: An Introduction." In *Arvo Pärt in Conversation*, ed. Enzo Restagno, trans. Robert Crow, 107–62. Champaign, IL: Dalkey Archive Press, 2012.

Briedis, Juris, ed. *Augstākās tehniskās izglītības vēsture Latvijā*. Vol. 3, *Rīgas Politehniskais institūts 1958–1990*. Riga: Rīgas Tehniskā universitāte, 2007.

Brossard, Jean-Pierre, ed. *Eduard Steinberg. Eine Monographie*. Moscow: Éditions d'En-Haut, 1992.

Brotbeck, Roman, and Roland Wächter. "Lernen, die Stille zu hören. Ein Gespräch mit dem estnischen Komponisten Arvo Pärt." *Neue Zeitschrift für Musik* 151, no. 3 (1988): 13–16.

Bryzgel, Amy. *Performance Art in Eastern Europe since 1960*. Manchester: Manchester University Press, 2017.

Cage, John. "The East in the West." *Asian Music* 1 (1968–69): 15–18.

Cateforis, Theo. *Are We Not New Wave? Modern Pop at the Turn of the 1980s*. Ann Arbor: University of Michigan Press, 2011.

Cherednichenko, Tat'iana. *Muzykal'nyi zapas. 70-e. Problemy. Portrety. Sluchai*. Moscow: Novoe literaturnoe obozrenie, 2002.

Chuikov, Ivan. "Navernoe, my byli i dissidentami." In *Eti strannye semidesiatye, ili Poteria nevinnosti*, ed. Georgii Kizeval'ter, 303–12. Moscow: Novoe literaturnoe obozrenie, 2010.

Crowley, David. "Sceny improwizowane/Scenes of Improvisation." In *Notatki z podziemia. Sztuka i muzyka alternatywna w Europie wschodniej 1968–1994/Notes from the Underground: Art and Alternative Music in Eastern Europe 1968–1994*, ed. David Crowley and Daniel Muzyczuk, 74–115. Łódź: Muzeum Sztuki, and London: Koenig Books, 2016.

Crowley, David, and Daniel Muzyczuk, eds. *Notatki z podziemia. Sztuka i muzyka alternatywna w Europie wschodniej 1968–1994/Notes from the Underground: Art and Alternative Music in Eastern Europe 1968–1994*. Łódź: Muzeum Sztuki, and London: Koenig Books, 2016.

Cushman, Thomas. *Notes from Underground: Rock Music Counterculture in Russia*. Albany: State University of New York Press, 1995.

Degot', Ekaterina. *Russkoe iskusstvo XX veka*. Moscow: Trilistnik, 2000.

Dohoney, Ryan. *Saving Abstraction: Morton Feldman, the de Menils, and the Rothko Chapel*. Oxford: Oxford University Press, 2019.

Dvoskina, Elena. "Tat'iana Grindenko: novyi put'." *Muzykal'naia akademiia* 2003, no. 2: 49–57.

Egorova, Tat'iana. *Vselennaia Eduarda Artem'eva*. Moscow: Vagrius, 2006.

Elste, Martin. "An Interview with Arvo Pärt." *Fanfare* 11 (1988): 337–41.

Engelhardt, Jeffers. "Perspectives on Arvo Pärt after 1980." In *The Cambridge Companion to Arvo Pärt*, ed. Andrew Shenton, 29–48. Cambridge: Cambridge University Press, 2012.

————. *Singing the Right Way: Orthodox Christians and Secular Enchantment in Estonia*. Oxford: Oxford University Press, 2015.

Eşanu, Octavian. *Transition in Post-Soviet Art: The Collective Actions Group before and after 1989*. Budapest: Central European University Press, 2013.

Fairclough, Pauline. "'Don't Sing It on a Feast Day': The Reception and Performance of Western Sacred Music in Soviet Russia, 1917–1953." *Journal of the American Musicological Society* 65 (2012): 67–111.

Fürst, Juliane. "Love, Peace and Rock 'n' Roll on Gorky Street: The 'Emotional Style' of the Soviet Hippie Community." *Contemporary European History* 23 (2014): 565–87.

Fürst, Juliane, and Josie McLellan, eds. *Dropping Out of Socialism: The Creation of Alternative Spheres in the Soviet Bloc.* Lanham, MD: Lexington Books, 2017.

Garšnek, Igor. "Uus ja vana—kakskümmend aastat hiljem." *Teater. Muusika. Kino* 1999, no. 2: 41–48.

Gillen, Eckhart. "Ungefähre Kunst in Riga." *Niemandsland: Zeitschrift zwischen den Kulturen* 2, no. 5 (1988): 32–50.

Gottschalk, Jennie. *Experimental Music since 1970.* New York: Bloomsbury, 2017.

Groys [Grois], Boris. *History Becomes Form: Moscow Conceptualism.* Cambridge, MA: MIT Press, 2010.

———. "Moscow Romantic Conceptualism." *A-Ya,* no. 1 (1979): 3–11; http://conceptualism.letov.ru/a-ya.pdf.

———. "Moskovskii romanticheskii kontseptualizm." *Tridtsat' sem',* no. 15 (August 1978): 50–65; https://samizdatcollections.library.utoronto.ca/islandora/object/samizdat%3A5423/pages.

Gürtelschmied, Walter. "Viele wissen noch nicht, daß ich hier bin." *Kurier,* August 17, 1980, 12–13.

Heikinheimo, Seppo. "As Kondrashin Defects, an Arvo Pärt Work Is Withdrawn from Tonight's Concert—There Are Dissident Soviet Composers Too." *Guardian,* December 6, 1978, 10.

———. "Matkustuskiellon syyt epäselvät; Pärtin poissaolo ei romuta konsertiia." *Heisingin Sanomat,* August 1, 1979, 18.

———. "Russische Musik-Avantgarde. Eine Woche für zeitgenössische Musik im estnischen Tallinn." *Allgemeine Zeitung Mainz,* December 23, 1978.

Hillier, Paul. *Arvo Pärt.* Oxford: Oxford University Press, 1997.

"Hortus Musicus." *Liesma,* June 1, 1979.

Iakovlev, A. "Diskoteki: vchera, segodnia, zavtra." *Jaunais Inženieris,* November 17, 1976.

Ījabs, Ivars. "Lediņš savos Rietumos." *Satori,* March 30, 2015; https://www.satori.lv/article/ledins-savos-rietumos.

Indra, P. "Septiņi priekšnojautas vakari. RPI diskotēkas avangarda mūzikas dekāde." *Dzimtenes Balss,* January 12, 1978.

IRWIN [collective], ed. *East Art Map: Contemporary Art and Eastern Europe.* London: Afterall Books, and Cambridge, MA: MIT Press, 2006.

Ivashkin, Alexander [Aleksandr]. *Alfred Schnittke.* London: Phaidon, 1996.

———, ed. *Besedy s Al'fredom Shnitke.* Moscow: RIK "Kul'tura," 1994.

Iverson, Jennifer. *Electronic Inspirations: Technologies of the Cold War Musical Avant-Garde.* Oxford: Oxford University Press, 2019.

Jackson, Matthew Jesse. *The Experimental Group: Ilya Kabakov, Moscow Conceptualism, Soviet Avant-Gardes*. Chicago: University of Chicago Press, 2010.

Jakelski, Lisa. *Making New Music in Cold War Poland: The Warsaw Autumn Festival, 1956–1968*. Oakland: University of California Press, 2017.

Juske, Ants. "Times of Transition." In *Forma Anthropologica*, ed. Ants Juske, seventh unnumbered page. Tallinn: Tallinn Art Hall, Art Hall Gallery, Gallery "Lumm," 1992.

Kabakov, Ilya [Ilia]. *60e-70e . . . Zapiski o neofitsial'noi zhizni v Moskve*. Vienna: Gesellschaft zur Förderung slawitischer Studien, 1999.

———. *On Art*. Ed. Matthew Jesse Jackson. Chicago: University of Chicago Press, 2018.

Kadile, D. "Tikāmies ar vārda un mūzikas daili." *Jaunais Inženieris*, April 29, 1976.

Kaplan, Isabelle R. "Comrades in Arts: The Soviet Dekada of National Art and the Friendship of Peoples." *RUDN Journal of Russian History* 19 (2020): 78–94.

Kareda, Saale. "'Dem Urknall entgegen': Einblick in den Tintinnabuli-Stil von Arvo Pärt." *Kirchenmusikalisches Jahrbuch* 84 (2000): 59–67.

Kārkliņa, I. "Decembris mūzikā." *Cīņa*, December 14, 1975.

Karnes, Kevin C. "Arvo Pärt, Hardijs Lediņš and the Ritual Moment in Riga, October 1977." *Res Musica* 11 (2019): 115–27.

———. *Arvo Pärt's Tabula Rasa*. Oxford: Oxford University Press, 2017.

———. "Arvo Pärt's Tintinnabuli and the 1970s Soviet Underground." In *Arvo Pärt: Sounding the Sacred*, ed. Peter C. Bouteneff, Jeffers Engelhardt, and Robert Saler, 68–85. New York: Fordham University Press, 2021.

———. "Disko kultūra un rituālais ceļojums Padomju Savienībā 20. gs. 80. gados." Trans. Anna Beļeviča. *Mūzikas Saule* 103 (2020): 42–48.

———. "Inventing Eastern Europe in the Ear of the Enlightenment," *Journal of the American Musicological Society* 72 (2018): 75–108.

———. "Soviet Musicology and the 'Nationalities Question': The Case of Latvia," *Journal of Baltic Studies* 39 (2008): 287–310.

Katunian, Margarita. "Unikal'nyi eksperiment so vremenem." *Muzykal'naia akademiia* 1999, no. 3: 1–9.

Kautny, Oliver. *Arvo Pärt zwischen Ost und West. Rezeptionsgeschichte*. Stuttgart: J. B. Metzler, 2002.

Kizeval'ter, Georgii [Georgy Kiesewalter], ed. *Eti strannye semidesiatye, ili Poteria nevinnosti. Esse, interv'iu, vospominaniia*. Moscow: Novoe literaturnoe obozrenie, 2010.

Klotiņš, Arnolds. "Mūzikas festivāls Tallinā." *Literatūra un māksla*, November 17, 1978, 3.

Kudu, Reet. "Collage teemal P–Ä–R–T." *Edasi*, November 19, 1978, 3.

Kurg, Andres. "Interview with Alexei Yurchak." *ARTMargins Online*, June 5, 2014; https://artmargins.com/interview-with-alexei-yurchak/.

Kushnir, Aleksandr. "Vkus magnitnogo khleba. Vvedenie v standarty sovetskoi magnitofonnoi kul'tury." In *100 magnitoal'bomov sovetskogo roka. 1977–1991: 15 let podpol'noi zvukozapisi*, ed. Aleksandr Kushnir, 8–55. Moscow: Kraft+, 2003.

———. *Zolotoe podpol'e. Polnaia illiustrirovannaia entsiklopediia rok-samizdata (1967–1994). Istoriia, antologiia, bibliografiia.* Nizhnii Novgorod: Izdatel'stvo "Dekom," 1994.

Kveberg, Gregory. "Shostakovich versus Boney M.: Culture, Status, and History in the Debate over Soviet *Diskoteki.*" In *Youth and Rock in the Soviet Bloc: Youth Cultures, Music, and the State in Russia and Eastern Europe*, ed. William Jay Risch, 211–27. Lanham, MD: Lexington Books, 2015.

Lediņš, Hardijs. "Disko. Disko? Disko!" *Padomju Jaunatne*, June 18, 1978.

———. "Mūzikas dekāde." *Padomju Jaunatne*, October 19, 1977.

———. "Vai esmu iegājis vēsturē kā mūziķis . . ." *Padomju Jaunatne*, October 21, 1989.

———. "Vai sasniegts viss?" *Padomju Jaunatne*, March 28, 1980.

Lediņš, Hardijs, and Normunds Lācis. "*HL*: NL." *Avots* 1988, no. 4: 50–55. Reprinted with an English translation in *Nebijušu sajūtu restaurēšanas darbnīca/ Workshop for the Restoration of Unfelt Feelings*, ed. Ieva Astahovska and Māra Žeikare, 138–48. Riga: Latvijas Laikmetīgas mākslas centrs, 2016.

Līdums, J. "Velvēs skan disko." *Dzimtenes Balss*, May 5, 1977.

Liepiņš, Viesturs. "Skanējumu sāk diskotēkas." *Jaunais Inženieris*, February 27, 1975.

Lindenbauma, Līga, ed. *Lediņš. Starp to un kaut ko citu.* Riga: Latvijas Nacionālā bibliotēka, 2015.

Lubimov, Alexei [Aleksei Liubimov]. "Keidzh (Cage) Dzhon." In *Muzykal'naia entsiklopediia*, ed. Iurii Keldysh, 2:768–69. Moscow: Sovetskaia entsiklopediia, 1974.

———. "Vremia radostnykh otkrytii." In *Eti strannye semidesyatye, ili Poterya nevinnosti*, ed. Georgii Kizeval'ter, 151–66. Moscow: Novoe literaturnoe obozrenie, 2010.

Maimets-Volt, Kaire. *Mediating the "Idea of One": Arvo Pärt's Pre-existing Music in Film.* Tallinn: Estonian Academy of Music and Theatre, 2009.

Manewitsch, Galina. "Eduard Steinberg. Eine biographische Skizze." In *Eduard Steinberg. Eine Monographie*, ed. Jean-Pierre Brossard, 17–36. Moscow: Éditions d'En-Haut, 1992.

Martynov, Vladimir. *Avtoarkheologiia (1952–1972).* Moscow: Klassika–XXI, 2011.

———. *Avtoarkheologiia (1978–1998).* Moscow: Klassika–XXI, 2012.

———. *Konets vremeni kompozitorov.* Moscow: Russkii put', 2002.

———. "Povorot 1974–1975 godov." In *Eti strannye semidesiatye, ili Poteria nevinnosti*, ed. Georgii Kizeval'ter, 167–79. Moscow: Novoe literaturnoe obozrenie, 2010.

———. *Zona opus posth, ili Rozhdenie novoi real'nosti.* Moscow: Klassika–XXI, 2011.

May, Christopher J. "Colorful Dreams: Exploring Pärt's Soviet Film Music." In *Arvo Pärt: Sounding the Sacred*, ed. Peter C. Bouteneff, Jeffers Engelhardt, and Robert Saler, 36–67. New York: Fordham University Press, 2021.

———. "System, Gesture, Rhetoric: Contexts for Rethinking Tintinnabuli in the Music of Arvo Pärt, 1960–1990." DPhil diss., University of Oxford, 2016.

————. "The Train to Brest: Mapping the Borders of Pärt Reception." *Res Musica* 11 (2019): 129–38.

McCarthy, Jamie. "An Interview with Arvo Pärt." *Musical Times* 130 (1989): 130–33.

McMichael, Polly. "'After All, You're a Rock and Roll Star (At Least, That's What They Say)': *Roksi* and the Creation of the Soviet Rock Musician." *Slavonic and East European Review* 83 (2005): 664–84.

Mets, Laine. "Rein Rannapi klaveriõhtult." *Sirp ja Vasar*, April 16, 1976, 10.

Mihkelson, Immo. "The Cradle of Tintinnabuli—40 Years since a Historic Concert"; https://www.arvopart.ee/en/the-cradle-of-tintinnabuli-40-years-since-a-historic-concert/.

"Mis on valmis, teoksil, kavas?" *Sirp ja Vasar*, October 13, 1978, 10.

Monastyrsky [Monastyrskii], Andrei. "Predislovie." In Monastyrskii, et al., *Poezdki za gorod: Kollektivnye deistviia*, 19–24. Moscow: Ad Marginem, 1998.

————, et al. *Poezdki za gorod: Kollektivnye deistviia*. Moscow: Ad Marginem, 1998.

Motte-Haber, Helga de la. "Struktur als Programm. Analytische Bemerkungen zur Komposition *Summa* von Arvo Pärt." In *Nähe und Distanz. Nachgedachte Musik der Gegenwart*, ed. Wolfgang Gratzer, 1:14–25. Hofheim: Wolke Verlag, 1996.

Munipov, Aleksei. "Vladimir Martynov o vrede progressa, Arvo Piarte i kompozitorakh budushchego." *Afisha*, April 24, 2013; https://daily.afisha.ru/archive/volna/archive/martynov_2013/.

Muzyczuk, Daniel. "Odcienie niezależności/Hues of Independence." In *Notatki z podziemia. Sztuka i muzyka alternatywna w Europie wschodniej 1968–1994/Notes from the Underground: Art and Alternative Music in Eastern Europe 1968–1994*, ed. David Crowley and Daniel Muzyczuk, 26–73. Łódź: Muzeum Sztuki, and London: Koenig Books, 2016.

Neue Gesellschaft für bildende Kunst, ed. *Riga: Lettische Avantgarde/Latviešu Avangards*. West Berlin: Elefanten Press, 1988.

Normet, Leo, and Arthur Vahter. *Soviet Estonian Music*. Tallinn: Eesti Raamat, 1967.

Oliņa, D. "Kāda celtne Vecrīgas panorāmā." *Padomju Jaunatne*, December 3, 1975.

Pärt, Arvo. "Aufzeichnungen." *Individualität: Europäische Vierteljahrsschrift* 28 (December 1990): 7–8.

————. "Greatly Sensitive: Alfred Schnittke in Tallinn." In *The Cambridge Companion to Arvo Pärt*, ed. Andrew Shenton, 198. Cambridge: Cambridge University Press, 2012.

————. "Tintinnabuli—Flucht in die freiwillige Armut." In *Sowjetische Musik im Licht der Perestroika*, ed. Hermann Danuser, Hannelore Gerlach, and Jürgen Köchel, 269–70. Laaber: Laaber-Verlag, 1990.

Pärt, Arvo, and Nora Pärt. "Arvo Pärt—*Tintinnabuli* (1976)." Trans. Shushan Avagyan. *Music and Literature* 1 (Fall 2012): 20–21.

Petrova, I. "Aizvadīta modernās mūzikas dekāde." *Jaunais Inženieris*, November 17, 1977.

Piekut, Benjamin. *Experimentalism Otherwise: The New York Avant-Garde and Its Limits*. Berkeley: University of California Press, 2011.

————. *Henry Cow: The World Is a Problem*. Durham, NC: Duke University Press, 2019.

————. "Pigeons." *Representations* 132 (2015): 112–20.

————, ed. *Tomorrow Is the Question: New Directions in Experimental Music Studies*. Ann Arbor: University of Michigan Press, 2014.

Piotrowski, Piotr. "No komunisma uz postkomunisma situāciju/From Communist to Post-Communist Condition." In *Atsedzot neredzamo pagātni/Recuperating the Invisible Past*, ed. Ieva Astahovska, 16–27. Riga: Latvijas Laikmetīgas mākslas centrs, 2012.

————. *In the Shadow of Yalta: Art and the Avant-garde in Eastern Europe, 1945–1989*. Trans. Anna Brzyski. London: Reaktion Books, 2009.

Prape, Gunta. "Diskotēka: Agrāk—Tagad." *Liesma*, April 1981, 7–8.

Pupa, Guntars. "Studenti oktobra 60. gadadienai." *Literatūra un Māksla*, October 21, 1977, 14.

Quillen, William. "After the End: New Music in Russia from *Perestroika* to the Present." PhD diss., University of California at Berkeley, 2010.

Rais, Mark. "Festival, festival." *Sirp ja Vasar*, November 17, 1978, 11.

————. "Nüüdismuusikafestival Riias." *Sirp ja Vasar*, January 6, 1978, 11.

Randalu, Ivalo. "Kontserdiafišš." *Noorte Hääl*, November 8, 1978, 4.

————. "Kontserdiafišš." *Noorte Hääl*, November 12, 1978, 3.

————. "Muutumised. Andres Mustonen Arvo Pärdist ja iseendast." *Teater. Muusika. Kino* 1995, no. 11: 33–40.

Rannap, Ines. "Festival on lõppenud, elagu festival!" *Sirp ja Vasar*, November 24, 1978, 10.

————. "Kontserdi päevik." *Kodumaa*, November 22, 1978, 5.

————. "Muusikasündmus TPI aulas." *Sirp ja Vasar*, October 21, 1977, 10.

Reed, S. Alexander. *Laurie Anderson's Big Science*. Oxford: Oxford University Press, 2021.

Remme, Anneli. "Ristirüütlid Brežnevi ajast." *Eesti Ekspress*, December 4, 2002.

Restagno, Enzo, ed. *Arvo Pärt im Gespräch*. Vienna: Universal Edition, 2010.

————, ed. *Arvo Pärt in Conversation*. Trans. Robert Crow. Champaign, IL: Dalkey Archive Press, 2012.

Rey, Anne. "Arvo Pärt, le saint excentrique." *Le Monde*, June 2, 1987, 11.

Reynolds, Simon. *Rip It Up and Start Again: Postpunk 1978–1984*. New York: Penguin, 2005.

Riese, Hans-Peter. *Eduard Steinberg. Monographie*. Cologne: Wienand, 1998.

————. "Wahrnehmung des Seins als ästhetische Einheit. Zu Eduard (Edik) Steinberg/The Perception of Existence as an Aesthetic Unity. On Eduard (Edik) Steinberg." In *Ost/West: Eduard Steinberg zwischen Moskau und Paris*, ed. Hans-Peter Riese and Roman Zieglgänsberger, 42–71. Cologne: Wienand, 2015.

Robinson, Thomas. "Analyzing Pärt." In *The Cambridge Companion to Arvo Pärt*, ed. Andrew Shenton, 76–110. Cambridge: Cambridge University Press, 2012.

Rosen, Steve. "King Crimson's Robert Fripp." *Guitar Player*, May 1974.

Rosma, Hedi, Kristina Kõrver, and Kai Kutman, eds. *In Principio: The Word in*

Arvo Pärt's Music. With an introduction by Toomas Siitan. Laulasmaa: Arvo Pärt Centre, 2014.

Rovner, Anton. "Riga—moe muzykal'noe prizvanie." *Muzyka i vremia* 2000, no. 5: 60–65.

Rudaks, Uldis. *Rokupācija. Latviešu rokmūzikas vēsture.* Riga: Dienas Grāmata, 2008.

Ryback, Timothy W. *Rock Around the Bloc: A History of Rock Music in Eastern Europe and the Soviet Union.* New York: Oxford University Press, 1990.

Samsons, Vilis, ed. *Latvijas PSR Mazā enciklopēdija.* 3 vols. Riga: Izdevniecība "Zinātne," 1967–70.

Šauriņš, A. "Šoruden—pirmā diskotēka." *Jaunais Inženieris,* September 25, 1975.

Savenko, Svetlana. "Maksimalizm Arvo Piarta." *Rossiiskaia muzykal'naia gazeta* 1990, no. 2: 11.

———. "Strogii stil' Arvo Piarta." *Sovetskaia muzyka* 1991, no. 10: 15–19.

———. "Vozvyshennoe i smirennoe. Arvo Piart: strikhi k portretu." *Muzykal'naia zhizn* 2005, no. 10: 17–20.

Schmelz, Peter J. *Alfred Schnittke's Concerto Grosso No. 1.* Oxford: Oxford University Press, 2019.

———. "From Skriabin to Pink Floyd: The ANS Synthesizer and the Politics of Soviet Music between Thaw and Stagnation." In *Sound Commitments: Avant-Garde Music and the Sixties,* ed. Robert Adlington, 254–77. Oxford: Oxford University Press, 2009.

———. *Sonic Overload: Alfred Schnittke, Valentin Silvestrov, and Polystylism in the Late USSR.* Oxford: Oxford University Press, 2021.

———. *Such Freedom, If Only Musical: Unofficial Soviet Music during the Thaw.* Oxford: Oxford University Press, 2009.

Scammel, Michael. "Art as Politics and Politics as Art." In *Nonconformist Art: The Soviet Experience, 1956–1986. The Norton and Nancy Dodge Collection,* ed. Alla Rosenfeld and Norton T. Dodge, 49–63. New York: Thames and Hudson, 1995.

Seiffarth, Carsten, Carsten Stabenow, and Golo Föllmer, eds. *Sound Exchange: Experimentelle Musikkulturen in Mittelosteuropa/Experimental Music Cultures in Central and Eastern Europe.* Saarbrücken: PFAU Verlag, 2012.

Semper, Aurora. "Varajase ja nüüdisaja muusika festival Tallinnas." *Rahva Hääl,* November 26, 1978, 3.

Shenton, Andrew, ed. *The Cambridge Companion to Arvo Pärt.* Cambridge: Cambridge University Press, 2012.

Siitan, Toomas. "Arvo Piart—pesni izgnannika." *Muzykal'naia akademiia* 1999, no. 10: 185–88.

———. "Introduction." Trans. Adam Cullen. In *In Principio: The Word in Arvo Pärt's Music,* ed. Hedi Rosma, Kristina Kõrver, and Kai Kutman, 9–15. Laulasmaa: Arvo Pärt Centre, 2014.

Solomon, Andrew. *The Irony Tower: Soviet Artists in a Time of Glasnost.* New York: Alfred A. Knopf, 1991.

"Soome muusika-arvustaja muljeid Tallinnast." *Vaba Eestlane,* January 23, 1979, 3.

Soomere, Uno. "Simfonizm Arvo Piarta." In *Kompozitori soiuznykh respublik. Sbornik statei,* vol. 2, ed. I. Bobykina, 161–221. Moscow: Sovetskii Kompozitor, 1977.

Taruskin, Richard. *The Oxford History of Western Music.* Vol. 5, *Music in the Late Twentieth Century.* Oxford: Oxford University Press, 2010.

Thiemann, Barbara, ed. *(Non)conform: Russian and Soviet Art, 1958–1995. The Ludwig Collection.* Munich: Prestel, 2007.

Toomistu, Terje. "The Imaginary Elsewhere of the Hippies in Soviet Estonia." In *Dropping Out of Socialism: The Creation of Alternative Spheres in the Soviet Bloc,* ed. Juliane Fürst and Josie McLellan, 41–62. Lanham, MD: Lexington Books, 2017.

Torn, Tina. "Varajase ja nüüdisaja muusika festival." *Õhtuleht,* November 4, 1978, 3.

Traumane, Māra. "NSRD pieturas punkti starptautiskajā mākslas un teorijas ainā/ NSRD: Points of Reference in International Art and Theory." In *Nebijušu sajūtu restaurēšanas darbnīca/Workshop for the Restoration of Unfelt Feelings,* ed. Ieva Astahovska and Māra Žeikare, 294–309. Riga: Latvijas Laikmetīgas mākslas centrs, 2016.

Troitsky, Artemy. *Back in the USSR: The True Story of Rock in Russia.* Boston: Faber and Faber, 1988.

———. *Subkultura: Stories of Youth and Resistance in Russia 1815–2017.* London: New Social, and Manchester: HOME, 2017.

Tupitsyn, Margarita. *Margins of Soviet Art.* Milan: Giancarlo Politi Editore, 1989.

———. "On Some Sources of Soviet Conceptualism." In *Nonconformist Art: The Soviet Experience, 1956–1986. The Norton and Nancy Dodge Collection,* ed. Alla Rosenfeld and Norton T. Dodge, 303–31. New York: Thames and Hudson, 1995.

———. "Some Russian Performances." *High Performance* 4, no. 4 (1981–82): 11–18.

Tupitsyn, Victor. "Immaculate Conceptualism." *Parkett* 83 (2008): 206–9.

———. *The Museological Unconscious: Communal (Post)Modernism in Russia.* Cambridge, MA: MIT Press, 2009.

Ulanova, Tat'iana. "Vladimir Martynov: 'Protivostoianie Rossii i Zapada vechnoe. Prosto seichas obostrenie.'" *Kul'tura,* December 12, 2014; https://www .classicalmusicnews.ru/interview/vladimir-martyinov-protivostoyanie-rossii -i-zapada-vechnoe-prosto-seychas-obostrenie/.

Vaitmaa, Merike. "Arvo Pärdi vokaallooming." *Teater. Muusika. Kino* 1991, no. 2: 19–27.

———. "Eesti muusika muutumises: viis viimast aastakümmet." In *Valgeid laike eesti muusikaloost,* ed. Urve Lippus, 135–81. Tallinn: Eesti Muusikaakadeemia, 2000.

———. "Hortus Musicus—muusika aed." *Sirp ja Vasar,* December 10, 1976, 10.

———. "*Tintinnabuli*—eluhoiak, stiil ja tehnika." *Teater. Muusika. Kino* 1988, no. 7: 37–47.

"Varajase ja nüüdisaegse muusika festival." *Sirp ja Vasar,* November 3, 1978, 10.

Vasiļjevs, Igors. "Tiesa." *Liesma* (1988), no. 4: 14–15.

Veiss, Aleksandrs. "Paldies par labu un aktīvu darbu." *Jaunais Inženieris,* November 3, 1977.

Viba, Ia. "Otkryt put' v tvorchestvo." *Jaunais Inženieris*, October 20, 1977.

Vīlipa, Daina. "A. Lubimova koncertā." *Rīgas Balss*, March 14, 1975.

Voss, Augusts. "Par republikas partijas organizācijas uzdevumiem, pildot PSKP CK lēmumu 'Par Lielās Oktobra sociālistiskās revolūcijas 60. gadadienu.'" *Literatūra un Māksla*, April 22, 1977, 2–4.

Yankilevsky [Iankilevskii], Vladimir. "Iz 1960-x v 1970-e." In *Eti strannye semidesiatye, ili Poteria nevinnosti*, ed. Georgii Kizeval'ter, 356–68. Moscow: Novoe literaturnoe obozrenie, 2010.

Yurchak, Alexei [Aleksei Iurchak]. *Eto bylo navsegda, poka ne konchilos'. Poslednee sovetskoe pokolenie*. Moscow: Novoe literaturnoe obozrenie, 2014.

———. *Everything Was Forever, Until It Was No More: The Last Soviet Generation*. Princeton, NJ: Princeton University Press, 2006.

———. "Necro-Utopia: The Politics of Indistinction and the Aesthetics of the Non-Soviet." *Current Anthropology* 49 (2008): 199–224.

———. "Suspending the Political: Late Soviet Artistic Experiments on the Margins of the State." *Poetics Today* 29 (2008): 713–33.

Zake, Ieva. "Soviet Campaigns against 'Capitalist Ideological Subversives' during the Cold War." *Journal of Cold War Studies* 12, no. 3 (2010): 91–114.

Zavadskaya, Yevgeniya [Evgeniia Zavadskaia]. *Kul'tura vostoka v sovremennom zapadnom mire*. Moscow: Izdatel'stvo "Nauka," 1977.

———. *Vostok na zapade*. Moscow: Izdatel'stvo "Nauka," 1970.

Žeikare, Māra. "Bolderājas stils mākslā." *Satori*, June 29, 2015; https://www.satori.lv/article/bolderajas-stils-maksla.

Žeikare, Māra, and Diāna Popova. "Hardija Lediņa diskotēkas." *Satori*, February 25, 2015; https://www.satori.lv/article/hardija-ledina-diskotekas.

Zelmane, Ieva. "Vai 'under' nozīmē 'zem'?" *Literatūra. Māksla. Mēs*, May 9, 1996.

Zhuk, Sergei I. *Rock and Roll in the Rocket City: The West, Identity, and Ideology in Soviet Dniepropetrovsk, 1960–1985*. Washington, DC: Woodrow Wilson Center Press, and Baltimore: Johns Hopkins University Press, 2010.

FILMS

Arvo Pärt: 24 Preludes for a Fugue. Dir. Dorian Supin. F-Seitse, 2001.

Arvo Pärt: Even If I Lose Everything. Dir. Dorian Supin. MinorFilm, 2015.

Arvo Pärt novembris 1978. Dir. Andres Sööt. Eesti telefilm, 1978; http://www.efis.ee/et/filmiliigid/film/id/1874/err-video.

Fantaasia C-dur. Dir. Andres Sööt. Eesti telefilm, 1979; http://www.efis.ee/et/filmiliigid/film/id/2435/err-video.

Manā mežā nav neviens. Dir. Kristīne Želve. Latvijas Televīzija, 2015.

Test Pilota Pirxa/Navigaator Pirx. Dir. Marek Piestrak. PRF-ZF and Tallinnfilm, 1979.

Värvilised unenäod. Dir. Virve Aruoja and Jaan Tooming. Tallinnfilm, 1974.

INDEX

Ābols, Juris, 93
abstraction, 16–17, 71–75, 77
Akvarium (band), 38
Amber Coast (radio program), 38, 103
Anderson, John, 37
Anderson, Laurie, 28
Artemyev, Eduard, 10, 92; *Solaris*, 149n24
Artusi, Giovanni, 100
Aurobindo, Sri, 20
avant-garde, musical, 4, 11–13, 17, 29, 36, 43, 60, 81, 98. *See also* experimentalism; modernism; polystylism, musical; serialism, musical
Avramecs, Boriss, 1, 5, 27, 29, 30, 43, 82–86, 89–91, 93, 97, 102, 104, 112
Axelrod, Gleb, 110
Aygi, Gennady, 5, 11

Bach, Johann Sebastian, 22–23, 49, 82–83, 101, 111
Baidin, Valery, 124–25
Balakauskas, Osvaldas, 93
Baltic capitals, distinctiveness of, 27–28, 153n80
Barthes, Roland, 11
Baušķenieks, Ingus, 133–34, 171n33

Berg, Alban, 40
Bērziņa, Aina, 39–40, 45, 102, 106
black market, 27, 38
Blyth, R. H., 20
Bogdanov, Yurii, 10, 83, 86, 99
Boiko, Juris, 32–33, 36–38, 91, 127–32. *See also* Lediņš, Hardijs; NSRD; Seque
Boiko, Martin, 38, 91–92, 102, 156n32, 165n52
Boomerang (band), 28, 83–84, 93
Boulez, Pierre, 40, 60
Bouteneff, Peter C., 69–70
Brezhnev, Leonid, 1, 4, 24
Brot & Salz (band), 49
Bulatov, Eric, *Dangerous (Opasno)*, 15–16
Bulldozer Exhibition (Moscow), 13–14
Byrd, William, 29

Cage, John, 2, 10, 17, 20–21, 29, 32, 40, 42, 60, 81–82, 109–10, 127; *4′33″*, 61, 130; *45′ for a Speaker*, 86; *Lecture on the Weather*, 86; *Silence*, 20
chant, Gregorian, 20, 23, 63, 74, 101
Cherednichenko, Tat'iana, 86, 149n26, 170n17

Chicago (band), 37

Christianity, 9, 20, 24, 62, 103–4, 124–25. *See also* chant, Gregorian; Christianity, Orthodox; mass, Latin; prayer; psalms; religion

Christianity, Orthodox, 4, 9–10, 61, 64, 66–67, 71, 101; apophatic knowledge, 70, 72–73, 75; *hesychasm* (silence), 69–70, 73, 98, 122; modal prototypes, 67, 170n17. *See also* Martynov, Vladimir; Pärt, Arvo

Chuikov, Ivan, 30, 32

Collective Actions (group), 17–19, 130

Communist Party: of the Estonian SSR, 108; of the Latvian SSR, 82, 89; of the USSR, 91

Composers' Union, Soviet, 27, 47, 135; of the Estonian SSR, 26, 76–77, 107–8; of the Latvian SSR, 25, 47, 49, 89–92, 102, 152n74

conservatories, Soviet, 43, 86; Latvian Conservatory, 38, 49, 90, 93, 103; Moscow Conservatory, 24, 98

Cushman, Thomas, 36

dancing, 35, 39, 41, 44, 48, 50, 134

Davis, Miles, 41

Davydova, Lydia, 80, 84, 93, 96

Debussy, Claude, 81

Deep Purple, 42

Degot', Ekaterina, 56, 72–73

Denisov, Edison, 109; *Singing of the Birds* (*Penie ptits*), 10, 92, 110

Derrida, Jacques, 11

disco: disco music, 41; discotheques, 27–28, 126–27; Soviet disco craze, 34–35, 47, 106. *See also* Lediņš, Hardijs; Riga Polytechnic Institute

dodecaphony. *See* serialism, musical

Dufay, Guillaume, 23

Dzeltenie Pastnieki (band). *See* Yellow Postmen, The

Dzimtenes Balss (newspaper). See *Voice of the Homeland*

Dzintarkrasts (radio program). See *Amber Coast*

early music, 23, 29, 43, 98, 100–101, 108. *See also* chant, Gregorian; Hortus Musicus; Madrigal

"East," imaginary, 12, 20, 99, 123

Eckhart, Meister, 20

emigration, 125, 136. *See also under* Pärt, Arvo

Engelhardt, Jeffers, 67, 70

Eşanu, Octavian, 15, 18

Estonia Concert Hall (Tallinn), 7, 110, 112, 145

Estonian Radio, 22, 149n24

estrada (genre), 40, 47, 49

Eurythmics (band), 133

experimentalism, 2, 12, 121, 130, 134. *See also* avant-garde, musical; modernism; polystylism, musical; postmodernism; serialism, musical

Feldman, Morton, 2

festivals: festival of contemporary music (Riga, 1976), 2–4, 6, 9, 25, 27, 30, 56, 79–81, 83–88, 121, 145; festival of contemporary music (Riga, 1977), 2–4, 6, 22, 30, 56, 68–69, 75, 79–81, 88–97, 102–6, 109, 112, 118, 121, 137, 140, 146; Festival of Early and Contemporary Music (Tallinn, 1978), 28, 61, 104, 106–16, 118, 124, 126, 128, 135, 139; Salzburg Festival, 110; Warsaw Autumn, 117; Wiener Festwochen, 139–40

film music, 23, 25, 52–54, 75–77, 98–99, 118–19, 126, 135

Fix (band), 47

Forpost (band). *See* Outpost

Fripp, Robert, 29, 39, 154n89

Gabriel, Peter, 37, 43

Gabrieli, Giovanni, 110

Genesis, book of, 9, 62

Gentle Giant (band), 42
Georgian, Karine, 139
glasnost, 102, 106
Glazunov, Alexander, 92
Gottschalk, Jennie, 12
Grebenshchikov, Boris, 38
Gregorian chant. *See* chant, Gregorian
Grindenko, Anatoly, 81, 110, 124
Grindenko, Tatiana, 8, 24, 28–29, 42,
    68, 80–83, 85, 110–11, 115–17, 126–27,
    134, 146
Groys, Boris, 19, 21
Gubaidulina, Sofia, 10, 24, 81; *Rumore e
    silenzio (Shum i tishina)*, 92; *Vivendi
    non vivendi*, 10
Gutman, Natalia, 81, 110–11, 139, 146

Handel, George Frideric, 23
Happenings (performance art), 39,
    86–88
Haydn, Joseph, 49, 135
Heikinheimo, Seppo, 112–13, 115
Henry Cow (band), 28, 39, 41
Henze, Hans Werner, 109, 111
Hilliard Ensemble, 139
Hillier, Paul, 69
Hindemith, Paul, 40
Hinduism, 19–20, 124
Hirvesoo, Avo, 162n80
Hortus Musicus, 7–8, 23, 43, 59, 68, 75,
    91–93, 95–96, 104, 108, 110, 113, 115,
    119, 138, 145–46

Iankilevskii, Vladimir, 1, 21
Ījabs, Ivars, 37
improvisation, 29, 39, 42, 86, 127–28
Ives, Charles, 40

Jackson, Matthew Jesse, 7, 149n28,
    150n36
Järvi, Neeme, 22, 117
jazz, 36, 40, 44, 47. *See also* Davis,
    Miles
Judaism, 71, 135

Kabakov, Ilya, 4–5, 14–15, 17, 19, 22, 24,
    72, 150n28, 162n81; *Graph of Hope
    and Fear*, 14
Kagan, Oleg, 110–11, 139, 146
Kaljuste, Tõnu, 25
Kalsons, Romualds, 83
Kangro, Raimo, 93, 107–8, 111
Karlsons, Juris, 41
Katkus, Donatus, 26, 81
KGB, 36, 38, 97, 102–3
Khlebnikov, Velimir, 85
Khrushchev, Nikita, 11, 13, 16, 31
Kiesewalter, Georgy, 9, 13
King Crimson, 10, 29, 32, 37, 42–43, 59,
    98; *Red*, 37, 39, 100. *See also* Fripp,
    Robert
Kivi, Inna, 108
Klas, Eri, 145–46
Klaus Renft Combo, 49
Knaifel, Alexander, 93
Komsomol (Soviet youth league), 28,
    35, 47; of the Estonian SSR, 109;
    of the Latvian SSR, 23, 79, 92, 102,
    106–7; of the Riga Polytechnic, 28,
    44–45, 47, 50, 83, 90–91
Kondrashin, Kirill, 134
Kremer, Gidon, 8, 68, 92, 110–11, 115–17,
    134–35, 139, 146, 167n15
Kutavičius, Bronius, 111
Kuulberg, Mati, 93

Laganovskis, Leonards, 170n19
Lake, Greg, 37
Lediņa, Rute, 37–38, 103–4
Lediņš, Hardijs, 6, 20, 25–30, 32,
    34–37, 50, 68, 75, 96, 102–3, 106,
    108, 112, 120–21, 137, 140, 145;
    Bolderāja walks, 128–33; as com-
    poser, 82, 127–28, 132–34; disco-
    theque lectures, 36, 41–43; as DJ,
    34–35, 40–41, 44, 104, 126–27, 133;
    Kuncendorf's China Notes, 20, 29,
    127–28. *See also* festivals; NSRD;
    Riga Polytechnic Institute; Seque

Lem, Stanisław, 76

Lianozovo Group. *See* Rabin, Oscar

Liepiņa, Anda, 45

Ligeti, György, 60

Lippus, Urve, 59

Lithuanian Chamber Orchestra, 110–11, 139, 146

Lubimov, Alexei, 1–2, 5–6, 9, 12, 19–20, 23, 68, 81–89, 91–92, 102–4, 108, 110, 115–16, 126–27, 140, 159n25, 162n11; performances of Cage, 20–21, 61

Lubotsky, Mark, 24

Lutosławski, Witold, 40

Macarius the Great, 64

Machaut, Guillaume de, 81

Madrigal (ensemble), 23, 93

magnitizdat, 29, 127, 133–34, 154n91, 170n20

Maksymiuk, Jerzy, 139

Malevich, Kazimir, 72

Manezh Exhibition (Moscow), 13–14

Mansuryan, Tigran, 93

Martynov, Ivan Ivanovich, 98, 165n56

Martynov, Vladimir, 6, 9–12, 15, 20–21, 28–29, 41–42, 60–61, 67, 83, 86, 89, 92–93, 97–101, 109, 114–15, 120–21; and Eastern spirituality, 99–100, 123–24; and Orthodox Christianity, 101, 123–26, 135, 170n17; and simulacra, concept of, 98, 100–101, 125, 170n17

Martynov, Vladimir, works: *Album-blatt* (*Listok iz al'boma*), 110, 130; *Asana*, 110, 124; *Ierarkhiia razumnykh tsennostei*, 85; *Opus posthumum* (*Opus posth*), 170n17; *Passionslieder*, 50, 96–98, 100, 103, 105, 125, 127; *Seraphic Visions of St. Francis of Assisi*, 109–13, 123, 126

Marxism-Leninism, 41

mass, Latin: ordinary, 2, 22, 25–26, 62–65, 75, 77, 80, 94, 96; requiem, 24–25, 28–29, 57–58, 62, 77, 139

May, Christopher J., 76, 136

McLaughlin, John, and Shakti (ensemble), 99

Melody Maker (magazine), 37–38

Mence, Selga, 93

Mentzer, Johann, 96–97

Messiaen, Olivier, 40

Mihkelson, Immo, 91, 107, 168n28

Mil'man, Mark, 159n25

Ministry of Culture, Soviet, 1, 5, 22, 135; of the Estonian SSR, 117, 119; of the Latvian SSR, 27, 91, 102

modernism, 9–10, 15–17, 41, 57, 59, 70–71, 98. *See also* avant-garde, musical; experimentalism; serialism, musical; polystylism, musical

Monastyrsky, Andrei, 17–18, 130. *See also* Collective Actions

Monighetti, Ivan, 110

Monteverdi, Claudio, 100

Moscow, art scene of, 9, 13, 30–31; Izmailovsky Park, 13–14, 17, 22. *See also* Bulldozer Exhibition; Manezh Exhibition; Moscow Conceptualism; Skriabin Museum

Moscow Conceptualism, 15–17, 71

Mozart, Wolfgang Amadeus, 23, 25, 49, 81, 101, 123

Murzin, Yevgeny, 10

Mustonen, Andres, 7, 23, 59, 68, 96, 104, 108–9, 111, 114–17, 138, 140, 145–46, 159n18

Myaskovsky, Nikolai, 26

new wave music, 104, 133–34, 171n32

Nicene creed. *See* mass, Latin

nostalgia, 32, 114

NSRD (band), 134, 172n36; *Medicine and Art*, 29, 172n35

Oktoberklub (band), 49

orientalism, 20. *See also* "East," imaginary

Orthodox Christianity. *See* Christianity, Orthodox
Outpost (band), 28–29, 125–26

Parsadanian, Boris, 107–9, 111
Pärt, Arvo, 26, 33–34, 93, 108–9, 114, 119–23; abstract work of, 73–75; algorithmic designs of, 55, 60, 63–66, 96, 158n9; emigration of, 5, 62, 66, 101, 122, 125, 135–40; faith of, 4, 9, 20, 21–24, 55–56, 59, 61–69, 77–78, 80, 89, 98, 101 (*see also* Christianity, Orthodox); musical diaries of, 4–5, 62–69, 83, 98, 159n29; relations with Soviet officials, 5, 77–78, 114, 118–20, 134–35; syllabic method of, 64–66, 68, 74, 98, 118; tintinnabuli style, 2, 4, 7, 22–23, 51–52, 55–57, 59–62, 69, 98
Pärt, Arvo, works: *An den Wassern zu Babel saßen wir und weinten*, 62–63; *Annum per annum*, 169n49; *Arbos*, 57, 68, 75, 93, 137, 146; *Calix*, 7, 25, 29, 57–58, 62–63, 67–68, 77, 93, 116, 137, 139, 145; *Cantate Domino*, 68, 75, 77, 80, 93, 118, 137, 139, 146; *Cantus in Memory of Benjamin Britten*, 57, 67, 116–17, 120, 134, 137, 145; *Collage über B-A-C-H*, 74; *Colorful Dreams* (*Värvilised unenäod*) film score, 52–55, 117; *Credo*, 22–23, 26, 55, 57–58, 61, 74, 78–79, 108, 117, 119, 139–40; *De Profundis*, 65, 160n41; *Footsteps in the Snow* (*Jäljed lumel*) film score, 118; *Fratres*, 63, 68, 75, 94, 110, 137, 146; *Für Alina*, 50, 53, 55, 59, 65, 73, 145–46, 147n4; *If Bach Had Kept Bees*, 59, 62, 76, 137, 145; *In spe*, 7, 62–63, 77, 94, 110, 137, 145–46; *Italian Concerto*, 107, 109–11, 116–18, 135, 139–40, 146; *Miserere*, 153n76, 158n14; *Missa Syllabica*, 2, 9, 25–26, 34, 64–66, 68, 73–76, 80, 95–98, 106, 113, 118, 127, 135, 137, 139, 146; *Modus*, 7, 9, 29, 52–55, 58–59, 62, 77, 80, 93, 145; *Nekrolog*, 74; *Pari intervallo*, 62, 94, 145–46; *Passio*, 65–67, 135, 139, 160n41; *Perpetuum mobile*, 74, 112, 117, 119; *Pro et contra*, 119; *Sarah Was Ninety Years Old*, 2, 10, 23, 25, 34, 50, 55, 62, 77, 80, 83–85, 106, 118, 139, 145; *Song to the Beloved* (*Laul Armastatule*), 57, 59, 98, 108; *Spiegel im Spiegel*, 118, 146; *Summa*, 26, 63–64, 68, 77, 80, 93, 137, 139, 146; *Tabula Rasa*, 7–8, 24, 63, 68, 73, 77, 79, 114–15, 117, 120, 122–23, 128, 134–35, 137, 145–46, 160n52; *Test*, 75–78, 95, 113, 139, 146, 168n29 (see also *Missa Syllabica*); *Test of Pilot Pirx* film score, 75–78, 118, 135; Third Symphony, 56–57, 74, 98, 117; *Tintinnabuli* (suite), 7–9, 23, 51, 56–59, 61–62, 74–75, 77, 79, 93–94, 116, 145–46; *Trivium*, 59, 62, 137, 145; *Variationen zur Gesundung von Arinuschka*, 146
Pärt, Nora, 59–61, 65–66, 74, 76–77, 116, 122–23, 128, 135–37
Pauls, Raimonds, 47
Pekarsky, Mark, 26, 81, 85, 91–92, 126
Pelēcis, Georgs, 29
Penderecki, Krzysztof, 40, 109–10
perestroika, 5, 21, 24, 31, 106, 116
Philharmonic, Soviet, 28; of the Estonian SSR, 4, 7, 22, 56, 75, 106–9, 145; of the Latvian SSR, 79, 81, 89, 92
Piekut, Benjamin, 7, 12, 121
Pink Floyd, 37
Põldmäe, Alo, 111
Police, The (band), 134
polystylism, musical, 7, 17, 59, 74
postmodernism, 21, 60, 89
prayer, 64, 69–70, 122
Prokofiev, Sergei, 92
Pro Musica (ensemble), 23
psalms, 63, 68–69, 80, 94, 140

Pupa, Guntars, 164n35
Pushkin, Alexander, 123

Queen (band), 39
Quillen, William, 20

Rabin, Oscar, 13
Rabinovitch, Alexandre, 125
Ramans, Ģederts, 47, 49
Randalu, Ivalo, 109–11, 115–17, 120, 123, 134, 139
Rannap, Innes, 112, 114, 122
Rannap, Rein, 145, 147n4
realism, Socialist, 4, 13, 15–16, 23, 43
religion, 4, 12, 19–23, 50, 76–77, 100, 102–4, 114, 124, 130; Soviet attitudes toward, 22, 24, 63, 77–78, 96, 113–14, 125. *See also* chant, Gregorian; Christianity; Hinduism; Judaism; mass, Latin; prayer; Zen
Riga Polytechnic Institute (RPI), 37, 89, 102; RPI discotheque, 4, 9, 25, 34–25, 39–40, 43, 46–48, 50, 52, 80, 121, 145; Student Club, 39–40, 44–47, 49, 79, 83–84, 90–92, 96–97, 102–3, 107, 120, 126–27. *See also* festivals; Komsomol; Lediņš, Hardijs
Riley, Terry, *In C*, 11, 82, 85
Robinson, Thomas, 55, 158n8
rock music, 27–29, 38, 41, 59; progressive rock, 10, 29, 36, 59, 99, 123; punk, 41. *See also individual bands and artists*
Roksi (journal), 38
Romanticism, 11, 41, 43
Roxy Music, 37
Rozhkov, Vladimir, 124
RPI. *See* Riga Polytechnic Institute

samizdat, 19, 36–38
Savenko, Svetlana, 22–23, 74, 81
Schiller, Friedrich, 25, 77
Schlee, Alfred, 112–13

Schmelz, Peter J., 16–17, 74
Schnittke, Alfred, 10, 24–26, 92, 109, 135, 139, 146; First Concerto Grosso, 68; *Moz-Art à la Haydn*, 111, 168n17; Requiem, 25, 28–29, 77; Second Violin Concerto, 24
Schoenberg, Arnold, 40, 81
Schubert, Franz, 49
Schulze, Klaus, 98
Semper, Aurora, 111–12, 115
Seque (collective), 82, 127–28, 147n5; *Best of Seque* 76, 127; *Bolderāja Style*, 133–34; *There's No One in My Forest (Manā mežā nav neviens)*, 134
serialism, musical, 7, 17, 56–57, 74
Sibelius, Jean, 123, 126
Siitan, Toomas, 22, 43, 66–67, 69–70, 136
silence, 122–23. *See also* Christianity, Orthodox
Silvestrov, Valentin, 1, 5, 9–10, 29, 83, 89, 91, 93, 103, 109; *Drama*, 82, 162n11; *Kitsch-Music*, 110; *Quiet Songs (Tikhie pesni)*, 9–10
Skriabin Museum (Moscow), 10, 28–29, 83, 99, 124
Slade (band), 39
Šmeļkovs, Kirils, 84–85
socialism, Soviet, 31–32, 43. *See also* USSR
Socialist realism. *See* realism, Socialist
Soft Cell (band), 133
Solomon, Andrew, 21, 32–33
Sondeckis, Saulius, 110, 146
Soomere, Uno, 56, 74
Sooster, Ülo, 150n28
Sööt, Andres, 115–17
Southey, Robert, 110
Soviet Union. *See* USSR
spirituality. *See* religion
Stalin, Joseph, 13, 32
Stalinism, 12, 23, 31, 164n36
Stanevičiūtė, Rūta, 21
Star Wars, 15

Steinberg, Arkady, 70
Steinberg, Eduard, 56, 70–73, 98; *Composition November-December*, 71
Stockhausen, Karlheinz, 2, 20, 29, 40–43, 82, 109, 127; *Aus den sieben Tagen*, 86, 130
Štreihfelds, Edmunds, 40, 43–44
Sumera, Lepo, 111
Suslin, Viktor, 93, 103
Süssmayr, Franz Xavier, 25
Suzuki, Daisetz, 20
synthesizer, 10, 29, 99, 134

Tallinn Chamber Choir, 7, 93, 145
Tangerine Dream, 10, 41
Tartu, University of, 9, 27, 75, 145–46
Taruskin, Richard, 60
Tchaikovsky, Pyotr Ilyich, 26
Theophan the Recluse, 68–69
tintinnabuli style. *See under* Pärt, Arvo
Toomistu, Terje, 99
Topmann, Monika, 162n80
Troitsky, Artemy, 35–36, 148n12, 153n80
T.U.M.S.A. (band), 172n36
Tupitsyn, Margarita, 15–16, 17, 150n36
Tupitsyn, Victor, 31, 147n9

Ultravox, 133
underground, Soviet, 4, 24, 81, 107, 119–21, 138–39. *See also* experimentalism; religion
Universal Edition, 112, 139
USSR, 1, 2, 4, 27, 37, 81, 103–4, 125, 135–36; alternative creative culture in, 5, 13–15, 99, 118. *See also* Christianity; Communist Party; Composers' Union, Soviet; conservatories, Soviet; experimentalism; Komsomol; Ministry of Culture,
Soviet; Philharmonic, Soviet; religion; underground, Soviet
utopianism, 32–33, 81, 89
Uusväli, Rolf, 145

Vaitmaa, Merike, 56–57, 59, 74
Varèse, Edgard, 81
Vasks, Pēteris, 93
Vilnius String Quartet, 26, 80–81, 91, 93, 103
Visocka, Asja, 45, 49, 102
Vivaldi, Antonio, 111
Voice of the Homeland (newspaper), 103–4
Volkonsky, Andrei, 23, 93, 125
Vorslavs, Lauris, 172n36
Voss, Augusts, 89

Wagner, Richard, 42, 49
Webern, Anton, 40
Who, The, 42
Wir (band), 49
Wyatt, Robert, *Rock Bottom*, 39, 42

Xenakis, Iannis, 109

Yankilevsky, Vladimir, 1, 21
Yellow Postmen, The (band), 133–34
Yes (band), 37
yoga, 10, 99, 124
Yurchak, Alexei, 5–6, 21, 24, 28, 30–32, 38, 42, 63, 109, 125, 147n9, 148n13

Zālītis, Edvīns, 93
Zavadskaya, Yevgeniya, 21, 99
Zemzare, Ingrīda, 164n35
Zemzaris, Imants, 93
Zen, 10, 17, 19–20
Zhuk, Sergei, 35, 39, 154n84
Žodžiks, Imants, 168n26, 171n24